D. H.
LAWRENCE

A COLLECTION OF CRITICAL ESSAYS

Edited by
Mark Spilka

A SPECTRUM BOOK

Prentice-Hall, Inc., *Englewood Cliffs, N. J.*

Acknowledgment is gratefully made to the following publishers for quotation from works under their copyright: The Viking Press, Inc., for material from *The Captain's Doll, Collected Poems, The Letters of D. H. Lawrence, England, My England, Phoenix, The Rainbow, Sons and Lovers, Touch and Go, The Widowing of Mrs. Holroyd, Women in Love;* Alfred A. Knopf, Inc., for material from *David, The Man Who Died, The Plumed Serpent, Pornography and Obscenity;* and William Heinemann, Ltd., for material from all these works in their English editions. Poems by D. H. Lawrence are reprinted by permission of Laurence Pollinger, Ltd., representing the D. H. Lawrence Estate, and the Viking Press, Inc.

Current printing (last digit):

12 11 10 9 8 7 6

© 1963 BY PRENTICE-HALL, INC.

ENGLEWOOD CLIFFS, N.J.

LIBRARY OF CONGRESS CATALOG CARD NO.: 63-9517

Printed in the United States of America

C

Table of Contents

D. H. LAWRENCE

Introduction

by Mark Spilka

I

Some thirty years after his death D. H. Lawrence enjoys more wide-spread popularity and esteem than he knew in his lifetime. His complete works are again in print, his tales and poems are widely anthologized, two books and a tale have been made into movies. His long-suppressed novel, *Lady Chatterley's Lover,* has been released in England and America, after considerable fanfare, and has quickly become a bestseller. A dozen critical studies, six biographies, and a dozen assorted texts—bibliographies, travel calendars, selected and collected letters, reception studies and comparisons—have appeared in the last decade, along with several hundred essays and unpublished dissertations. In sum, his literary and popular stock has risen. He is now generally recognized as the foremost English novelist of his generation, and he begins to take his place among the important modern novelists: Joyce, Mann, Proust, Faulkner, Kafka. In terms of popular audience he even begins to exceed more famous masters.

Much of his success recalls the notoriety of the Twenties, when *Lady Chatterley* was banned in England and America and his exhibited paintings were seized by London police. But the critical renaissance, which seems to have sparked the popular revival, remains more durable and substantial. It falls within a larger shift in critical study by which methods first devised for poetry were applied to modern novels. This new approach has rescued Lawrence from the possessive memorialists, sex cultists, hostile liberals, and religious purists who destroyed his reputation in the Thirties. From that early free-for-all (which followed hard upon his death) Lawrence emerged a sex-mad homosexual fascist, a mindless and misguided genius scarcely worthy of attention. By the early Forties the number of books and essays on him had noticeably dwindled. Then, in the mid-Fifties, the new flood of entries began.

The new commentary was itself part of a larger movement toward contextual study. Late in the Thirties, when Lawrence's stock was falling, a movement called the New Criticism was gaining strength in the academies. It advocated close textual analysis as opposed to biographical and ideological studies, subordinating life to text and approaching ideas as formal elements. Since the attacks on Lawrence as man and ideologist had nearly overshadowed his work, this approach was potentially beneficial. But New Critics also favored "tradition," conscious and impersonal artistry, and tenable contextual beliefs, and Lawrence fell short (or so it seemed) on all these counts. T. S. Eliot attacked him as a religious heretic in sensibility, the product of "vague hymn-singing pietism" or decaying Protestantism. He found him ignorant and untrained, snobbish and humorless, insensitive to "ordinary social morality," and given to "distinct sexual morbidity" and extreme individualism. "The point is," he wrote, "that Lawrence started life wholly free from any restriction of tradition or institution, that he had no guidance except the Inner Light, the most untrustworthy and deceitful guide that ever offered itself to wandering humanity." Misguided by that light, Lawrence's vision was intensely spiritual, but also "spiritually sick," and likely to mislead unwary readers. I. A. Richards attacked him too for holding magical beliefs in an age of science instead of plunging into the destructive element of unbelief. Whether religious or scientific, then, the fathers of New Criticism found Lawrence's views misleading or untenable in context. Still another contextualist, R. P. Blackmur, attacked Lawrence for favoring inspiration at the expense of craft in poetry. Converting Eliot's religious terms into formal equivalents, he wrote: "When you depend entirely upon the demon of inspiration, the inner voice, the inner light, you deprive yourself of any external criterion to show whether the demon is working or not." The deceitful inner guide—inspiration—needs external support from craft or "rational imagination." By abandoning such guides, he argued, Lawrence had committed formal heresy, or "the fallacy of expressive form," and had left us with poetic "ruins."

These objections are so famous as to suggest a historical fallacy in ascribing Lawrence's rise to New Critical ministrations. Yet within the last decade latent tendencies have emerged among New Critics which have made them more receptive to "heretical" achievements. They have finally made their peace with Lawrence, chiefly through the persuasive work of F. R. Leavis, his leading English advocate. Close reader and renegade moralist, Leavis combines the qualities of two American critics, Cleanth Brooks and Yvor Winters. His early works, *New Bearings in English Poetry* (1932) and *Revaluation: Tradition and Development in English Poetry* (1936), have been aptly compared to Brooks's proselytizing texts, *Modern Poetry and the Tradition* (1939) and *The Well Wrought Urn* (1947). His books on education and culture, which promoted detailed literary study, may be compared to Brooks and Warren's *Understanding Poetry* (1938) in academic impact. Thus Leavis has played a vital role in the spread of English formalism. But like Yvor Winters (whom he sometimes quotes with approval), Leavis stresses the moral value of literature, especially in his treatment of fiction. As the editor of *Scrutiny*, Leavis gathered around him a group of critics for whom, says David Daiches, "a great work of literature was one in which a genuine moral vision of experience was communicated through a fully particularized, fully realized imaginative rendering of life. Every detail in a novel had to be freshly imagined and had to spring from the true depths of the writer's moral being." In his book, *The Great Tradition* (1948), Leavis himself led the way in applying this moral version of formalism to fiction. In the field of fiction, he held, "some challenging discriminations are very much called for; the field is so large and offers such insidious temptations to complacent confusions of judgment and to critical indolence." Leavis' immediate targets were those literary histories in which minor and major figures were lumped together as "classical novelists." He brought to his attack the same discriminating tests which New Critics had applied to poetry, and so pioneered in the historic shift from poetry to fiction. The title of his book is exemplary here: in fiction as in poetry, there is a tradition of mature, serious, and complex writing which makes for greatness. The tradition is formal, in the sense that forms are modes of exploring life, but its writers chiefly show "a vital capacity for experience, a kind of reverent openness before life, and a marked moral intensity." In Leavis' view these writers, in the field of the English novel, are Jane Austen, George Eliot, Henry James, Joseph Conrad— and D. H. Lawrence. Lawrence is not discussed in *The Great Tradition*, except as a capstone for the opening chapter. But by 1950 Leavis had begun to write those essays, published in *Scrutiny* and later gathered into book form, which largely induced the Lawrence revival.

In establishing his private tradition, Leavis employed tactics of exclusion and comparative evaluation learned from Eliot; but his inclusions derived from an essentially Protestant morality which Eliot had opposed. Leavis' tradition was characterized by vigorous moral individualism, not by reliance on external guides. His divergence from Eliot was nowhere so apparent as with Lawrence, whom he defended from Eliot's charges with polemical fervor. Eliot himself, in a later recantation, had modified those charges but, as Leavis rightly saw, he still considered Lawrence an example of "the crippling effect upon men of letters of not having been brought up in the environment of a living and central tradition." As a bona fide Englishman, Leavis now charged Eliot with ignorance of English culture. Far from being uneducated and untrained, he argued, Lawrence had led "an extraordinarily active intellectual life" among youthful friends; he had read widely and had made the most of later training at Nottingham University. As for "vague hymn-singing pietism," which Eliot had deplored, Leavis cited the "strong intellectual tradition" among Congregationalists, their stimulation of strenuous inquiry and moral seriousness, which Lawrence had transposed to his work. Thus, against Eliot's orthodoxy and urban gentility, Leavis cited "heretic" vitality and provincial vigor. By New Critical polemics he placed Law-

rence in the "great tradition" of intelligent moral sensibilities from
Austen through Conrad—a tradition, paradoxically, of individualistic
moralists. We have only just begun to gauge the effect of that grouping
upon young English redbrick scholars, for whom Leavis and Lawrence
are culture heroes.

The Lawrence essays in *Scrutiny* were part of a series Leavis called
"The Novel as Dramatic Poem." The New Critical tactic here is obvious:
all literature is seen as poetry, or read as if it were poetry, often at the
expense of genre characteristics. There is much to be said against the
practice, but for Leavis there were immediate advantages. His guiding
simile, the novel as dramatic poem, allowed him to examine fiction with
the care and "scrutiny" which he brought to poetry: to quote and analyze
long passages, to demonstrate the operative function of ideas, and to
develop symbolic and experiential patterns. Then, too, by insisting on
the dramatic nature of such fiction, he could keep fidelity with rendered
life and temporal progression and avoid excessive symbol-hunting.

Later critics, notably William York Tindall, Eliseo Vivas and Angelo
Bertocci, would treat Lawrence's symbols as implicative networks in the
symboliste tradition, and so freeze the novels into intellectual patterns or
"symbolic poems." Although Lawrence clearly works through implication, his chief mode of progression is dramatic, and symbols merely
integrate and focus that progression. Leavis' simile is more apt, and more
likely to promote the kind of formal study Lawrence needs, given his
fluid sense of relatedness and change. With his lone aesthetic guide,
Leavis has been sensitive to such distinctions and has done exemplary
work within their limits. His long interpretations of *The Rainbow* and
Women in Love remain definitive; his readings of *The Captain's Doll,
St. Mawr,* and "Daughters of the Vicar" and his discriminating work with
other tales have helped to establish something like a Lawrence canon.
He has been instrumental, in fact, in another New Critical process: the
creation of new hierarchies of accepted texts. Largely through Leavis'
efforts, *Women in Love* and *The Rainbow* are now recognized as Lawrence's greatest novels; *Sons and Lovers* has slipped to third place, *Lady
Chatterley* to fourth, and *The Plumed Serpent* makes a dubious fifth
(Leavis himself dislikes the last two novels); then come the longer tales
—*The Captain's Doll, The Fox, St. Mawr, The Man Who Died, The
Virgin and the Gypsy*—in what constitutes an impressive body of major
fiction. The exclusion here of weaker novels, and the inclusion of more
integral achievements, begins with Leavis' essays.

Most important of all, Leavis brought to the novels his amazing
powers of critical penetration. His readings are, for the most part, extraordinarily persuasive; they illuminate meaning and order where previous
readers found impenetrable chaos. In *Women in Love,* for instance, Leavis
demonstrates an integrative intelligence in Lawrence, and a place for
intelligence per se, which few critics had allowed. Its critique of the mind

which tries to dominate and exploit life-sources, as opposed to the mind used instrumentally to define and abet conditions for organic life, was first explained by Leavis. It was Leavis too who replaced the erroneous label, "religion of sex," with "full spontaneous being" as Lawrence's chief concern. But his clarification of Lawrence's concepts needs no documentation: what is often missed is his demonstration of their dramatic function in context, his convincing account of the integration of cultural and psychological conflicts by a novelist once dismissed as hopelessly abstruse and foggy. Time and familiarity alone might have clarified concepts: but the contextual approach to ideas has revealed, more profoundly, the power and force of a major creative intelligence. Finally, Leavis has shown the richness of rendered life in Lawrence, the normative value of his dramatized distinctions, his neglected powers of characterization, the vitality of wit in his shorter tales, and other attributes denied or submerged by early detractors. With characteristic firmness, he has judged and discarded works which fail to meet his exacting standards. We may quarrel with his exactions, we may question his inclusions and exclusions, we may deplore his ardors and recriminations: but Leavis remains, for all that, the ablest of Lawrence critics and the chief progenitor of his revival.

The American scholar, Harry T. Moore, has also helped to promote that revival. Moore's contribution is not primarily critical; but his indefatigable industry, uncommon sense, and temperate judgment have served critical goals. In the doldrum Forties, Moore spoke of Lawrence as "The Great Unread" and raised the forlorn cry, "Why Not Read Lawrence Too?" His belief that Lawrence should be *read,* that his works provide "one of the richest reading experiences of our time," suggests the nature of his service. In 1951 Moore published *The Life and Works of D. H. Lawrence,* a critical biography which subordinated "life" to "works," and which made "the fullest survey yet . . . of Lawrence's writings." Moore brought to his task an incomparable advantage: he had never met the author, had no memories to record, no personal stake in possessing or effacing him. His ability to take in stride his aberrations and follies, and to measure them against compensatory charms, was cleansing and corrective. That same ability, applied to the whole sweep of Lawrence's works, placed them in perspective for other critics. The biographical advance has culminated, in recent years, with Edward Nehls' three volumes of memorial perspectives, *D. H. Lawrence: A Composite Biography* (1957-59). Nehls achieves a check-and-balance effect through shifting points of view; he arranges brief memoirs as lenses on the author's life, or as multiple perspectives through which Lawrence becomes rounder, deeper, more complex. No longer the flat, fixed victim of the single memorial, Lawrence emerges as a many-sided genius, growing, changing, lapsing, and reviving—an emergence which begins, in effect, with Moore's biography. By the same token, Moore's critical work has fostered further study. Graham Hough's comprehensive survey, *The Dark Sun* (1956), owes much to Moore's example; and other critics have profited from his balanced readings. Perceptive as well as balanced, Moore was the first to connect *The Rainbow* and *Women in Love* with *symbolisme* as an enriching technique. His chief contribution consists, however, in his amazing output of useful texts for Lawrence scholars: *D. H. Lawrence's Letters to Bertrand Russell* (1948); *The Life and Works* (1951); a group of Lawrence's essays, called *Sex, Literature and Censorship* (1953); a second biography, *The Intelligent Heart* (1954), with new material on Lawrence's youth; *Poste Restante: A Lawrence Travel Calendar* (1956); two anthologies of critical essays on Lawrence, *The Achievement of D. H. Lawrence* (1953) with Frederick Hoffman, and *A D. H. Lawrence Miscellany* (1959); and finally *The Collected Letters* (1962) in two volumes.

II

Through the ministrations, then, of a great critic and an industrious scholar, the Lawrence revival has gathered force. Its New Critical aspects can be seen in the kind of morally-committed formalism it fosters. Mark Schorer provides an important case in point. In his famous essay, "Technique as Discovery" (1948), Schorer attacked Lawrence for failing to allow technique to fathom meaning in *Sons and Lovers,* for using it instead in confused and contradictory ways, in his private attempt to master sickness. Yet, in an introduction to that novel (1951), he modified these charges and arrived at friendlier judgments. By 1953 he had become absorbed with Lawrence's formal problems, not as attempts to master sickness which somehow failed, but as attempts to extend the novel to encompass new material which tested (and perhaps shattered) its dimensions—material, moreover, of tremendous moral consequence. Writing of *Women in Love,* Schorer says:

> The intention . . . is so tremendous, so central to our lives, that we must for our own sakes make an effort to tolerate it. I say tolerate for the reason that I have known almost no readers who, on *first* reading, did not find it either opaque beyond endurance, or tiresome, or revolting. This has been the response even of readers who can agree with Lawrence when he in effect equates plot as we have known it with a morality that has lost its relevance [for the modern novelist], even its reality. Yet is it not the fact that the reason the novel is difficult to judge is that it will not accept the disciplines of plot but does not quite find some new limitation that will *contain* this material, so that we are repeatedly asked to love Lawrence the man in order to accept Lawrence the novelist? . . . And the question is whether a novelist has the right to impose himself to this extent on his reader, even when his reader is eager to accept as much as he can, even when his reader, like the

present writer, cannot, after eight or ten readings of this novel, imagine being without it. It is possible that *Women in Love* attempts to do more than the novel as we know it and even as Lawrence developed it itself knows how to do. This does not for a moment mean that the attempt must not be made. No novelist speaks more directly to us than Lawrence, and if we can't hear him, we are, I quite believe, lost.

Here Schorer has moved considerably beyond the puristic formalism of "Technique as Discovery." He is still preoccupied with generic problems ("the question is: What is a novel?"); but his own commitment to the novel's intention, its morally significant matter, allows him to tolerate flaws, to value partial success, to insist that the attempt to contain such matter must be made. He seems aware, moreover, that much of the novel's inaccessibility lies in its newness, its strangeness, its educative burden in providing readers with new grounds for aesthetic judgment. He delineates himself the new conception of "character as fate" in the novel, the new structure of "fluid, dance-like movement," the new theme of integration and disintegration of being which suits that structure, and the incantatory prose which makes for visionary effects. Granting the general strength of these developments, he questions *only* the integration theme, which moves away from social reality toward purely psychic drama. The disintegration theme, which stays in social context, is more effective, he believes, since the genre normally deals with individuals in that context. Indeed, he grants to the rendering of that theme "the real Russian bang," forgetting how much that bang depends upon "dance-like" contrast with the integration theme, whatever its social texture. We can agree with Schorer that Birkin, the integrated hero, is less successfully characterized than death-directed Gerald Crich (though scarcely blanched into sainthood, as Schorer later holds); but without the psychic drama of Birkin's integration, Gerald's life and death would lose immeasurably in significance. Schorer's curious lapse on this point may be traced, I think, to our modern skittishness before prophetic quests. His sense of commitment has its limits, and he retreats for the moment toward generic purism; but by 1959, in his Introduction to the famous Grove edition of *Lady Chatterley's Lover,* he seems more confident of his ground. He agrees with Father Tiverton (Martin Jarrett-Kerr), an English critic who connects Lawrence with Christian thought, that Lawrence had "reached the point in imaginative being at which the preacher and the poet coincide, since the poem is the sermon." "The *whole* poem," adds Schorer, "or the *whole* story, or the *whole* novel, not any set of extractable words or scenes that exist only as a portion of those wholes. This primary axiom of all reading and all criticism applies nowhere more drastically than to *Lady Chatterley's Lover.*" Schorer's commitment to this novel is based on its combination of "a solid and sustained social context" with "a clear and happily developed plot" and pervasive symbolism, by which the

novel itself "finally forms one great symbol." Within these more or less
conventional generic lines, he finds his own version of moral formalism.

In *The English Novel: Form and Function* (1953), Dorothy Van Ghent
provides a similar instance of hesitations and commitments. She begins
that volume with a credo on "the critical approach to literature as a
search for the principle of form in the work and implicitly as a search
for form in the self." Given that humane view of formalism, she is
troubled at first by Lawrence's apparent neglect of formal niceties. "D. H.
Lawrence's sensitivity to twentieth century chaos was peculiarly intense,"
she writes, "and his passion for order was similarly intense; but this
sensitivity and this passion did not lead him to concentrate on refinements and subtleties of novelistic technique in the direction laid out, for
instance, by James and Conrad." She implies, however, that Lawrence
eludes this art tradition and finds his own techniques for exploring vital
problems: "We need to approach Lawrence with a good deal of humility
about 'art,' and a good deal of patience for the disappointments he
frequently offers as an artist, for it is only thus that we shall be able to
appreciate the innovations he actually made in the novel as well as the
importance and profundity of his vision of modern life." Here, certainly, there is an abandonment of puristic qualms and a willingness to
explore imperfect triumphs in a new aesthetic vein. The novel in question is *Sons and Lovers*. She examines it, not in Freudian terms, but
through the Lawrencean idea of "an organic disturbance in the relationships of men and women . . . first seen in the disaffection of mother and
father, then in the mother's attempt to substitute her sons for her husband, finally in the sons' unsuccessful struggle to establish natural manhood." Such transgressions against "the natural life-directed condition
of the human animal" lead to twisted desires to "possess" other persons,
to violate their natural integrity, their "otherness" of being or separate
selfhood—an offense which Lawrence sees "as a disease of modern life in
all its manifestations." In the novel itself, says Miss Van Ghent, the disease is probed through new (and apparently "adequate") techniques.
Beyond conventional narrative logic, there is the book's poetic logic, its
extensively developed imagery, which replaces episode and discursive
analysis and assumes their expressive function; it does so, she asserts,
because Lawrence must make us sensitively aware of vital individuality
in things or people—or, to apply her own credo, because his "principle
of form" must convey his sense of the normative forms of selfhood. His
concrete imagery is an expression, then, of "his vision of life as infinitely
creative of individual identities, each whole and separate and to be
reverenced as such." That vision illuminates all major relations and
events, and points through these toward such modern betrayals as "possessorship" and death-worship. Miss Van Ghent believes that the novel
itself concludes with the modern death-drift (though the text shows
otherwise); yet, along with Stephen Spender, she finds Lawrence "the

most hopeful modern writer, because he looks beyond the human to the nonhuman, which can be discovered within the human." By foregoing formal niceties and Freudian expectations, by relating form instead to Lawrence's assumptions, Miss Van Ghent discovers what other critics often overlook: as early as *Sons and Lovers* Lawrence was using new techniques to fathom meanings of enormous consequence.

To younger critics those meanings have appealed with something like refreshing force. Young Leavisites in England like Martin Green (*A Mirror for Anglo-Saxons*, 1960) and Raymond Williams (*Culture and Society*, 1958), oppose genteel sterility and industrial pressures with Lawrencean virtues, such as "decency" and "close spontaneous living," which they trace to his working class origins. Their approach coincides, significantly, with that of emerging writer-spokesmen for lower and lower-middle class vitality, like Amis, Braine, and Sillitoe. Young American critics, raised on puristic formalism, now turn to Lawrence in their attempts to go beyond it. Thus Richard Foster, in a virtual call to critical arms, finds Lawrence's "fierce integrity" as a critic exemplary, "because in our time critics characteristically choose or are taught to be less than he is: a man alive who illuminates literature in an infinity of directions with his powerful vision of its moral relationship to all our human experience." This dissatisfaction with puristic limitations helps to explain why Marvin Mudrick finds *The Rainbow* original, not on formal grounds, but as "the first English novel to record the normality and significance of physical passion," and "the only English novel to record . . . the social revolution whereby Western man lost his sense of community"; or why Julian Moynahan acclaims "the deed of life" in *Lady Chatterley's Lover*, the exploration of vital possibilities, as opposed to cerebral and abstract perspectives; or why the young American poet, W. D. Snodgrass, moves from "symbol" and "pattern" in "The Rocking-Horse Winner" to "the Way to Live." Finally, there is my own book, *The Love Ethic of D. H. Lawrence* (1955), the first official thesis to emerge from that New Critical (though eclectic) outpost, the Indiana School of Letters, and thus a sign of changing times.

My intention, in that book, was to illuminate the Lawrencean idea of responsibility for the quality of one's being, and for its development through love, friendship, and creative labor. I held that in five important novels—*Sons and Lovers, The Rainbow, Women in Love, Lady Chatterley's Lover* and *The Man Who Died*—Lawrence had developed a concrete vision of experience with normative value for his readers; that he had tried to set forth the conditions of manhood, womanhood, and marriage as they make for individual and, in the case of *The Man Who Died*, for social regeneration; that the attempt was decidedly artistic, but in the vein of prophetic art which enables us to grasp new moral possibilities. I would agree, then, with Harry Moore, that Lawrence is most successful when his prophetic side "is best realized in the expressional."

My position may be compared with that of an older critic, Eliseo Vivas, a late convert to New Criticism who seems both attracted and repelled by the notion of prophetic art. In *D. H. Lawrence: The Failure and the Triumph of Art* (1960) Vivas argues for an essentially negative Lawrence, who "charts our world" in two or three symbolic novels which present (beyond paraphrase) "the specific process of disintegration of which we are the victims." Since these novels are conceived by Vivas as "constitutive symbols"—symbolic forms through which we grasp the world—our positions differ chiefly with respect to positive and negative stress on values and dramatic and symbolic stress on forms. Vivas tends to efface or neutralize every positive value in Lawrence, and to accept him only as a maker of wasteland novels. In *Women in Love*, for instance, Vivas negates *Blutbrüderschaft* as homosexuality, throws out the love of Birkin and Ursula as the novel's norm, and, like Schorer, settles for the deathward drift in Gerald Crich as the novel's great achievement. Yet again I would insist that the "drift" acquires its force from its alternatives. If Lawrence makes an impressive indictment of the modern wasteland, he does so through his engagement with neglected values or new possibilities of value, like *Blutbrüderschaft* and "star-equilibrium." His novels test and explore such values, submit them to the qualifying purge of concrete situations, substantiate them in the double sense of giving them substance and of proving them against complex experience. We cannot separate his indictments from these provings: they are integral to his peculiarly prophetic art and, from my own point of view, the real source of his vitality and importance. Though elsewhere in his book Vivas isolates and accepts such value-possibilities, he rejects their textual integration, their informing role in "constitutive symbols" through which we grasp the modern wasteland. A strict New Critic, his fear of prophetic quests seems to subvert even the affirmations allowed by his negative approach. On the whole, our younger critics seem less morally hamstrung.

III

The revival which I have been describing has largely concentrated on the novels—has indeed been generated by recovery of the novels—as Lawrence's chief *métier*. And here the title of Leavis' collected essays, *D. H. Lawrence: Novelist* (1955), seems definitive. In the meantime, the tales and longer stories have failed to attract distinctive criticism, except from Leavis and (less evenly) Graham Hough, who treat them as subordinate triumphs. But to subordinate the tales is itself significant. Writing in 1942, H. E. Bates made this prediction: "Later generations will react to the novels of Lawrence much as we now react to the novels of Hardy. The philosophical rumblings will date; the wonderful pictures, the life directly projected, will remain. From such a test the short stories will emerge as the more durable achievement."

The prediction still seems premature. The emergence of moral formalism has made the novels, imperfect as they often are, seem more durable and important than more perfectly finished tales. How much rendered life can a story offer, say "The Prussian Officer" or "The Blind Man," compared with novels like *The Rainbow* or like *Women in Love*, whose "intention is so tremendous, so central to our lives," says Schorer, that we must learn to tolerate their flaws? We can agree with Leavis when he calls the tales a body of creative work which would alone insure greatness. But we must agree too with Hough that they are byproducts of the novels—not the "growing points" of Lawrence's fiction, but surplus creations, more compact and fully realized than the novels, less preachy and repetitious. Yet, as Hough points out, "simply to prefer them probably implies some reduction in the importance of Lawrence as a whole." Certainly those who prefer them have failed to produce distinctive criticism, and may continue to fail, unless they are willing to consider those "philosophic rumblings" in the novels, and the techniques employed to insure their integration, as they relate to creation of the tales. Yet the tales can lead to provocative conclusions. The poet Snodgrass treats the financial, social, and sexual implications of the rocking-horse symbol, as it applies to modern modes of self-enclosure and vicarious life, with refreshing vigor. By relating the tale to Lawrence's essays and letters (themselves byproducts or forerunners of the novels), he arrives at principles of self-development and reciprocity which are denied the young rider by his money-obsessed mother. Though Snodgrass tends to force the meshing of his materials, and to impose a pattern of ironies which may not exist, he deserves credit for establishing the psychological base (in onanism) for "mechanical riding" in the tale, and for discussing in moral terms (terms of self-development and emotional growth) a modern maladjustment with far-reaching implications. Unlike most symbol-hunters, he is willing to pursue and expound such matters for their normative value.

Many recent critics of Lawrence have shifted their attention to his poetry. Taking Blackmur's attack as their point of departure, these critics either defend "expressive form" as a poetic mode or show that Lawrence goes beyond it. Expressive form, says Blackmur, is directly communicated feeling, unmediated by form; it springs from the belief "that if a thing is only intensely enough felt its mere expression in words will give it satisfactory form." For English critics like A. Alvarez and V. de S. Pinto, however, expressive form in Lawrence transcends the level of personal outburst and requires "instinctive" craftsmanship. Pinto places it in the romantic tradition of "organic form," by which poems are shaped from within so as to capture living moments of experience rather than perfected bygone moments or static moments in futurity. Three American critics, Karl Shapiro, Bernice Slote, and James E. Miller, Jr., have pro-

posed an extreme version of this "heretic" tradition, one which begins
with Whitman and includes Lawrence, Dylan Thomas, and Hart Crane
as its modern exponents, and which rivals the dominant modern school
of Eliot and Pound. Yet Crane and Thomas are tainted by the cerebral
tactics and formal restraints of the dominant school; and, as other critics
have shown, Lawrence himself uses wit, irony, intelligence, and rational
imagination in his poetry. The game of new traditions apparently has its
hazards, but also its rewards, if we can accept the break with Blackmur's
views as final. Adopting a middle ground, Graham Hough retains those
views but holds that "something impressive remains" in Lawrence's
poetry which eludes them. That something can be found, he says, by reading Lawrence's poetry as a whole, as "work poetically felt and conceived,
whose individual units rarely reach perfection or self-subsistence," but
whose honest, poignant, and powerfully expressive fragments can be sal-
vaged. Reading the poems in this way, he recovers wholes as well as parts,
affirms their value as creative insights, and grants them final justification
"as successive stages in the building of [the poet's] ship of death."

Hough's method testifies to the willingness of many recent critics to
accept and appraise imperfect triumphs, to measure form by its moral
function, and to relate literature organically to life. Here the latent
moralism, the covert humanism of early formalists, becomes manifest,
drawn forth perhaps by Lawrence's fierce engagement with wasteland culture, his urgent sense of the modern death-drift, and his creative attempts
to transcend it. In the abundant thoughtless Twenties, his urgency
seemed exorbitant. In the crisis-ridden Sixties, we find it more commensurate with reality. As Neil Myers notes, Lawrence's rage against modern
dehumanization derives from a vision of what has since emerged "in the
corruption of slayer and slain at Auschwitz and Hiroshima." More than
any other modern novelist, he indicts our degradations, tests and explores
alternative values, arrives at normative possibilities. Critics today are exploring his novels, tales, and poems, and beyond that, his plays, criticism,
letters, travel books—even his philosophical excursions—so as to comprehend his moral vision of the age. If, as Vivas holds, that vision enables us
to grasp "the specific process of disintegration of which we are the victims," it may also help us, individually if not collectively, to reverse that
process. The moral formalists, those who have rescued Lawrence from
comparative oblivion, suggest that it will. More important, the works
themselves suggest it through images of quickness, aloneness, wholeness,
balance, tenderness, communion, resurrection and restoration—through
images, that is, of promise.

IV

The essays in this volume chiefly represent the moral-formalist trend
which I have noted. All are from the last decade; eight are by younger

critics. Without question the best criticism on Lawrence appears within that period, much of it by younger men influenced by Leavis, or schooled in the New Criticism and pushing onward. A fuller sample of Lawrence criticism might prove less rewarding. During his lifetime there was little intelligent recognition. In the Thirties, Aldous Huxley, Francis Fergusson, Max Wildi, Horace Gregory, and others wrote perceptive essays, but their work was lost in the destructive hassle over Lawrence's bones; in any case, it scarcely constitutes a ripe or deeply unified approach. The Forties were decidedly quiescent. Then, a quarter century after his death, when his life and ideology were assimilated, Lawrence emerged as a major English novelist. Today his hostile critics (Anthony West, Katherine Anne Porter, assorted censors, new Freudians and old formalists) repeat the hassles of the Thirties in a minor key: the breakthrough has been made in criticism and biography, and Lawrence seems likely to remain a great prophetic artist.

He is, of course, a problematic artist, driven by strong beliefs on sex, religion, and politics, hence likely to attract indiscriminate hostility or praise. Yet his severest and most clinical admirers (e.g., Diana Trilling) fail to do him justice. By elaborating and maximizing faults they freeze and minimize his virtues. What Lawrence needs, and what he receives from most of the contributors to this volume, is intelligently sympathetic criticism which concentrates on his achievements without blinking at his faults, and which is formally imaginative and acute yet amenable to the prophetic possibilities of art. Marvin Mudrick and Julian Moynahan seem exemplary here, in their essays on *The Rainbow* and *Lady Chatterley's Lover* in the section on major novels. Mark Schorer on *Women in Love,* Dorothy Van Ghent on *Sons and Lovers,* exhibit the hesitant commitments of older formalists. Harry T. Moore, writing on *The Plumed Serpent,* places that still unplaced creation in thematic perspective and defines its failure with characteristic saneness. As with all other critics, its imaginative force eludes him: he attributes it to Lawrence's descriptive powers, as distinct from his objectionable beliefs, though it seems to me the descriptions invoke one set of beliefs (cosmic and religious) which fail to jibe with others (political and programmatic). In the section on the tales, Graham Hough discerns a more effective fusion of religious and programmatic beliefs in *The Man Who Died*—"an allegory of the course of Christian civilization" in which the old dispensation dies and the new emerges from its ashes. A sense of cultural continuity persists here which *The Plumed Serpent* lacks. In still other essays, Monroe Engel makes an interesting case for formal continuity in the short novels, which first appear when the longer novels falter; W. D. Snodgrass explores the moral implications of the rocking-horse symbol; and, as an antidote to symbolic, mythic, and poetic definitions of Lawrencean structure, I present my own definition of ritual or emotional form in "The Blind Man."

The section on other genres includes Vivian de Sola Pinto's defense of

Lawrence's poetry, Richard Foster's appraisal of Lawrence's morally-engaged criticism, Arthur Waterman's analysis of Lawrence's plays (which were apparently used as testing-grounds for variant ideas) and Raymond Williams' view of the social writings. This section might be expanded, if space permitted, to include criticism of the letters, travel books, and "pollyanalytics" on psychology and cosmology. Ideally, a fourth section might be added on controversial issues: censorship, fascism, *Blutbrüder-schaft*, phallic vs. romantic marriage. But Lawrence's versatility (there are forty books in seven genres) and iconoclasm per se seem less relevant now than his prophetic fiction, to which I have given fullest weight. Most conspicuously missing from this volume is, finally, F. R. Leavis, whose refusal to contribute leaves this critical *Hamlet* without its Prince: yet, for better or worse, his spirit haunts the whole anthology.

On *Sons and Lovers*

by Dorothy Van Ghent

Novels, like other dramatic art, deal with conflicts of one kind or another—conflicts that are, in the work of the major novelists, drawn from life in the sense that they are representative of real problems in life; and the usual urgency in the novelist is to find the technical means which will afford an ideal resolution of the conflict and solution of the living problem—still "ideal" even if tragic. Technique is his art itself, in its procedural aspect; and the validity of his solution of a problem is dependent upon the adequacy of his technique. The more complex and intransigent the problem, the more subtle his technical strategies will evidently need to be, if they are to be effective. The decade of World War I brought into full and terrible view the collapse of values that had prophetically haunted the minds of novelists as far back as Dostoevsky and Flaubert and Dickens, or even farther back, to Balzac and Stendhal. With that decade, and increasingly since, the problems of modern life have appeared intransigent indeed; and, in general, the growth of that intransigence has been reflected in an increasing concern with technique on the part of the artist. D. H. Lawrence's sensitivity to twentieth century chaos was peculiarly intense, and his passion for order was similarly intense; but this sensitivity and this passion did not lead him to concentrate on refinements and subtleties of novelistic technique in the direction laid out, for instance, by James and Conrad. Hence, as readers first approaching his work, almost inevitably we feel disappointment and even perhaps shock that writing so often "loose" and repetitious and such unrestrained emotionalism over glandular matters should appear in the work of a novelist who is assumed to have an important place in the literary canon. "There is no use," Francis Fergusson says, "trying to appreciate [Lawrence] solely as an artist; he was himself too often impatient of the demands of art, which seemed to him trivial compared with the quest he followed." [1] And Stephen Spender phrases the problem of Lawrence in

[1] "D. H. Lawrence's Sensibility," in *Critiques and Essays in Modern Fiction*, edited by John W. Aldridge (New York: The Ronald Press Company, 1952), p. 328.

this way: what interested him "was the tension between art and life, not the complete resolution of the problems of life within the illusion of art. . . . For him literature is a kind of pointer to what is outside literature. . . . This outsideness of reality is for Lawrence the waters of baptism in which man can be reborn." [2] We need to approach Lawrence with a good deal of humility about "art" and a good deal of patience for the disappointments he frequently offers as an artist, for it is only thus that we shall be able to appreciate the innovations he actually made in the novel as well as the importance and profundity of his vision of modern life.

⌊*Sons and Lovers* appears to have the most conventional chronological organization; it is the kind of organization that a naïve autobiographical novelist would tend to use, with only the thinnest pretense at disguising the personally retrospective nature of the material.⌉We start with the marriage of the parents and the birth of the children. We learn of the daily life of the family while the children are growing up, the work, the small joys, the parental strife. ⌊Certain well-defined emotional pressures become apparent: the children are alienated from their father, whose personality degenerates gradually as he feels his exclusion; the mother more and more completely dominates her sons' affections, aspirations, mental habits. Urged by her toward middle-class refinements, they enter white-collar jobs, thus making one more dissociation between themselves and their proletarian father. As they attempt to orient themselves toward biological adulthood, the old split in the family is manifested in a new form, as an internal schism in the characters of the sons; they cannot reconcile sexual choice with the idealism their mother has inculcated. This inner strain leads to the older son's death. The same motif is repeated in the case of Paul, the younger one.⌉Paul's first girl, Miriam, is a cerebral type, and the mother senses in her an obvious rivalry for domination of Paul's sensibility. The mother is the stronger influence, and Paul withdraws from Miriam; but with her own victory Mrs. Morel begins to realize the discord she has produced in his character, and tries to release her hold on him by unconsciously seeking her own death. Paul finds another girl, Clara, but the damage is already too deeply designed, and at the time of his mother's death he voluntarily gives up Clara, knowing that there is but one direction he can take, and that is to go with his mother. At the end he is left emotionally derelict, with only the "drift toward death."

⌊From this slight sketch, it is clear that the book is organized not merely on a chronological plan showing the habits and vicissitudes of a Nottinghamshire miner's family, but that it has a structure rigorously controlled by an idea: an idea of an organic disturbance in the relationships of men

[2] "The Life of Literature," in *Partisan Review,* December, 1948.

and women—a disturbance of sexual polarities that is first seen in the
disaffection of mother and father, then in the mother's attempt to substitute her sons for her husband, finally in the sons' unsuccessful struggle to
establish natural manhood. Lawrence's development of the idea has certain major implications: it implies that his characters have transgressed
against the natural life-directed condition of the human animal—against
the elementary biological rhythms he shares with the rest of biological
nature; and it implies that this offense against life has been brought
about by a failure to respect the complete and terminal individuality of
persons—by a twisted desire to "possess" other persons, as the mother tries
to "possess" her husband, then her sons, and as Miriam tries to "possess"
Paul. Lawrence saw this offense as a disease of modern life in all its manifestations, from sexual relationships to those broad social and political
relationships that have changed people from individuals to anonymous
economic properties or to military units or to ideological automations.

The controlling idea is expressed in the various episodes—the narrative logic of the book. It is also expressed in imagery—the book's poetic
logic. Perhaps in no other novelist do we find the image so largely
replacing episode and discursive analysis, and taking over the expressive
functions of these, as it does in Lawrence. The chief reason for the extraordinary predominance of the image as an absolute expressive medium
in Lawrence lies in the character of the idea which is his subject. He
must make us aware—sensitively aware, not merely conceptually aware—
of the profound life force whose rhythms the natural creature obeys; and
he must make us aware of the terminal individuality—the absolute
"otherness" or "outsideness"—that is the natural form of things and of
the uncorrupted person. We must be made aware of these through the
feelings of his people, for only in feeling have the biological life force and
the sense of identity—either the identity of self or of others—any immediacy of reality. He seeks the objective equivalent of feeling in the image.
As Francis Fergusson says, Lawrence's imagination was so concrete that he
seems not "to distinguish between the reality and the metaphor or symbol
which makes it plain to us." [3] But the most valid symbols are the most
concrete realities. Lawrence's great gift for the symbolic image was a function of his sensitivity to and passion for the meaning of real things—for
the individual expression that real forms have. In other words, his gift
for the image arose directly from his vision of life as infinitely creative of
individual identities, each whole and separate and to be reverenced as
such.

Let us examine the passage with which the first chapter of *Sons and
Lovers* ends—where Mrs. Morel, pregnant with Paul, wanders deliriously
in the garden, shut out of the house by Morel in his drunkenness. Mrs.

[3] Fergusson, *op. cit.*, p. 335.

Morel is literally a vessel of the life force that seems to thrust itself at
her in nature from all sides, but she is also in rebellion against it and the
perfume of the pollen-filled lilies makes her gasp with fear:

> The moon was high and magnificent in the August night. Mrs. Morel,
> seared with passion, shivered to find herself out there in a great white light,
> that fell cold on her, and gave a shock to her inflamed soul. She stood for a
> few moments helplessly staring at the glistening great rhubarb leaves near
> the door. Then she got the air into her breast. She walked down the garden
> path, trembling in every limb, while the child boiled within her. . . .
>
> She hurried out of the side garden to the front, where she could stand as
> if in an immense gulf of white light, the moon streaming high in face of
> her, the moonlight standing up from the hills in front, and filling the valley
> where the Bottoms crouched, almost blindingly. There, panting and half
> weeping in reaction from the stress, she murmured to herself over and over
> again: "The nuisance! the nuisance!"
>
> She became aware of something about her. With an effort she roused her-
> self to see what it was that penetrated her consciousness. The tall white lilies
> were reeling in the moonlight, and the air was charged with their perfume,
> as with a presence. Mrs. Morel gasped slightly in fear. She touched the big,
> pallid flowers on their petals, then shivered. They seemed to be stretching
> in the moonlight. She put her hand into one white bin: the gold scarcely
> showed on her fingers by moonlight. She bent down to look at the binful
> of yellow pollen; but it only appeared dusky. Then she drank a deep
> draught of the scent. It almost made her dizzy.
>
> Mrs. Morel leaned on the garden gate, looking out, and she lost herself
> awhile. She did not know what she thought. Except for a slight feeling of
> sickness, and her consciousness in the child, herself melted out like a
> scent into the shiny, pale air.

She finally arouses Morel from his drunken sleep and he lets her in. Un-
fastening her brooch at the bedroom mirror, she sees that her face is
smeared with the yellow dust of the lilies.

The imagery of the streaming moonlight is that of a vast torrential
force, "magnificent" and inhuman, and it equates not only with that
phallic power of which Mrs. Morel is the rebellious vessel but with the
greater and universal demiurge that was anciently called Eros—the power
springing in plants and hurling the planets, giving the "glistening great
rhubarb leaves" their fierce identity, fecundating and stretching the lilies.
The smear of yellow pollen on Mrs. Morel's face is a grossly humorous
irony. This passage is a typifying instance of the spontaneous identification Lawrence constantly found between image and meaning, between
real things and what they symbolize.

Our particular culture has evolved deep prohibitions against the expression, or even the subjective acknowledgment of the kind of phallic
reality with which Lawrence was concerned—and with which ancient
religions were also concerned. Certainly one factor in the uneasiness that

Lawrence frequently causes us is the factor of those cultural prohibitions.
But these prohibitions themselves Lawrence saw as disease symptoms,
though the disease was far more extensive and radical than a taboo on the
phallus. It was a spiritual disease that broke down the sense of identity,
of "separate selfhood," while at the same time it broke down the sense of
rhythm with universal nature. Paul Morel, working his fairly unconscious, adolescent, sexual way toward Miriam, finds that rhythm and that
selfhood in the spatial proportions of a wren's nest in a hedge:

> He crouched down and carefully put his finger through the thorns into
> the round door of the nest.
> "It's almost as if you were feeling inside the live body of the bird,"
> he said, "it's so warm. They say a bird makes its nest round like a cup with
> pressing its breast on it. Then how did it make the ceiling round, I
> wonder?"

When Paul takes his first country walk with Clara and Miriam, the appearance of a red stallion in the woods vividly realizes in unforced symbolic dimension the power which will drive Paul from Miriam to Clara,
while the image also realizes the great horse itself in its unique and mysterious identity:

> As they were going beside the brook, on the Willey Water side, looking
> through the brake at the edge of the wood, where pink campions glowed
> under a few sunbeams, they saw, beyond the tree-trunks and the thin hazel
> bushes, a man leading a great bay horse through the gullies. The big red
> beast seemed to dance romantically through that dimness of green hazel
> drift, away there where the air was shadowy, as if it were in the past, among
> the fading bluebells that might have bloomed for Deirdre. . . .
> The great horse breathed heavily, shifting round its red flanks, and
> looking suspiciously with its wonderful big eyes upwards from under its
> lowered head and falling mane. . . .

A simple descriptive passage like the following, showing a hen pecking at
a girl's hand, conveys the animal dynamics that is the urgent phase of the
phallic power working in the boy and the girl, but its spontaneous symbolism of a larger reality is due to its faithfulness to the way a hen does
peck and the feeling of the pecking—due, that is, to the actuality or
"identity" of the small, homely circumstance itself:

> As he went round the back, he saw Miriam kneeling in front of the hen-
> coop, some maize in her hand, biting her lip, and crouching in an intense
> attitude. The hen was eyeing her wickedly. Very gingerly she put forward
> her hand. The hen bobbed for her. She drew back quickly with a cry, half
> of fear, half of chagrin.
> "It won't hurt you," said Paul.
> She flushed crimson and started up.

"I only wanted to try," she said in a low voice.

"See, it doesn't hurt," he said, and, putting only two corns in his palm, he let the hen peck, peck, peck at his bare hand. "It only makes you laugh," he said.

She put her hand forward, and dragged it away, tried again, and started back with a cry. He frowned.

"Why, I'd let her take corn from my face," said Paul, "only she bumps a bit. She's ever so neat. If she wasn't, look how much ground she'd peck up every day."

He waited grimly, and watched. At last Miriam let the bird peck from her hand. She gave a little cry—fear, and pain because of fear—rather pathetic. But she had done it, and she did it again.

"There, you see," said the boy. "It doesn't hurt, does it?"

There is more terse and obvious symbolism, of the kind typical in Lawrence, in that sequence where Clara's red carnations splatter their petals over her clothes and on the ground where she and Paul first make love, but we acquire the best and the controlling sense of Lawrence's gift for the image, as dramatic and thematic expression, in those passages where his urgency is to see *things* and to see them clearly and completely in their most individualizing traits, for the character of his vision is such that, in truly seeing them as they are, he sees through them to what they mean.

We frequently notice the differentiating significance of a writer's treatment of nature—that is, of that part of "nature" which is constituted by earth and air and water and the nonhuman creatures; and we find that attitudes toward nature are deeply associated with attitudes toward human "good," human destiny, human happiness, human salvation, the characteristic problems of being human. One might cite, for instance, in *Tom Jones,* Fielding's highly stylized treatment of outdoor nature (as in the passage in which Tom dreams of Sophia beside the brook, and Mollie Seagrim approaches): here nature has only generalized attributes for whose description and understanding certain epithets in common educated currency are completely adequate—brooks murmur, breezes whisper, birds trill; nature is really a linguistic construction, and this rationalization of nature is appropriate in Fielding's universe since everything there exists ideally as an object of *ratio,* of reasoning intelligence. We notice in Jane Austen's *Pride and Prejudice* (in the description of Darcy's estate, for example) that outdoor nature again has importance only as it serves to express rational and social character—wherefore again the generalized epithet that represents nature as either the servant of intelligence or the space where intelligence operates. In George Eliot's *Adam Bede,* where there is relatively a great deal of "outdoors," nature is man's plow-field, the acre in which he finds social and ethical expression through work; this is only a different variety of the conception of nature as significant by virtue of what man's intelligential and social character makes of it for his ends.

With Emily Brontë, we come nearer to Lawrence, though not very near. In *Wuthering Heights,* nature's importance is due not to its yielding itself up to domestication in man's reason, or offering itself as an instrument by which he expresses his conscience before God or society, but to its fiercely unregenerate difference from all that civilized man is—a difference that it constantly forces on perception by animal-like attacks on and disruptions of human order. In Hardy, nature is also a daemonic entity in its own right, and not only unrationalizable but specifically hostile to the human reason. It is worth noting that, among all English novelists, Hardy and Lawrence have the most faithful touch for the things of nature and the greatest evocative genius in bringing them before the imagination. But there are certain definitive differences of attitude. Both Emily Brontë's and Hardy's worlds are dual, and there is no way of bringing the oppositions of the dualism together: on the one side of the cleavage are those attributes of man that we call "human," his reason, his ethical sensibility; and on the other side is "nature"—the elements and the creatures and man's own instinctive life that he shares with the nonhuman creatures. The opposition is resolved only by destruction of the "human": a destruction that is in Emily Brontë profoundly attractive, in Hardy tragic. But Lawrence's world is multiple rather than dual. Everything in it is a separate and individual "other," every person, every creature, every object (like the madonna lilies, the rhubarb plants, the wren's nest, the stallion); and there is a creative relationship between people and between people and things so long as this "otherness" is acknowledged. When it is denied—and it is denied when man tries to rationalize nature and society, or when he presumptuously assumes the things of nature to be merely instruments for the expression of himself, or when he attempts to exercise personal possessorship over people—then he destroys his own selfhood and exerts a destructive influence all about him.

In *Sons and Lovers,* only in Morel himself, brutalized and spiritually maimed as he is, does the germ of selfhood remain intact; and—this is the correlative proposition in Lawrence—in him only does the biological life force have simple, unequivocal assertion. Morel wants to live, by hook or crook, while his sons want to die. To live is to obey a rhythm involving more than conscious attitudes and involving more than human beings—involving all nature; a rhythm indifferent to the greediness of reason, indifferent to idiosyncrasies of culture and idealism. The image associated with Morel is that of the coalpits, where he descends daily and from which he ascends at night blackened and tired. It is a symbol of rhythmic descent and ascent, like a sexual rhythm, or like the rhythm of sleep and awaking or of death and life. True, the work in the coalpits reverses the natural use of the hours of light and dark and is an economic distortion

of that rhythm in nature—and Morel and the other colliers bear the spiritual traumata of that distortion; for Lawrence is dealing with the real
environment of modern men, in its complexity and injuriousness. Nevertheless, the work at the pits is still symbolic of the greater rhythm governing life and obedience to which is salvation. Throughout the book, the
coalpits are always at the horizon:

> On the fallow land the young wheat shone silkily. Minton pit waved its
> plumes of white steam, coughed, and rattled hoarsely.
> "Now look at that!" said Mrs. Morel. Mother and son stood on the road
> to watch. Along the ridge of the great pit-hill crawled a little group in
> silhouette against the sky, a horse, a small truck, and a man. They climbed
> the incline against the heavens. At the end the man tipped the waggon.
> There was an undue rattle as the waste fell down the sheer slope of the
> enormous bank. . . .
> "Look how it heaps together," [Paul says of the pit] "like something
> alive almost—a big creature that you don't know. . . . And all the trucks
> standing waiting, like a string of beasts to be fed. . . . I like the feel of
> *men* on things, while they're alive. There's a feel of men about trucks,
> because they've been handled with men's hands, all of them."

Paul associates the pits not only with virility but with being alive. The
trucks themselves become alive because they have been handled by men.
The symbolism of the pits is identical with that of Morel, the father, the
irrational life principle that is unequally embattled against the death
principle in the mother, the rational and idealizing principle working
rhythmlessly, greedily, presumptuously, and possessively.
The sons' attitude toward the father is ambivalent, weighted toward
hate because the superior cultural equipment of the mother shows his
crudeness in relief; but again and again bits of homely characterization of
Morel show that the children—and even the mother herself—sense, however uncomfortably, the attractiveness of his simple masculine integrity.
He has, uninjurable, what the mother's possessiveness has injured in the
sons:

> "Shut that doo-er!" bawled Morel furiously.
> Annie banged it behind her, and was gone.
> "If tha oppens it again while I'm weshin' me, I'll ma'e thy jaw rattle,"
> he threatened from the midst of his soapsuds. Paul and the mother frowned
> to hear him.
> Presently he came running out of the scullery, with the soapy water
> dripping from him, dithering with cold.
> "Oh, my sirs!" he said. "Wheer's my towel?"
> It was hung on a chair to warm before the fire, otherwise he would have
> bullied and blustered. He squatted on his heels before the hot baking-fire
> to dry himself.
> "F-ff-f!" he went, pretending to shudder with cold.

"Goodness, man, don't be such a kid!" said Mrs. Morel. "It's *not* cold."

"Thee strip thysen stark nak'd to wesh thy flesh i' that scullery," said the miner, as he rubbed his hair; "nowt b'r a ice-'ouse!"

"And I shouldn't make that fuss," replied his wife.

"No, tha'd drop down stiff, as dead as a door-knob, wi' thy nesh sides."

"Why is a door-knob deader than anything else?" asked Paul, curious.

"Eh, I dunno; that's what they say," replied his father. "But there's that much draught i' yon scullery, as it blows through your ribs like through a five-barred gate."

"It would have some difficulty in blowing through yours," said Mrs. Morel.

Morel looked down ruefully at his sides.

"Me!" he exclaimed. "I'm nowt b'r a skinned rabbit. My bones fair juts out on me."

"I should like to know where," retorted his wife.

"Iv-ry-wheer! I'm nobbut a sack o' faggots."

Mrs. Morel laughed. He had still a wonderfully young body, muscular, without any fat. His skin was smooth and clear. It might have been the body of a man of twenty-eight, except that there were, perhaps, too many blue scars, like tattoo-marks, where the coal-dust remained under the skin, and that his chest was too hairy. But he put his hands on his sides ruefully. It was his fixed belief that, because he did not get fat, he was as thin as a starved rat.

Paul looked at his father's thick, brownish hands all scarred, with broken nails, rubbing the fine smoothness of his sides, and the incongruity struck him. It seemed strange they were the same flesh.

Morel talks the dialect that is the speech of physical tenderness in Lawrence's books.[4] It is to the dialect of his father that Paul reverts when he is tussling with Beatrice in adolescent erotic play (letting the mother's bread burn, that he should have been watching), and that Arthur, the only one of the sons whom the mother has not corrupted, uses in his lovemaking, and that Paul uses again when he makes love to Clara, the uncomplex woman who is able for a while to give him his sexual manhood and his "separate selfhood." The sons never use the dialect with their mother, and Paul never uses it with Miriam. It is the speech used by Mellors in *Lady Chatterley's Lover;* and, significantly perhaps, Mellors' name is an anagram on the name Morel.

Some of the best moments in the children's life are associated with the father, when Morel has his "good" periods and enters again into the intimate activity of the family—and some of the best, most simply objective writing in the book communicates these moments, as for instance the passage in Chapter 4 where Morel is engaged in making fuses:

. . . Morel fetched a sheaf of long sound wheat-straws from the attic. These he cleaned with his hand, till each one gleamed like a stalk of gold, after

[4] This observation is made by Diana Trilling in her Introduction to *The Portable D. H. Lawrence* (New York: The Viking Press, Inc., 1947).

which he cut the straws into lengths of about six inches, leaving, if he could, a notch at the bottom of each piece. He always had a beautifully sharp knife that could cut a straw clean without hurting it. Then he set in the middle of the table a heap of gun-powder, a little pile of black grains upon the white-scrubbed board. He made and trimmed the straws while Paul and Annie filled and plugged them. Paul loved to see the black grains trickle down a crack in his palm into the mouth of the straw, peppering jollily downwards till the straw was full. Then he bunged up the mouth with a bit of soap—which he got on his thumb-nail from a pat in a saucer—and the straw was finished.

There is a purity of realization in this very simple kind of exposition that, on the face of it, resists associating itself with any *symbolic* function —if we tend to think of a "symbol" as splitting itself apart into a thing and a meaning, with a mental arrow connecting the two. The best in Lawrence carries the authenticity of a faithfully observed, concrete actuality that refuses to be so split; its symbolism is a radiation that leaves it intact in itself. So, in the passage above, the scene is intact as homely realism, but it radiates Lawrence's controlling sense of the characterful integrity of objects—the clean wheat straws, the whitely scrubbed table, the black grains peppering down a crack in the child's palm, the bung of soap on a thumbnail—and that integrity is here associated with the man Morel and his own integrity of warm and absolute maleness. Thus it is another representation of the creative life force witnessed in the independent objectivity of things that are wholly concrete and wholly themselves.

The human attempt to distort and corrupt that selfhood is reflected in Miriam's attitude toward flowers:

Round the wild, tussocky lawn at the back of the house was a thorn hedge, under which daffodils were craning forward from among their sheaves of grey-green blades. The cheeks of the flowers were greenish with cold. But still some had burst, and their gold ruffled and glowed. Miriam went on her knees before one cluster, took a wild-looking daffodil between her hands, turned up its face of gold to her, and bowed down, caressing it with her mouth and cheeks and brow. He stood aside, with his hands in his pockets, watching her. One after another she turned up to him the faces of the yellow, bursten flowers appealingly, fondling them lavishly all the while. . . .

"Why must you always be fondling things!" he said irritably. . . . "Can you never like things without clutching them as if you wanted to pull the heart out of them? . . . You're always begging things to love you. . . . Even the flowers, you have to fawn on them—"

Rhythmically, Miriam was swaying and stroking the flower with her mouth. . . .

"You don't want to love—your eternal and abnormal craving is to be loved. You aren't positive, you're negative. You absorb, absorb, as if you must fill yourself up with love, because you've got a shortage somewhere."

The relationship of the girl to the flowers is that of a blasphemous possessorship which denies the separateness of living entities—the craving to break down boundaries between thing and thing, that is seen also in Miriam's relationship with Paul, whom she cannot love without trying to absorb him. In contrast, there is the flower imagery in Chapter 11, where Paul goes out into the night and the garden in a moment of emotional struggle:

> It grew late. Through the open door, stealthily, came the scent of madonna lilies, almost as if it were prowling abroad. Suddenly he got up and went out of doors.
>
> The beauty of the night made him want to shout. A half-moon, dusky gold, was sinking behind the black sycamore at the end of the garden, making the sky dull purple with its glow. Nearer, a dim white fence of lilies went across the garden, and the air all round seemed to stir with scent, as if it were alive. He went across the bed of pinks, whose keen perfume came sharply across the rocking, heavy scent of the lilies, and stood alongside the white barrier of flowers. They flagged all loose, as if they were panting. The scent made him drunk. He went down to the field to watch the moon sink under.
>
> A corncrake in the hay-close called insistently. The moon slid quite quickly downwards, growing more flushed. Behind him the great flowers leaned as if they were calling. And then, like a shock, he caught another perfume, something raw and coarse. Hunting round, he found the purple iris, touched their fleshy throats and their dark, grasping hands. At any rate, he had found something. They stood stiff in the darkness. Their scent was brutal. The moon was melting down upon the crest of the hill. It was gone; all was dark. The corncrake called still.

The flowers here have a fierce "thereness" or "otherness" establishing them as existences in their own right—as separate, strange selves—and the demiurgic Eros is rudely insistent in their scent. Paul's perception of that independent life puts him into relation with himself, and the moment of catalytic action is marked by the brief sentence: "At any rate, he had found something." The "something" that he finds is simply the iris, dark, fleshy, mysterious, alien. He goes back into the house and tells his mother that he has decided to break off with Miriam.

Darkness—as the darkness of this night in the garden—has in Lawrence a special symbolic potency. It is a natural and universal symbol, but it offers itself with special richness to Lawrence because of the character of his governing vision. Darkness is half of the rhythm of the day, the darkness of unconsciousness is half of the rhythm of the mind, and the darkness of death is half of the rhythm of life. Denial of this phase of the universal tide is the great sin, the sin committed by modern economy and modern rationalism. In acceptance of the dark, man is renewed to himself —and to light, to consciousness, to reason, to brotherhood. But by refusal to accept that half of the rhythm, he becomes impotent, his reason becomes destructive, and he loses the sense of the independence of others which is essential to brotherhood. In Chapter 13 of *Sons and Lovers* there is a passage that realizes something of what we have been saying. It occurs just after Paul has made love to Clara in a field:

> All the while the peewits were screaming in the field. When he came to, he wondered what was near his eyes, curving and strong with life in the dark, and what voice it was speaking. Then he realized it was the grass, and the peewit was calling. The warmth was Clara's breathing heaving. He lifted his head, and looked into her eyes. They were dark and shining and strange, life wild at the source staring into his life, stranger to him, yet meeting him; and he put his face down on her throat, afraid. What was she? A strong, strange, wild life, that breathed with his in the darkness through this hour. It was all so much bigger than themselves that he was hushed. They had met, and included in their meeting the thrust of the manifold grass-stems, the cry of the peewit, the wheel of the stars. . . .
> . . . after such an evening they both were very still. . . . They felt small, half afraid, childish, and wondering, like Adam and Eve when they lost their innocence and realized the magnificence of the power which drove them out of Paradise and across the great night and the great day of humanity. It was for each of them an initiation. . . . To know their own nothingness, to know the tremendous living flood which carried them always, gave them rest within themselves. If so great a magnificent power could overwhelm them, identify them altogether with itself, so that they knew they were only grains in the tremendous heave that lifted every grass-blade its little height, and every tree, and living thing, then why fret about themselves? They could let themselves be carried by life, and they felt a sort of peace each in the other. There was a verification which they had had together. Nothing could nullify it, nothing could take it away; it was almost their belief in life.

But then we are told that "Clara was not satisfied. . . . She thought it was he whom she wanted. . . . She had not got him; she was not satisfied." This is the impulse toward personal possessorship that constantly confuses and distorts human relationships in Lawrence's books; it is a denial of the otherness of people, and a denial, really, of the great inhuman life force, the primal "otherness" through which people have their independent definition as well as their creative community. Paul had felt that "his experience had been impersonal, and not Clara"; and he had wanted the same impersonality in Clara, an impersonality consonant with that of the manifold grass stems and the peewits' calling and the wheel of the stars. André Malraux, in his preface to the French translation of *Lady Chatterley's Lover,* says that this "couple-advocate," Lawrence, is concerned not with his own individuality or that of his mate, but with "being": "Lawrence has no wish to be either happy or great,"

Malraux says; "he is only concerned with being." [5] The concern with
being, with simple being-a-self (as distinguished from imposing the ego or
abdicating selfhood in the mass), can be understood only in the context of
twentieth century man's resignation to herd ideologies, herd recreations,
herd rationalizations. Lawrence's missionary and prophetic impulse, like
Dostoevsky's, was to combat the excesses of rationalism and individualism,
excesses that have led—paradoxically enough—to the release of mon-
strously destructive irrationals and to the impotence of the individual. He
wanted to bring man's self-definition and creativity back into existence
through recognition of and vital relationship with the rhythms that men
share with the nonhuman world; for he thought that thus men could find
not only the selves that they had denied, but also the brotherhood they
had lost.

The darkness of the phallic consciousness is the correlative of a passionate life assertion, strong as the thrust of the grass stems in the field where
Paul and Clara make love, and as the dynamics of the wheeling stars. "In
the lowest trough of the night" there is always "a flare of the pit." A
pillar of cloud by day, the pit is a pillar of fire by night: and the Lord is
at the pit top. As a descent of darkness and an ascent of flame is associated
with the secret, essential, scatheless maleness of the father, so also the
passionate self-forgetful play of the children is associated with a fiery light
in the night—an isolated lamppost, a blood-red moon, and behind, "the
great scoop of darkness, as if all the night were there." It is this understanding of the symbolism of darkness in Lawrence that gives tragic
dignity to such a scene as that of the bringing home of William's coffin
through the darkness of the night:

> Morel and Paul went, with a candle, into the parlour. There was no gas
> there. The father unscrewed the top of the big mahogany oval table, and
> cleared the middle of the room; then he arranged six chairs opposite each
> other, so that the coffin could stand on their beds.
> "You niver seed such a length as he is!" said the miner, and watching
> anxiously as he worked.
> Paul went to the bay window and looked out. The ash-tree stood mon-
> strous and black in front of the wide darkness. It was a faintly luminous
> night. Paul went back to his mother.
> At ten o'clock Morel called:
> "He's here!"
> Everyone started. There was a noise of unbarring and unlocking the front
> door, which opened straight from the night into the room.
> "Bring another candle," called Morel. . . .
> There was the noise of wheels. Outside in the darkness of the street
> below Paul could see horses and a black vehicle, one lamp, and a few pale
> faces; then some men, miners, all in their shirt-sleeves, seemed to struggle in

[5] In *Criterion,* XII:xlvii (1932-33), 217.

the obscurity. Presently two men appeared, bowed beneath a great weight. It was Morel and his neighbour.

"Steady!" called Morel, out of breath.

He and his fellow mounted the steep garden step, heaved into the candle-light with their gleaming coffin-end. Limbs of other men were seen strug-gling behind. Morel and Burns, in front, staggered; the great dark weight swayed.

"Steady, steady!" cried Morel, as if in pain. . . .

The coffin swayed, the men began to mount the three steps with their load. Annie's candle flickered, and she whimpered as the first men appeared, and the limbs and bowed heads of six men struggled to climb into the room, bearing the coffin that rode like sorrow on their living flesh.

Here the darkness appears in another indivisible aspect of its mystery—as the darkness of death. Perhaps no other modern writer besides Rilke and Mann has tried so sincerely to bring death into relationship with life as Lawrence did, and each under the assumption that life, to know itself creatively, must know its relationship with death; a relationship which the ethos of some hundred and fifty years of rationalism and industrialism and "progress" have striven to exorcise, and by that perversion brought men to an abject worship of death and to holocausts such as that of Hiro-shima. *Sons and Lovers* ends with Paul a derelict in the "drift toward death," which Lawrence thought of as the disease syndrome of his time and of Europe. But the death drift, the death worship, is for Lawrence a hideous distortion of the relationship of death to life. In the scene in which William's coffin is brought home, the front door "opened straight from the night into the room." So, in their rhythmic proportions, life and death open straight into each other, as do the light of consciousness and the darkness of the unconscious, and the usurpation of either one is a per-version of the other. Stephen Spender calls Lawrence "the most hopeful modern writer." His "dark gods," Spender says,

> . . . are symbols of an inescapable mystery: the point of comprehension where the senses are aware of an otherness in objects which extends beyond the senses, and the possibility of a relationship between the human individ-ual and the forces outside himself, which is capable of creating in him a new state of mind. Lawrence is the most hopeful modern writer, because he looks beyond the human to the nonhuman, which can be discovered within the human.[6]

[6] "The Life of Literature," *op. cit.*

The Originality of *The Rainbow*

by Marvin Mudrick

Manners and morals: they are, critics agree, what novels properly
concern themselves with; and the specialist in the English novel can readily demonstrate the English novelist's expert attention to both from *Moll
Flanders* to the latest thriller by Graham Greene. Certainly, fiction is of
all literary genres the most intractable to description or definition, and
we are grateful for any indices to its nature. We are also proud of our
language and literature; and the novel in English has an illustrious history, no doubt about it. So the manners and morals, and the fiction, we
are specially interested in are English and American. It may not, then,
seem chauvinistic to us when Caroline Gordon[1] discovers the world history of the novel to be a triumphant progress toward apotheosis in the
work of the Anglo-American, Henry James, who was obliging enough to
scrutinize, with the tact of an exquisite sensibility, Anglo-Saxon manners
and morals—of only a few social groups, to be sure—on *both* sides of the
Atlantic. Even Dr. Leavis, who demotes or dismisses Richardson, Fielding,
Sterne, Smollett, Dickens, Thackeray, Hardy, and Joyce, expresses much
admiration for Hawthorne, and finds a great tradition in Jane Austen,
George Eliot, James, Conrad, and Lawrence, in whose work, as it seems to
him, manners are so chosen and placed as to reflect on their particular
surfaces the image of that sober absolute morality, essentially secular and
embattled, which for two centuries has been the strength of England if
not of the entire civilized world.

It is just here, regarding the rest of the world, that a doubt arises. Compare, for instance, George Eliot and Tolstoy, or Conrad and Dostoevsky
—comparisons that Dr. Leavis, at any rate, ought to accept as fair, since
one great tradition ought to be able to stand up against another, and
since George Eliot and Tolstoy share a preoccupation with the social and
ordinary as Conrad and Dostoevsky share a preoccupation with the psychological and extraordinary. Or compare Stendhal and Jane Austen, or

"The Originality of *The Rainbow*" by Marvin Mudrick. From *Spectrum*, III (Winter,
1959), 3-28. Copyright © 1959 by *Spectrum*. Appeared also in *A D. H. Lawrence Miscellany* edited by Harry T. Moore (Carbondale: Southern Illinois University Press, 1959).
Reprinted by permission of the author and *Spectrum*.

[1] In *How to Read a Novel* (New York: The Viking Press, Inc., 1957).

Turgenev and James, or almost any nineteenth century French or Russian novelist and Hawthorne.

Fiction, and a tradition of fiction, may be genuine without being great. Greatness is, after all, relative, and when we compare George Eliot and Tolstoy we are aware of such differences in magnitude that to describe the two of them by the same honorific epithet is to do no service to either. Nor is George Eliot a feeble representative of the tradition Dr. Leavis singles out: *Middlemarch,* at least, is a very impressive novel; with a breadth of intelligent sympathy it fixes for all time the manners and morals of its own place and time, and it is perhaps the only English novel that sensitively registers something like a whole society. Yet it is, as the author notes, "A Study of Provincial Life." There is, in fact, no English novel that registers a whole society; and, in the balance with Continental fiction, there is almost no English novel that cannot fairly be described as provincial.

It is not, of course, merely a question of subject: a novelist may be as cosmopolitan as he pleases in treating provincial life—as are Flaubert or Galdós, for example. The point is that for the English novelist a provincialism of temperament is likely to go along with his provincialism of subject. Mme. Bovary, not to mention Bouvard and Pécuchet, has written some of the better known English novels, and the sturdy pragmatism of the English petty bourgeoisie has penetrated and sustained English fiction since those redoubtable self-made innovators and moral men of practical affairs, Defoe and Richardson. The English novel has characteristically been partisan, either protective or rebellious; and the standard of conduct —of manners and morals—which it lavishly illustrates, and by which it measures itself, is the middle-class standard. *Wuthering Heights* and *Tristram Shandy* are as pertinent to the case as *Pamela,* and together they exemplify the three major modes of English fiction: romance as protest, satire as protest, and sentiment as affirmation. Perhaps Dr. Leavis recoils with such a spasm of distaste from Sterne because *Tristram Shandy* is the most subversive protest in English fiction against the bourgeois imperatives that Dr. Leavis, by implication, finds so congenial to the flowering of a great artistic tradition.

These imperatives are, of course, overwhelmingly materialistic. Tom Jones in the hay (sowing his wild oats) with a pretty chambermaid, Scrooge converted to the obsession of giving rather than withholding smiles and crowns and guineas, Pamela indignantly rejecting premarital advances for the sake of wealth and rank later—all of them are enjoying the satisfactions of a morality that ultimately, despite its solemn façade, repays its adherents and sinks human problems in cash and Christmas pudding, a morality of trivial appetites. Whether the English novelist is examining, with intelligence or sentimentality or cynicism, the manners and squeamishness of the cultivated provinces, or the local color of urban and rural low life, or the sinister fascinations of the *haut monde,* or the convulsive freakishness of grand supersexual and asexual passions, or the palpitating idealism of young women who—not having been told what they can importantly do—are looking for something important to do: whatever the English novelist tries, the manners and morals of the earliest and most oppressively successful middle class in history are breathing down his neck and directing his pen into the official view of a life that is in any case considerably less exhilarating than the life visible to the great Continental novelists. Or, for that matter, to Chaucer and Shakespeare.

We must come to it at last, the bourgeois imperative which has defended the materialist order against its gravest threat, and which Anglo-Saxon fiction had perforce to accept for two centuries: the imperative against human normality. You may, the imperative declares, transcend sex by the rhetoric of a grand passion, you may cheapen it as by Fielding's characteristic resort to comic-strip prurience, you may ignore it or jeer at it, you may even in extremity be clinical about it, but you may not regard it as a serious, normal, central preoccupation of mankind, and you may not attempt to understand it.

The first literary effect of such a proscription was to deprive English fiction of normal women. The sphere of decision for women, in Western civilization at least, has always been love and marriage; and if the woman is not permitted to take into account the most serious impulse of her private existence, she may surrender to domesticity or the vapors and become one of Dickens' brave Biddys or dumb Doras, or she may be encouraged to transcend sex before going to the trouble of learning what it is, like George Eliot's Dorothea or Emily Brontë's Cathy or any other Gothic or Romantic heroine. There are even relatively few *interesting* women in English fiction, and most of these are interesting because their authors understand and document the pathology of their reduction: Jane Austen's Emma, Dickens' Estella (his only powerful insight into a woman's sensibility). And there are a very few whose normality has the protective coloration of intelligence and so passes undetected: Jane Austen's Elizabeth Bennet and Anne Elliot, for example. Generally speaking, however, the heroine of English fiction is likely to be a dead loss—think of all the unrememberable Amelias hung like decorative albatrosses round the necks of the heroes of Victorian novels. And then think of Tolstoy's Natasha and Anna, Dostoevsky's women supreme in their passionate abnormality, the whole range of unapologetic women in Stendhal and Balzac and Flaubert, the gallery of unhurried female sensuality in Colette: not only a definable *sex* in contrast to the poor sticks of English heroines, but almost a different species. The English hero, true, has always been allowed some scope of heroic action in adventure (often commercial), in working his way up, in "becoming a success." Still, to eradicate half the human race, and to confine the energies of the other half mainly within the bounds of materialistic aspiration—this is not to survey, through morals and manners, the limits of human possibility. It was this order of things that D. H. Lawrence confronted when he began writing the novel the first part of which eventually became *The Rainbow*.

Literary revolutions are as various and frequent as political elections: some are important, most are not. When what has been called the Flaubertian tradition (a French import which, though it deeply influenced two representatives of his own "native" tradition, Dr. Leavis regards with a somewhat xenophobic distaste) was introduced into English fiction, and such novelists as James, Conrad, Ford, and Joyce adopted and developed the techniques available to a conscious craftsmanship in fiction, one important and irreversible revolution had occurred—the most important, some critics believe, in the history of English fiction. Certainly, it produced important and original work, even though it has inflicted upon us, unavoidably, all the gimmickry of craft-consciousness and myth-mongering and symbolifying criticism, as well as some of the doleful justification for such criticism in those pointless manipulations of technique into which the tradition may tempt the novelist: Conrad, for example, somberly picking his way through the underbrush of half a dozen intervening points of view, in that disastrous virtuoso exercise, *Chance,* to report on a man's tying a shoelace.

To this tradition, and to the revolution it achieved, Lawrence does not belong. Joyce belonged to them, but he participated in another literary revolution, the revolution against the Anglo-Saxon (and Irish) censor; and here he and Lawrence may be said to have stood in a common cause. Joyce's publishing and distributing difficulties with *Dubliners* and *Ulysses* strikingly resemble Lawrence's with *The Rainbow* and *Lady Chatterley's Lover.* Nevertheless, there is censorship and censorship. When Judge Woolsey issued his celebrated decision admitting *Ulysses* into the United States, he remarked, in denying that it came within the legal definition of obscenity, that its effect on the reader was more likely to be "emetic" than "aphrodisiac." The interesting judicial principle was thus established that, for the Anglo-Saxon commonwealth, to vomit is, if not positively healthier, at least less baneful than to engage in sexual intercourse. The judge rightly inferred that Joyce's sexual imagery and naughty language were no vital threat at all to Anglo-Saxon mores, but only the signs by which a whole culture manifested its nausea and self-disgust. The Joycean Revolution of the Word has brought freedom, it is now obvious, mainly for cynical clinicians and cautious pornographers, the freedom to spit and hiss (and leads directly to such a May-fly oddity of literary entomology as the San Francisco Renaissance). Today, a quarter-century after the canonization of Molly Bloom, the Woolseyan principle has been challenged: *Lady Chatterley's Lover,* which audaciously attempted to rehabilitate sexual imagery and the old Anglo-Saxon words as signs of health and tenderness (and which, by the way, succeeded), has at last been legally published in both the United States and the United Kingdom.

Still, *Lady Chatterley's Lover* is, by the pressures of its subject and of the lateness of its hour, as close to being hortatory as a work of art can afford to be; even without its four famous words (all of them used more frequently, of course, in *Ulysses* and in almost any current popular novel), its radical extraliterary intent is clear. *The Rainbow*—which marked the outbreak of the Lawrencean revolution—is in fact a more dangerous work because it is less open to philistine retaliation, because it bases itself confidently on no exhortation at all, only on the assumption that sex is a serious, normal, central preoccupation of mankind. After its early skirmish with suppression (which showed, not how acutely prescient, but how very silly, English censors could be in 1915), *The Rainbow* has been widely accessible in print, and is even becoming generally accepted—at least the first half of it—as a brilliant record of English manners and morals over three generations, a *really* great English family-chronicle novel, not less respectable and beyond comparison better than anything in this line by Arnold Bennett.

True enough, there is, beside it, no family-chronicle novel in English that deserves mention; and anything that will certify the respectability of *The Rainbow* is to be prized, just as we ought to prize Lawrence's subliterary reputation as a sensational novelist for making more of his fiction accessible in cheap paperback American reprints than that of any other major English author. *The Rainbow* is not, after all, so respectable as Galsworthy: there are reasons for Lawrence's notoriety, as well as for his boring and disappointing the common reader, to whom he is notorious; and the reasons are all in *The Rainbow*. Nothing promises to be more, and proves on inspection to be less, sensational than this family-chronicle novel which assumes not only that generations are generated, but that the relationship between husband and wife is the central fact of human existence, that the living nucleus of this relationship is the act of sexual union, that the act of sexual union is infinitely serious, complex, and difficult, and that an act of such radiant significance must be fairly treated by the honest novelist.

Graham Hough, however, disapproves of Lawrence's candor: "As for physical passion . . . no one should try to present it as . . . [Lawrence] does, and traditional literary good sense has always known it." [2] This appeal to timeless good taste would be plausible if it were not for the very special conditions against which Lawrence had to contend. Most authors of the past, and of other cultures, who have dealt with physical passion have not, indeed, presented it directly. Chaucer did not, nor did Colette; but the reason is that neither needs to: for Chaucer, the sacramental nature of passion, and for Colette, the various joys of an indulged sensuality are self-evident and unchallenged; medieval Catholic humanism and modern French hedonism meet in their conviction of the power

---

* In *The Dark Sun* (London: Gerald Duckworth & Co., 1956), p. 63.

of sexual gratification, which can bring to peace and stillness men and women alike. Lawrence, very much on the other hand, has a unique problem: he must reassert this life-renewing power against two centuries of a culture and literature that have muffled and denied its very existence, and he can reassert it only by presenting its actuality as a reminder to the deaf and blind. Lawrence's terrible candor is necessary only because there has been so mendacious and destructive a silence; and yet, because it is so peremptorily called for, it not only reclaims old truths but rushes on to make discoveries. The long reign of English philistinism—in both life and letters—is Lawrence's provocation and his unexampled opportunity.

Of course Lawrence has the advantage of springing from the country community of English workingmen-farmers, a community not bound or even much influenced by the shopkeeper code, and he comes to maturity at a time when the whole structure of class and community is about to encounter the disintegrating shock of World War I. In his historic moment, Lawrence has before him the life of the last English community: not the manners of the province (which are in any case the manners of the provincial petty bourgeoisie and minor gentry), but a life rich in productive labor and in continuity with the passing seasons, rooted in the earthly and physical, inarticulate without grossness or stupidity, a life seemingly permanent yet fated to pass away in the general breakdown of codes and communities and to be replaced or transcended—if by anything —by individual aspiration. It is this process, over three generations, which is the subject and theme of *The Rainbow*; the process is the most momentous human fact of the past century; and it is a process which, in *The Rainbow*, discloses itself poignantly and most crucially in the sexual histories of individuals. The revolutionary nature of *The Rainbow* is, then, twofold: it is the first English novel to record the normality and significance of physical passion; and it is the only English novel to record, with a prophetic awareness of consequences, the social revolution whereby Western man lost his sense of community and men—more especially, women—learned, if they could, that there is no help any longer except in the individual and in his capacity for a passional life.

As soon as the critic of Lawrence begins to favor such terms as *community* and *passion*, he risks being suspected of imagining, obsequiously on cue from his author, a unanimity of social feeling that never was and a potency of personal feeling that never could be, under idyllic and perpetually recurring circumstances in the rural districts of the English Midlands up to, say, the turn of our century. But Lawrence presents no idylls. The community in *The Rainbow*, like every other, is an abstraction from its individuals, who are its only embodiment; and it lives as more than a mere term of discourse only so long as it provides forms and sanctions for the abiding impulses of their separate natures. These impulses are, besides, not all of them communal and sympathetic: Lawrence's individuals are just that, different and distinct from one another except when a strength of sympathy draws them together for moments out of the reciprocal alienations of individuality; and every relationship in *The Rainbow* testifies, not how easy and renewable, but how hard to come by, how precarious, and how irrecoverably unique each instance of passion is, even in a nature as faithful to itself and as sensitively patient as Tom Brangwen's:

. . . Then she said:
"You will be good to me, won't you?"
She was small and girlish and terrible, with a queer, wide look in her eyes. His heart leaped in him, in anguish of love and desire, he went blindly to her and took her in his arms.
"I want to," he said as he drew her closer and closer in. She was soothed by the stress of his embrace, and remained quite still, relaxed against him, mingling in to him. And he let himself go from past and future, was reduced to the moment with her. In which he took her and was with her and there was nothing beyond, they were together in an elemental embrace beyond their superficial foreignness. But in the morning he was uneasy again. She was still foreign and unknown to him. Only, within the fear was pride, belief in himself as mate for her. And she, everything forgotten in her new hour of coming to life, radiated vigour and joy, so that he quivered to touch her.
It made a great difference to him, marriage. Things became remote and of so little significance, as he knew the powerful source of his life, eyes opened on a new universe, and he wondered in thinking of his triviality before. A new, calm relationship showed to him in the things he saw, in the cattle he used, the young wheat as it eddied in a wind.
And each time he returned home, he went steadily, expectantly, like a man who goes to a profound, unknown satisfaction. At dinnertime, he appeared in the doorway, hanging back a moment from entering, to see if she was there. He saw her setting the plates on the white-scrubbed table. Her arms were slim, she had a slim body and full skirts, she had a dark, shapely head with close-banded hair. Somehow it was her head, so shapely and poignant, that revealed her his woman to him. As she moved about clothed closely, full-skirted and wearing her little silk apron, her dark hair smoothly parted, her head revealed itself to him in all its subtle, intrinsic beauty, and he knew she was his woman, he knew her essence, that it was his to possess. And he seemed to live thus in contact with her, in contact with the unknown, the unaccountable and incalculable.
They did not take much notice of each other, consciously.
"I'm betimes," he said.
"Yes," she answered.
He turned to the dogs, or to the child if she were there. The little Anna played about the farm, flitting constantly in to call something to her mother, to fling her arms round her mother's skirts, to be noticed, perhaps caressed, then, forgetting, to slip out again.
Then Brangwen, talking to the child, or to the dog between his knees, would be aware of his wife, as, in her tight, dark bodice and her lace fichu, she was reaching up to the corner cupboard. He realized that he lived by

her. Did he own her? Was she here for ever? Or might she go away? She was
not really his, it was not a real marriage, this marriage between them. She
might go away. He did not feel like a master, husband, father of her children. She belonged elsewhere. Any moment, she might be gone. And he was
ever drawn to her, drawn after her, with ever-raging, ever-unsatisfied desire.
He must always turn home, wherever his steps were taking him, always to
her, and he could never quite reach her, he could never quite be satisfied,
never be at peace, because she might go away.

At evening, he was glad. Then, when he had finished in the yard, and
come in and washed himself, when the child was put to bed, he could sit
on the other side of the fire with his beer on the hob and his long white
pipe in his fingers, conscious of her there opposite him, as she worked at her
embroidery, or as she talked to him, and he was safe with her now, till morning. She was curiously self-sufficient and did not say very much. Occasionally
she lifted her head, her grey eyes shining with a strange light, that had nothing to do with him or with this place, and would tell him about herself. She
seemed to be back again in the past, chiefly in her childhood or her girlhood,
with her father. She very rarely talked of her first husband. But sometimes,
all shining-eyed, she was back at her own home, telling him about the
riotous times, the trip to Paris with her father, tales of the mad acts of the
peasants when a burst of religious, self-hurting fervour had passed over the
country.

Tom Brangwen's apprehensions are not, after all, merely the customary
timeless ones of husbands, but unprecedented seismic shocks: *The Rainbow* is recording a community in its last flare of vitality and gradual
dying away, and all relationships and feelings are shaken by the great
change. The foreignness of Tom's wife represents, disturbingly enough,
the essential distance between all men and especially between the sexes;
but it is already a terrifying difference beyond natural difference. Tom
is no simple farmer: his aspiration toward the irreducibly alien woman
is an inarticulate but not unconscious aspiration toward the experience
of a life beyond the receding satisfactions of a community in process of
dissolution. Until he meets Lydia he refuses, in drink and solitude, the
only life his community offers him. Now, his dissatisfactions are new, and
the brave chances he takes are new.

It was the coming of the colliery, years before, bringing canal and
railway through the Brangwen land, which cut across the past and
offered a promise of the future:

> As they drove home from town, the farmers of the land met the blackened
> colliers trooping from the pit-mouth. As they gathered the harvest, the west
> wind brought a faint, sulphurous smell of pit-refuse burning. As they pulled
> the turnips in November, the sharp clink-clink-clink-clink-clink of empty
> trucks shunting on the line, vibrated in their hearts with the fact of other
> activity going on beyond them.

Tom, the young farmer awakened to a troubled sense of the restrictions of the Brangwen life, comes eventually into his own vision of a life beyond, once he has had his encounter with the complaisant pretty girl and his little talk with her Frenchman escort, the "ageless" and "monkey-like" gracious and imperial gentleman from elsewhere. When Tom sees the foreign lady walking toward him on the road, he knows that she is the awful chance he must take, and the best he can do. Yet the impulse outward moves, necessarily, more rapidly than the possibility of comprehending and fulfilling it: the breakup of the community is too sudden and unanticipated as railways and canals cut across the enclosed spaces of the mind, and the individual is freed from traditional unquestioned preoccupations in order to think and do—what? Tom Brangwen seeks out and lives with strangeness; but his satisfaction and his anguish remain equally resistant to statement or analysis, shy of words, still therefore plausibly connected with the old inarticulate traditional world. His steadiness, halfway between two worlds, is constantly in danger from the incompleteness of its commitment to either; it can be shaken, as by his stepdaughter, Anna, whom he desperately loves but who has come too far from the past to rest in mute suspensions of judgment:

> . . . She tried to discuss people, she wanted to know what was meant. But her father became uneasy. He did not want to have things dragged into consciousness. Only out of consideration for her he listened. And there was a kind of bristling rousedness in the room. The cat got up and, stretching itself, went uneasily to the door. Mrs. Brangwen was silent, she seemed ominous. Anna could not go on with her fault-finding, her criticism, her expression of dissatisfactions. She felt even her father against her.

Individual aspiration, once it is released, has no certain or obvious goal; and how can it be held in check somewhere, how can one keep it from making all action or repose seem premature and insufficient, how can the skeptical analytic mind be quieted? In fact, even for Tom these questions have force, the speechless remoteness of his marriage—for all of its passion—is finally not enough, his pathetic paternal jealousy of his stepdaughter's choice of a husband poisons even as it recalls to him his sense of his own life:

> What was missing in his life, that, in his ravening soul, he was not satisfied? He had had that friend at school, his mother, his wife, and Anna? What had he done? He had failed with his friend, he had been a poor son; but he had known satisfaction with his wife, let it be enough; he loathed himself for the state he was in over Anna. Yet he was *not* satisfied. It was agony to know it.
> Was his life nothing? Had he nothing to show, no work? He did not count

his work, anybody could have done it. What had he known, but the long, marital embrace with his wife! Curious, that this was what his life amounted to! At any rate, it was something, it was eternal. He would say so to anybody, and be proud of it. He lay with his wife in his arms, and she was still his ful-fillment, just the same as ever. And that was the be-all and the end-all. Yes, and he was proud of it.

But the bitterness, underneath, that there still remained an unsatisfied Tom Brangwen, who suffered agony because a girl cared nothing for him. He loved his sons—he had them also. But it was the further, the creative life with the girl, he wanted as well. Oh, and he was ashamed. He trampled himself to extinguish himself.

So Tom Brangwen dies, drunk as Noah to forget the wearying puzzles of his middle age, drowned in the flood of rain, and his women mourn him:

. . . They cleared and washed the body, and laid it on the bed.

There, it looked still and grand. He was perfectly calm in death, and, now he was laid in line, inviolable, unapproachable. To Anna, he was the majesty of the inaccessible male, the majesty of death. It made her still and awe-stricken, almost glad.

Lydia Brangwen, the mother, also came and saw the impressive, inviolable body of the dead man. She went pale, seeing death. He was beyond change or knowledge, absolute, laid in line with the infinite. What had she to do with him? He was a majestic Abstraction, made visible now for a moment, inviolate, absolute. And who could lay claim to him, who could speak of him, of the him who was revealed in the stripped moment of transit from life into death? Neither the living nor the dead could claim him, he was both the one and the other, inviolable, inaccessibly himself.

"I shared life with you, I belong in my own way to eternity," said Lydia Brangwen, her heart cold, knowing her own singleness.

"I did not know you in life. You are beyond me, supreme now in death," said Anna Brangwen, awe-stricken, almost glad.

This is Everyman, not at all the conventional individualist hero of English fiction; and Lawrence, anticipating perplexity, provided his critics with a long peg on which to hang their theories about *The Rainbow* and *Women in Love*. "You mustn't look," he wrote to Edward Garnett, who had been disappointed to find no trace of *Sons and Lovers* in the new work, ". . . for the old stable *ego* of the character. There is another ego, according to whose action the individual is unrecognizable, and passes through, as it were, allotropic states which it needs a deeper sense than any other we've been used to exercise, to discover are states of the same single radically unchanged element." And he goes on to make obligingly explicit the analogy of diamond-carbon to the mode of char-acterization he has just begun to feel at home in. Now this tip from the essentially kindly Lawrence to his bewildered English friend is a useful

one, for the elucidation of *Women in Love* especially, as Mark Schorer
has pointed out.[3] It is nevertheless not so simple, or perhaps even so
accurate, as it looks; and it does not indicate anything nearly so unprecedented—if one takes into account Continental fiction—as Lawrence
appears to think.

The trouble is that, in this formulation, Lawrence does not yet seem
to have made clear to himself why the old mode of characterization is
being discarded and how the new mode functions, and what sort of
novel employs one or the other. *Sons and Lovers* is—like *A Portrait of the
Artist as a Young Man*—a willful and confused post-Victorian novel of
youthful longing and self-discovery, written by a young man whose *parti
pris* rejects or ignores the values of the community which has helped to
make him; *The Rainbow,* on the other hand, is an elegiac novel about
the dissolution of a community whose values, even as these pass away, the
author neither rejects nor ignores but seeks to understand and somehow,
for his characters' sake, to transcend. The characters (Mr. Morel excepted)
in *Sons and Lovers* are post-Victorian individualists colliding with an
angry young individualist of a hero; the characters in *The Rainbow*
breathe and move, as long as they can, in the large atmosphere of a
community. Not that Tom Brangwen is less *individual* than, say, Paul
Morel; quite the contrary, he is more honestly and totally imagined, and
therefore more human and more of a man. If the novelist creates his
characters as more or less aggressive bundles of recognizable traits, as egos
stabilized by manners and morals, and his novel as a sequence of colli-
sions between such bundles, he will produce the kind of novel that
Lawrence is now giving up, the novel preoccupied—whether in affirmation or in protest—with manners and morals, the class novel, the standard
English novel. If, however, the novelist creates his characters in a life-
size medium, fictional and communal, which nurtures, provokes, and
makes room for the strength of impulse, he will produce a novel like *The
Rainbow*—or *Anna Karenina,* or *The Idiot,* or *The Red and the Black.*
Characters in novels like these are not caricatures or even conventional
heroes, mere victims or arbiters of manners and morals, they are passions
and first principles; and they are all the more human and individual for
being so. Nor, of course, is Lawrence's new mode of characterization
unprecedented or revolutionary, it is only not very English.

What *is* revolutionary in *The Rainbow*—what makes Lawrence, in
perhaps the most important sense, the only modern novelist—is not the
mode of characterization, but the new awareness which finds this mode
necessary: the awareness that with the dying away, in the age of technol-
ogy, of genuine communal relations between men, with the inevitable

---

[3] See the next essay in this text, "*Women in Love* and Death," by Schorer, especially
pp. 51-54 [Ed.].

thwarting of what Lawrence was later to call "the societal impulse," the only hope for man lies in those remaining potentialities of human relationship which depend for their realization on the fullest (not necessarily the most various or complicated) possible realization of the sexual impulse. Lawrence, being English, had in this respect no choice but to be revolutionary. English novelists, as spokesmen for the most advanced middle class in the world, had since Defoe been advocating the simplest escape from the intolerable human problems posed by industrialism—the escape into materialist success, the pursuit of what Dickens' Wemmick poignantly euphemizes under the phrase "portable property"; but with the end of the expansive romantic phase of English industrialism, no serious English writer could any longer believe in this escape and pursuit, as Dickens and others before and after could believe in it once it had been sweetened by contrition, materialist benevolence, and marital union with another form of portable property. (We cannot imagine a French or an Italian or a Russian Lawrence, just as we cannot imagine an English Dostoevsky, though the awareness of which Lawrence is both creator and instrument has, finally, as much to say to the Continent as Dostoevsky has to say to the English.) For Lawrence, then, the hope—in fact the last resort—of modern man is—the unhappy word stares at us as it did at Lawrence's censors—sex: not as cold appetite, not as self-imposed exile from the teeming world, not as the exploiting of sensation or the temporary allaying of an itch, but as the bond of tranquillity and faith between man and woman, those polar opponents, and the last renewable proof of human community.

The Rainbow is midpassage and arrival. Tom Brangwen still has roots, connections, the virtue of quietness in solitude; of these vestiges of community Anna and Will still keep something by, as it were, barely remembering them, Anna in her slovenly cheerful maternity, Will in his mute satisfaction with manual labor or minor artisanship. Only Ursula—modern woman and therefore, in her unforeseen and disastrously unprepared-for homelessness, true representative of modern mankind—has nothing at all of what, outside themselves, sustained the two generations before her. And for all three generations the unmapped territory to be explored, with increasing desperation and hope, is sex.

Tom Brangwen has a real marriage, notwithstanding its ultimate vulnerability to the stress of uncomprehended change; his apparently unwarrantable youthful waiting for a strangeness beyond his ordinary experience is rewarded and vindicated, and his life is transfigured by the reality of passion. If his marriage fails to give him everything, it nevertheless gives him much, even enough to make him at length unhappily sensitive to the unknown vibrations of what he must do without.

For Anna and Will, on the other hand, marriage seems at first sunnier and more simple. They have moved very far out of the shadow of the old

Brangwen world; Anna, at least, is impatient with established sanctities; and both of them rejoice on their prolonged honeymoon in an uninhibited mutual exploration of sexuality, day after day of vital time-dissolving ease:

As they lay close together, complete and beyond the touch of time or change, it was as if they were at the very centre of all the slow wheeling of space and the rapid agitation of life, deep, deep inside them all, at the centre where there is utter radiance, and eternal being, and the silence absorbed in praise: the steady core of all movements, the unawakened sleep of all wakefulness. They found themselves there, and they lay still, in each other's arms; for their moment they were at the heart of eternity, whilst time roared far off, forever far off, towards the rim.

Then gradually they were passed away from the supreme centre, down the circles of praise and joy and gladness, further and further out, towards the noise and the friction. But their hearts had burned and were tempered by the inner reality, they were unalterably glad.

Gradually they began to wake up, the noises outside became more real. They understood and answered the call outside. They counted the strokes of the bell. And when they counted midday, they understood that it was midday, in the world, and for themselves also.

It dawned upon her that she was hungry. She had been getting hungrier for a lifetime. But even yet it was not sufficiently real to rouse her. A long way off she could hear the words, "I am dying of hunger." Yet she lay still, separate, at peace, and the words were unuttered. There was still another lapse.

And then, quite calmly, even a little surpised, she was in the present, and was saying:

"I am dying with hunger."

"So am I," he said calmly, as if it were of not the slightest significance. And they relapsed into the warm, golden stillness. And the minutes flowed unheeded past the window outside.

Then suddenly she stirred against him.

"My dear, I am dying of hunger," she said.

It was a slight pain to him to be brought to.

"We'll get up," he said, unmoving.

And she sank her head on to him again, and they lay still, lapsing. Half consciously, he heard the clock chime the hour. She did not hear.

"Do get up," she murmured at length, "and give me something to eat."

"Yes," he said, and he put his arms round her, and she lay with her face on him. They were faintly astonished that they did not move. The minutes rustled louder at the window.

"Let me go then," he said.

She lifted her head from him, relinquishingly. With a little breaking away, he moved out of bed, and was taking his clothes. She stretched out her hand to him.

"You are so nice," she said, and he went back for a moment or two.

Then actually he did slip into some clothes, and, looking round quickly at her, was gone out of the room. She lay translated again into a pale, clearer peace. As if she were a spirit, she listened to the noise of him down-stairs, as if she were no longer of the material world.

In such moments as Lawrence here presents, there can be no "charac-ters" in the conventional fictional sense: the mode of characterization is dictated by the focus of attention, which here is on a core of impulse anterior to personality. It is, of course, easy to misunderstand such a passage in the context of English fiction, especially that sort of woman's fiction of which *Jane Eyre* is a quasi-serious instance: the emotion of romantic love reduces heroine (or hero) to a fluttering impotency—espe-cially in anticipation—that may resemble a reduction to impulse. But the conjugal satisfactions of Tom Brangwen, or Anna, or Will, are not reductive at all; they liberate universal human powers; far from making romantic victims they make those relations between people without which there are only egos in collision and no persons. Nobody, it is true, can live indefinitely at such a depth of impulse; and the comic ascension of Anna and Will to the level of a more mundane appetite testifies not only to the existence of a daylight world in which we are all, more or less, scrupulously differentiated fictional characters, but also to that respect for full human truth which disciplines even the most rhapsodic utter-ances in this novel. The careful reader never forgets that *The Rainbow* is, in one large and traditional aspect, a great realistic novel: Tom Brangwen's life outside marriage, for example, is registered with an immediacy and resonance that would establish him as one of the great figures in English fiction even if he were nothing more; and one thinks of such superb set-pieces as Tom's efforts at comforting the child Anna while Lydia is bearing his first child, Tom's drunkenly inspired eulogy of marriage, his death in the flood—a luminous pertinence of detail, a fidelity to locale, a sternness of pathos not readily matched in any other fiction. Nevertheless, as the rhythm of the style—always near, when not actually, the rhythm of rhapsodic utterance—persists in implying, life is renewable only and perpetually at the springs of impulse, in celebration and praise, where we are less unique than human; and only to the degree to which we have renewed ourselves there, can we breathe and move as individuals in the daylight world.

Renewal, the gift and aim of life, becomes in modern marriage less and less the gift of repose, more and more pressingly the aim of conscious and personal exploration: woman is less passive and man more anxious, approaching an uneasy identity of roles. Lydia is still withdrawn and enigmatic, a woman of the old dispensation, unharried, immured in domesticity and unamenable to self-questioning; so Tom is the explorer —joyous or baffled—in this first marriage, moving doubtfully at the rim of awareness. Anna, on the other hand, has come awake, because the invasion of all things by mechanism and the conscious mind has made Lydia the last possible woman of her kind: having lost what her mother unquestionably had, Anna must make up for it by becoming explorative in her own right, the free companion of her husband. But, after the shared bliss of the honeymoon, the difficulties of the new dispensation become gradually manifest. When the communal sanction for marriage is dissipated and only free and equal individuals remain, the burden on accidents of personality grows suddenly enormous. The temperamental differences between Lydia and Tom were unbridgeable, and of no significance to Lydia. Yet Will's soft inarticulateness drives the skeptical articulate Anna wild, and Anna's attacks on her husband's temperament drive him into retaliatory fury:

> She . . . clung to the worship of human knowledge. Man must die in the body but in his knowledge he was immortal. Such, somewhere, was her belief, quite obscure and unformulated. She believed in the omnipotence of the human mind.
> He, on the other hand, blind as a subterranean thing, just ignored the human mind and ran after his own dark-souled desires, following his own tunnelling nose. She felt often she must suffocate. And she fought him off.
> Then he, knowing he was blind, fought madly back again, frantic in sensual fear. He did foolish things. He asserted himself on his rights, he arrogated the old position of master of the house.
> "You've a right to do as I want," he cried.
> "Fool!" she answered. "Fool!"
> "I'll let you know who's master," he cried.
> "Fool!" she answered. "Fool! I've known my own father, who could put a dozen of you in his pipe and push them down with his finger-end. Don't I know what a fool you are!"

In the perilous colloidal tension of modern marriage, too much depends on merely personal qualities. And—at least for persons living in the delusive afterglow of the old world, still unalert to the swarming problems of consciousness—too much depends on the increasingly elaborate and conscious satisfactions of sexuality: the man, having lost his inherited mastery, comes to depend on these as on a drug, and the woman comes to resent what she will eventually regard as his infantile male weakness. Variety, the avoidance of monotony, becomes more and more a brutal conjugal compulsion. At length, reciprocally excited by Will's brush with infidelity, Anna and Will give themselves to the pleasures of a sort of democratic sexual cannibalism, to the fetishistic daylight fevers of sensuality, the manipulation of bodies as instruments for pleasure; and if Lawrence's imagery in this passage plainly obliges us to find the experience analogous to the Fall, it obliges us also to see the new experiences as a necessary expansion of man's knowledge in the time of another forced departure from the garden. Still, Anna and Will never reclaim their honeymoon fulfillment of passion or seem capable of the reconciliation between passion and sensuality; and their lives dwindle away in subtle disorganization, in the minor consummations and complaints of Anna's role as the fecund housewife and Will's as a woodwork teacher for the town, "very happy and keen in his new public spirit." Since their imperfect truce is the first modern marriage, it is appropriate that they bring into being the first complete modern woman, totally dispossessed and therefore totally explorative.

The child Ursula still has her father's environing and sometimes overpowering love; and she has, also, in conversation with her grandmother, a window on the certainties of the past even as the thought of growing up without such certainties begins to trouble her:

> . . . Ursula asked her deepest childish questions of her grandmother.
> "Will somebody love me, grandmother?"
> "Many people love you, child. We all love you."
> "But when I am grown up, will somebody love me?"
> "Yes, some man will love you, child, because it's your nature. And I hope it will be somebody who will love you for what you are, and not for what he wants of you. But we have a right to want what we want."
> Ursula was frightened, hearing these things. Her heart sank, she felt she had no ground under her feet. She clung to her grandmother. Here was peace and security. Here, from her grandmother's peaceful room, the door opened on to the greater space, the past, which was so big, that all it contained seemed tiny; loves and births and deaths, tiny units and features within a vast horizon. That was great relief, to know the tiny importance of the individual, within the great past.

Lydia's wisdom in old age is wasted on her granddaughter, and reverberates outward into the large implications of the novel. One of the dangers of marriage in the time of a breaking of bonds is, as Lydia suggests, that a man may be driven to seek in a mate not a distinct and different person as generous and needy as himself, but only what will compensate him, somehow, for his sense of loss—though, tragically, he must have both in order to have either. The marriage of Anna and Will is, at last, a deadlock because neither wife nor husband has the generosity and wisdom to acknowledge and accept the unbreakable differentness of the other; and Tom's response to Lydia's strangeness—at the beginning so compelling an attraction for him—is, at last, to drift back into confusion and the oblivion of drink. Moreover, the grandmother's words to the child Ursula are a prophecy; for Skrebensky will desperately seek in Ursula (as Will sought in Anna) only what might make up for his unmanning sense of loss, and Ursula herself will not understand, not at least till very late, that her promiscuity with Skrebensky is no generous gift of love but only a confession of mutual weakness, no passionate resolution but an increasingly unsatisfactory escape into sex from the unprecedented problems of the modern consciousness.

In the new world there are no landmarks or guideposts, the great past is no longer even a memory, everyone is free and dispossessed; so Ursula's life becomes, necessarily enough, a kind of adventure in limbo. Yet it is this concluding section—in bulk, more than half—of the novel that has been most vexatious and unrewarding for readers; and any effort to assess *The Rainbow* bumps hard against it. No doubt, the section is less satisfying than most of what has come before: it is unduly repetitive, it is occasionally content to make points by assertion rather than by incident, it sometimes mistakes mere detailed documentation for thematic illustration and development, its tone sometimes verges on stridency. There are, after all, too many and too similar descriptions of Ursula and Skrebensky making hopeless love; the career of Ursula as a teacher, how-ever interesting it may be in its own right, is recorded at too much length and with too little relevance to the theme of the novel; and when Law-rence, in his haste to dismiss dry book-learning, tries to palm off on us so trivially literary a truism about college life as this:

> College was barren, cheap, a temple converted to the most vulgar, petty commerce. Had she not gone to hear the echo of learning pulsing back to the source of the mystery?—The source of mystery! And barrenly, the pro-fessors in their gowns offered commercial commodity that could be turned to good account in the examination-room; ready-made stuff too, and not really worth the money it was intended to fetch; which they all knew.

When Lawrence settles for this sort of thing, we are persuaded that he is no longer, for the time being at any rate, attending to the seriousness of his theme. It is perhaps more to the point to agree with Dr. Leavis that Lawrence, his mind already on the very different second novel which had detached itself from his original conception of a single novel on marriage, was trying to finish *The Rainbow* with less sympathy than conscientiousness: in this view, the frustrating account of Ursula's long and strenuous career of frustration may be taken as the result of Law-rence's prudent desire to save her consummation for *Women in Love*.

Still, *The Rainbow* is, finally, not about consummation but about promise. The rainbow that Ursula sees at the very end of the novel need not be dismissed as a despairing symbolic stroke to allow a nominal con-clusion and to release Lawrence for *Women in Love*; though the two novels are obviously related in ways more important than the continuance of several characters through the second, it may be that those readers who find the end of *The Rainbow* wanting have turned their minds prematurely to the next book, and are expecting what it is not in the

theme of the earlier novel to give. No doubt Lawrence's original intention was to write a single novel which would encompass and illustrate in
the lives of a family the great social and psychological change of our
century, and which would conclude with a treatment of such individual
problems and individual solutions as, indeed, are treated in *Women in
Love.* But it must have become eventually clear to him that the breakdown of community was a subject in itself, and that it culminated appropriately in the coming to consciousness of emancipated, modern
woman. If Lawrence had ended the novel with modern woman numbed
in her grimace of freedom, he would have been merely cynical; if he
had ended with Ursula still unsure of her feelings for Skrebensky, the
novel would trail off in a puzzle. The novel does, in fact, end as Ursula,
having freed herself of her struggle with Skrebensky, is for the first time
genuinely free not only of the unrevivable past but of those false ties she
has tentatively accepted in place of it. To require any more—at least
schematically—is to require an unequivocal happy ending, and even in
Women in Love or *Lady Chatterley's Lover* Lawrence is not that obliging.

The fault is, then, not of scheme but of execution: much of the last
half of *The Rainbow* seems to have been written with a slackening of
Lawrence's attention to proportion and detail. Yet much is finely done.
Something as difficult, for instance, as the relationship between Ursula
and Miss Inger comes off without damage to our sympathy for Ursula,
and with strong pertinence to the theme. In a time when the injunctions
of community and family have been broken, when the individual is
responsible only to himself and to his own impulses, why should not
Ursula first admire and then fiercely love the handsome, independent
woman who so resembles what she herself wishes to be? And why should
the warmth and physical responsiveness of her feelings be curbed? No
mere prohibition will do, for sanctions and prohibitions alike have gone
under. It is only by living through the experience that Ursula can judge
its sinister misleadingness for her: to be free like Winifred Inger is to take
pleasure only in the thrill of physiological or mechanical process, to
handle and reject, to give nothing, to hate one's humanness and to deny
the possibility of relationship—as Ursula discovers during the visit to
her uncle's colliery:

> His real mistress was the machine, and the real mistress of Winifred was
> the machine. She too, Winifred, worshipped the impure abstraction, the
> mechanisms of matter. There, there, in the machine, in service of the ma-
> chine, was she free from the clog and degradation of human feeling. There,
> in the monstrous mechanism that held all matter, living or dead, in its serv-
> ice, did she achieve her consummation and her perfect unison, her immor-
> tality.

The narcissistic delights of homosexuality are not enough, even for Winifred Inger; even she must make a commitment to something outside herself, and she finds her consummation and her unison, her immortality, in the machine. But Ursula continues to seek hers in the flesh. Perhaps the repetitive savageries of Ursula's sexual encounters with Skrebensky are partly justifiable on the ground that with Skrebensky Ursula's attempt is so much more plausible and at the same time so much more exacerbating: at least Skrebensky is a man and no narcissistic projection of herself, though she can master and break him; at least Skrebensky is not positively evil, though he is weak and inchoate. If we do not lose sympathy with Ursula for her annihilating cruelty toward Skrebensky, it is because we are convinced that she suffers in the grip of an impulse which is, if it can ever be fulfilled, the sanest and most healing impulse accessible to her; if she appears at moments in the guise of a female spider devouring her sexually spent and useless mate, she is in any case obeying a brute instinct more vital than Skrebensky's attachment to political abstractions or Miss Inger's attachment to mechanism. Ursula's quest is desperate, so therefore are her feelings often; but the discoveries she must make cannot be arrived at by theorem, and she has no immediately recognizable allies. To contain and to be blocked from fulfilling so mastering an impulse is, finally, punishment and promise enough, as Lawrence indicates in the marvelous passage in which Ursula has her heart-stopping encounter with the stampeding horses, hallucination or reality:

> She knew they had not gone, she knew they awaited her still. But she went on over the log bridge that their hoofs had churned and drummed, she went on, knowing things about them. She was aware of their breasts gripped, clenched narrow in a hold that never relaxed, she was aware of their red nostrils flaming with long endurance, and of their haunches, so rounded, so massive, pressing, pressing, pressing to burst the grip upon their breasts, pressing forever till they went mad, running against the walls of time, and never bursting free. Their great haunches were smoothed and darkened with rain. But the darkness and wetness of rain could not put out the hard, urgent, massive fire that was locked within these flanks, never, never.

The new woman is too strong, and the new man is too weak, the woman suddenly conscious of long-sleeping powers and the man suddenly confronted with a rival. It is as if, for the new broken reed of a man like Skrebensky, all the long history of patriarchal Western civilization—its dream of wholeness and community, its exaltation of the family and of romantic love—has been man's dogged postponement of woman's inevitable supremacy. It all leads to Skrebensky, totally dependent, beaten child and rejected lover, hearing his doom on the final morning-after:

He tapped at her bedroom door at the last minute. She stood with her umbrella in her hand. He closed the door. He did not know what to say.

"Have you done with me?" he asked her at length, lifting his head.

"It isn't me," she said. "You have done with me—we have done with each other."

He looked at her, at the closed face, which he thought so cruel. And he knew he could never touch her again. His will was broken, he was seared, but he clung to the life of his body.

"Well, what have I done?" he asked, in a rather querulous voice.

"I don't know," she said, in the same dull, feelingless voice. "It is finished. It has been a failure."

In this contest—though Skrebensky thinks otherwise—there is no kindness and cruelty, only life and death, all and nothing; the issue is beyond the condescensions of charity, and the time is very late. There must be, somewhere, men to face up to the new dispensation: men like Tom Brangwen, who did much and might have done more had he known better what had overtaken him. Anna, in paralyzing contempt of Will when he tried to assert an authority he had already yielded by his un-manly surrender to her flesh, cried out that her stepfather "could put a dozen of you in his pipe and push them down with his finger-end." The new woman is strong in her power to wound and even to kill man's spirit if she has no male counterforce to match her. Yet life somehow continuously renews itself: in a time of human degradation, the unique powers of woman have at last asserted themselves; and such powers, coming so unexpectedly out of the very sources of life, cannot be without a commensurate object and response. What remains, in the compulsive ugliness of modern industrialism, as all values except those preservable by the conscious individual are swept away, is promise:

In everything she saw she grasped and groped to find the creation of the living God, instead of the old, hard barren form of bygone living. Sometimes great terror possessed her. Sometimes she lost touch, she lost her feeling, she could only know the old horror of the husk which bound in her and all mankind. They were all in prison, they were all going mad.

She saw the stiffened bodies of the colliers, which seemed already enclosed in a coffin, she saw their unchanging eyes, the eyes of those who are buried alive: she saw the hard, cutting edges of the new houses, which seemed to spread over the hillside in their insentient triumph, the triumphs of hor-rible, amorphous angles and straight lines, the expression of corruption tri-umphant and unopposed, corruption so pure that it is hard and brittle: she saw the dun atmosphere over the blackened hills opposite, the dark blotches of houses, slate roofed and amorphous, the old church-tower standing up in hideous obsoleteness above raw new houses on the crest of the hill, the amorphous, brittle, hard edged new houses advancing from Beldover to meet the corrupt new houses from Lethley, the houses of Lethley advancing to mix with the houses of Hainor, a dry, brittle, terrible corruption spreading over the face of the land, and she was sick with a nausea so deep that she perished as she sat. And then, in the blowing clouds, she saw a band of faint iridescence colouring in faint colours a portion of the hill. And forgetting, startled, she looked for the hovering colour and saw a rainbow forming itself. In one place it gleamed fiercely, and, her heart anguished with hope, she sought the shadow of iris where the bow should be. Steadily the colour gathered, mysteriously, from nowhere, it took presence upon itself, there was a faint, vast rainbow. The arc bended and strengthened itself till it arched indomitable, making great architecture of light and colour and the space of heaven, its pedestals luminous in the corruption of new houses on the low hill, its arch the top of heaven.

And the rainbow stood on the earth. She knew that the sordid people who crept hard-scaled and separate on the face of the world's corruption were living still, that the rainbow was arched in their blood and would quiver to life in their spirit, that they would cast off their horny covering of disintegration, that new, clean, naked bodies would issue to a new germination, to a new growth, rising to the light and the wind and the clean rain of heaven. She saw in the rainbow the earth's new architecture, the old, brittle corruption of houses and factories swept away, the world built up in a living fabric of Truth, fitting to the over-arching heaven.

The pledge of the future is Ursula's knowledge of what is terrible about the present, and her knowledge derives from a power of passion which must at length be consummated because it would otherwise have had no cause to spring into being. Dostoevsky called the Russians the "god-bearing" people, those who carry the secret of life within them and preserve it for that remote apocalypse when all the world will be fit to receive it. At the conclusion of *The Rainbow* Ursula is the single god-bearing person left in the world. It is a tribute to the prodigious optimism and persuasiveness of Lawrence's vision that the secret she holds seems worth the keeping until the world is fit to receive it.

Women in Love and Death

by Mark Schorer

In Lawrence's little read, brilliantly extended Introduction to
Maurice Magnus' *Memoirs of the Foreign Legion*, we encounter this
passage:

> "Why!" I said. "Is it you?"
> "Yes," he replied. "A terrible thing has happened."
> He waited on the stairs, and I went down. Rather unwillingly, because
> I detest terrible things, and the people to whom they happen.

The people to whom they happen. Put this phrase beside an early exchange between Birkin and Gerald in *Women in Love*:

> "You think people should just do as they like."
> "I think they always do."

Put these two together, and we are at the very center of the startling
development that the old idea that "character is fate" achieves in Lawrence, and particularly here, in *Women in Love*. If we consider this
development in relation to uses of the same idea in earlier novels, we will
see just how it is startling. Over a third of *The Portrait of a Lady*, for
example, is "taken up with brushwork," according to Stephen Spender's
mistaken reading, "that has nothing to do with the story." Really, James
is painting in all the features of Isabel Archer's lovely, candid intelligence
which is yet an intelligence where every virtue shades off into not, perhaps, a vice, but at least a false perception—all this so that we can recognize the inevitability of her renunciation of the right to ignorance once
her education in corruption is completed, and she gains her moral freedom in the paradox of social slavery. This is among our finest demon-
strations in fiction of the belief in the freedom of the will and the responsibilities of that freedom—a belief that necessarily selects for its emphasis
the concept *character* from the whole phrase *character is fate*. Take, now,

"*Women in Love* and Death" by Mark Schorer. From *The Hudson Review*, VI
(Spring, 1953), 34-47. Copyright 1953 by *The Hudson Review*. Revised by the author
and reprinted by permission of the author and *Hudson Review*.

Joseph Conrad's understanding of the proposition as it is implied by his title, *Chance,* and as this implication pervades all his novels. Chance is accident, and in accident lies opportunity, *that* kind chance: determinism and free will, the will operating out from the ground that accident allows it. And here, of course, the emphasis falls upon *fate* in that whole phrase *character is fate.* In Lawrence, the two terms become equivalents, the emphasis distributed with complete equality and balance. The new development in Lawrence is found most clearly in his theme of the victim who invites the victimizer, the murderee who invites the murderer. Because the equivalence of these terms had not previously been handled in fiction, and because of the extremity with which Lawrence felt the urgency of his interpretation for the modern world, the idea that we can and constantly do choose our fate, not only our social or our psychological fate, but our final fate, our *destiny,* choose life or death—because of the novelty of this interpretation in fiction and the extremity with which Lawrence felt it, he abandoned the kind of novel he had been writing and the kinds of novel that had been written by others, and attempted instead to write the novel as psychic drama. He first became aware of the alteration in his aims as he was writing *The Rainbow*; he became completely aware of it as he was writing *Women in Love.* The change can be seen in four ways:

First, characterization. The whole notion of character in fiction undergoes an alteration. He will now create more *essential* beings, will be concerned first of all not with the "ego" that interests the traditional novelist, but with the "primal forces" that are prior to "character."

. . . I don't think the psychology is wrong, it is only that I have a different attitude to my characters, and that necessitates a different attitude in you, which you are not prepared to give. As for its being my cleverness which would pull the thing through—that sounds odd to me, for I don't think I am so very clever, in that way. I think the book is a bit futuristic—quite unconsciously so. But when I read Marinetti—"The profound intuitions of life added one to the other, word by word, according to their illogical conception, will give us the general lines of an intuitive physiology of matter"— I see something of what I am after. I translate him clumsily, and his Italian is often obfuscated—and I don't care about physiology of matter—but somehow—that which is physic—non-human, in humanity, is more interesting to me than the old-fashioned human element—which causes one to conceive a character in a certain moral scheme and make him consistent. The certain moral scheme is what I object to. In Turgenev, and in Tolstoi, and in Dostoevsky, the moral scheme into which all the characters fit—and it is nearly the same scheme—is, whatever the extraordinariness of the characters themselves, dull, old, dead. When Marinetti writes: "It is the solidity of a blade of steel that is interesting by itself, that is, the uncomprehending and inhuman alliance of its molecules in resistance to, let us say, a bullet. The heat of a piece of wood or iron is in fact more passionate, for us, than the laughter or tears of a woman"—then I know what he means. He is stupid, as

an artist, contrasting the heat of the iron and the laugh of the woman. Because what is interesting in the laugh of the woman is the same as the bind-
ing of the molecules of steel or their action in heat: it is the inhuman will,
call it physiology, or like Marinetti—physiology of matter, that fascinates
me. I don't so much care about what the woman *feels*—in the ordinary usage
of the word. That presumes an ego to feel with. I only care about what the
woman *is*—what she is—inhumanly, physiologically, materially—according
to the use of the word: but for me, what she *is* as a phenomenon (or as representing some greater, inhuman will), instead of what she feels according
to the human conception. That is where the futurists are stupid. Instead of
looking for the new human phenomenon, they will only look for the phe-
nomena of the science of physics to be found in human beings. They are
crassly stupid. But if anyone would give them eyes, they would pull the right
apples off the tree, for their stomachs are true in appetite. You mustn't look
in my novel for the old stable *ego* of the character. There is another ego,
according to whose action the individual is unrecognizable, and passes
through, as it were, allotropic states which it needs a deeper sense than any
other we've been used to exercise, to discover are states of the same single
radically unchanged element. (Like as diamond and coal are the same pure
single element of carbon. The ordinary novel would trace the history of the
diamond—but I say, "Diamond, what! This is carbon." And my diamond
might be coal or soot, and my theme is carbon.) . . . Again, I say, don't
look for the development of the novel to follow the lines of certain characters: the characters fall into the form of some other rhythmic form, as when
one draws a fiddle-bow across a fine tray delicately sanded, and sand takes
lines unknown.[1]

In the novel itself, Birkin tells us that personalities are not very interesting, that there are only a few great ideas that animate all individuals:
these are the basic elements, the carbon: life and death, the two possible
allegiances. And these are the psychic engagements that the novelist wishes
to explore, just as they are the elements beneath the social character that
interest Birkin in forming his personal relationships:

> He looked at her, to see if he felt that she was good-looking.
> "I don't *feel* that you're good-looking," he said.
> "Not even attractive?" she mocked, bitingly.
> He knitted his brows in sudden exasperation.
> "Don't you see that it's not a question of visual appreciation in the least,"
> he cried. "I don't *want* to see you. I've seen plenty of women, I'm sick and
> weary of seeing them. I want a woman I don't see."
> "I'm sorry I can't oblige you by being invisible," she laughed.
> "Yes," he said, "you are invisible to me, if you don't force me to be
> visually aware of you. But I don't want to see you or hear you."
> "What did you ask me to tea for, then?" she mocked.
> "I want to find you, where you don't know your own existence, the you

[1] D. H. Lawrence, in a letter to Edward Garnett, June 5, 1914.

that your common self denies utterly. But I don't want your good looks, and I don't want your womanly feelings, and I don't want your thoughts nor opinions nor your ideas—they are all bagatelles to me."

"You are very conceited, Monsieur," she mocked. . . . "I think you want to tell me you love me, and you go all this way round to do it."

"All right," he said, looking up with sudden exasperation. "Now go away then, and leave me alone. I don't want any more of your meretricious persiflage."

"Is it really persiflage?" she mocked, her face really relaxing into laughter.

This quotation is even more helpful than Lawrence's letter to an understanding of the change that has come over his intention since *Sons and Lovers,* and certainly it points to his new problem as a novelist. *I want to find you, where you don't know your own existence, the you that your common self denies utterly.* And all the rest, all that attaches to the conscious, social character, is it, for a novelist, "really persiflage," "meretricious persiflage"? If it is, then the novel as it was written before Lawrence had been built on persiflage, since its generic character depends on the development of conflict out of social materials, and if we took Lawrence's letter with complete literalness, or Birkin's ambition as a true equivalent to the ambition of Lawrence, the novelist, he would be directed toward such a novelistic disaster as Virginia Woolf's *The Waves,* albeit in his terms. So we may say at once that in the novel, the *pure* psychic drama is an impossibility, and that we do not have that attempt here.

What we have, in fact, are several different orders of characterization, the orders that traditionally appear in the novel. We have a group of "free" characters, and a group of "bound" characters. The free characters are limited to four, the four who actively seek out their fate through the plot movement; the rest are all fixed in their social roles, and in rigid social scenes, and, except perhaps for Hermione and the elder Criches, are caricatures whose fate is sealed before the outset. These have all taken the way of death, and therefore they exist at the level of the social personality alone, and they are characterized by means of the familiar technique of caricature, maximum selection. But the free characters, the four, are compounded of a double drive, and it is here that the method of characterization is new and unfamiliar. They have their social existence and they have their psychic existence; the first is inevitably an expression of the second, but in the second lies their whole motivation. As two take the way of death, their social role becomes more and more important ("Civilized society is insane," reflects Constance Chatterley). And as the two others take the way of life, their social role becomes less important, ceases, in fact, to exist. This has been Birkin's ambition and struggle throughout, the need to isolate himself on the cliff of self-responsibility, outside society yet not outside human relationship.

"If I find I can live sufficiently by myself," he continued, "I shall give up my work altogether. It has become dead to me. I don't believe in the humanity I pretend to be part of, I don't care a straw for the social ideals I live by, I hate the dying organic form of social mankind—so it can't be anything but trumpery, to work at education. I shall drop it as soon as I am clear enough—tomorrow perhaps—and be by myself."

"What I want is a strange conjunction with you—" he said quietly; "—not meeting and mingling;—you are quite right:—but an equilibrium, a pure balance of two single beings:—as the stars balance each other."

The attempt is by no means an entire success, as the final pages of the novel make quite clear, but because of the nature of the attempt, the characterization of Birkin is not an entire success, either. He, more exclusively than any of the others, embodies Lawrence's ambition to handle the carbon in character, his drama comes nearest to being the pure psychic drama, but for the very reason that his sufferings and his struggle have no social objectification and cannot have, he tends to elude us as a novelistic being. The contrast with Gerald is instructive.

The second large difference between *Women in Love* and the traditional novel is in the notion of structure. The book is to have no mechanical plot (or only the shadow of a mechanical plot), it is to have no "story" in the conventional sense; instead, it is developed in separate episodes, and these only sporadically developed as "scenes." Yet these are meant to form a pattern of psychic relationships ("the form of some other rhythmic form"), a pattern of psychic movement with a large *general* rhythm, but without the objective or rationalized frame of the old novel.

Because it does not have this rationalized frame, *Women in Love* gives a first impression of much greater looseness and even aimlessness than it actually has, and if we can begin reading it, not as what it begins by seeming—a realistic novel—but as a drama of primal compulsions, a psychic symbolization, it will be seen to have its own kind of coherence, its own kind of organized—indeed, highly and complexly organized—structural presentation of theme. It is a different kind of structure from Conrad's or James's or Hardy's, bearing, perhaps, a more immediate relationship to the art of dance than to the traditional art of fiction. As in dance, it develops through the shifting allegiances between the members, and the configuration of characters, their thematic signifying, is perhaps the strictest of all English novels.

The basic pattern is established at once: Gudrun feels drawn to Gerald; Ursula feels drawn to Birkin. Each of these males is presently seen in another relationship with females: Gerald with the Pussums, whom he destroys, as she wishes; Birkin with Hermione, who is determined to dominate him by force of her will. In the second chapter, Birkin enunciates the theme. There are no accidents, he says; death seeks death; individuation is life; between the two is a perilous balance. From this discussion emerges presently the double idea: of Will—victim and victimizer, and of Death, symbolized socially in the coal mines, intellectually in Bohemia, the two finally brought together in Loerke, the industrial artist; and of Being—wholeness of function, symbolized first in the African statue, and throughout the novel by the natural order—flowers, animals.

Through this quartet of characters this theme will sound. We might glance at some of its variations. For it is of the essence of Lawrence's intuition that these two poles are not fixed or static; they are fluid forces in perpetual conflict, of dissolution and resolution; so that he creates a kind of psychical dialectic, and his relationships are not for a minute rigid. The pattern is fluid, as these two forces and their derivatives attract and repel.

Birkin and Hermione, for example, have had a long relationship; from its opiates to his being, Birkin is now feebly trying to detach himself; the conflict bursts into the open and Hermione beats him with a chunk of lapis. The next scene, the two girls at the railroad crossing and Gerald on his horse, demonstrates their allegiance, Gudrun's fascination, Ursula's horror at Gerald's cruel domination. Next, we find Birkin in a deathy mood still, and Ursula attracted by but resisting the "life" he offers, and it is in that resistance that she moves toward Hermione. The big scene of "The Water Party" clarifies issues momentarily: it is an experience of literal death, and it pushes both Gerald and Birkin, in their differing responses, toward their own destinies; the two women respond accordingly. In Chapter XV, which follows, Ursula yearns toward real death as an escape from a living death in society, and, being at death's door, not life's, she now hates Birkin. Birkin turns away, and in the next chapter, he invites Gerald to enter a pact of *Blutbrüderschaft*—a complete commitment, one to the other. Gerald declines this invitation, and in the next chapter, the great pivotal chapter, "The Industrial Magnate," we are reminded why. This is at once an interlude and a keystone, a projection of individual failure into the fabric of the social structure. The old man (impotent love) is here opposed to Gerald (abstract hate) and between them is the defeated will of the mother. This is a superb image of industrial society in its psychic terms, all its self-defeating pulls exposed. In industry, harmony becomes organzation, and Gerald, as "God of the machine," "converted the industry into a new and terrible purity"—which is death itself. An immediate contrast with the mechanical image is found in the next chapter, "Rabbit"—the image of the vital, wholly single, wholly self-possessed animal life. To Gerald and Gudrun, the creature is "mad," yet in their observation of it, they feel their own bond in some recognized "obscenity." Again, in this chain-like structure, a contrast follows. The chapter called "Moony" shows us Ursula's conflict of despair and desire, to yield or to will; and Birkin's conflict between desire and destructiveness, in the elaborate moon image, reflected on the water, which he attempts to destroy. But like life, it persists in reasserting itself. The conclusion is Birkin's decision to propose marriage to Ursula, but the proposal is a fiasco, and once more he withdraws. Meantime, however, because the larger form of the "process" is working in both Ursula and Gudrun, through and above these variations, they draw apart, begin to feel their alienation. As they draw apart, Birkin once more turns to Gerald, having been denied by Ursula, and if we feel anything legitimate to the novel's purpose in the chapter called "Gladiatorial," we feel Lawrence's own sense of the desperateness of his psychic dialectic in this symbolic conflict. "Woman to Woman" is a counterpart to the chapter called "Man to Man" and shows us Ursula and Hermione in momentary allegiance against Birkin. The Ursula-Birkin climax comes in the chapter called "Excurse," in Birkin's self-recognition, and in the achievement of their "polarity" in relationship.

The other side of the story now develops contrariwise. In "Death and Love," the death of Gerald's father drives him to Gudrun, by way of the graveyard; he brings the clay of his father's new grave into her bedroom. This is love *as* death, and the process now need only resolve itself, as it quickly does. The four go abroad. Ursula and Birkin find the cold Alps uncongenial and leave; Gudrun pits her will against Gerald. She is on the way to becoming a Hermione, but because hers is the death-seeking, not the life-seeking antagonist, Gudrun wins: she kills him, which is also what he has sought. And the novel ends on the partial resolution found by Ursula and Birkin. It seems to say that they have found as much as can be expected by any two individuals unless more individuals will make their effort.

It is instructive to compare this fluid, dance-like movement with the characteristic structure of Thomas Hardy, as, for example, in *Jude the Obscure*. The scheme here is a kind of rigidly counterpointed interchange of character that Hardy much enjoyed. He begins with Jude and Arabella. Then he sets up Sue and Philotson. Then Jude and Sue reverse their roles, and at the end, they reverse them yet again, returning to their original partners. It is like a folk-dance figure, and Hardy's interest is in making it come full circle; it is perfectly expressive of the iron morality that obsessed his imagination. "The certain moral scheme is what I object to," Lawrence declared, and referred, of course, not to Hardy, but to that social morality with which most novelists, including Hardy, have generally been concerned, and of which the traditional notion of plot is an expression. Lawrence wishes to explore a deeper life, a life that seethes and boils beneath institutions as it seethes and boils beneath "personalities."

This is the third great difference between *Women in Love* and other novels, the theme and subject themselves. The structure of the novel is so precisely and so richly expressive of this theme that, after even a cursory examination of the structure, little more need be said of theme. But

we should observe how explicit Lawrence is in enunciating it. Halfway
through the novel we come upon this exact antithesis:

> Birkin thought of Gerald. He was one of those strange white wonderful
> demons from the north, fulfilled in the destructive frost mystery. And was he
> fated to pass away in this knowledge, this one process of frost-knowledge,
> death by perfect cold? Was he a messenger, an omen of the universal dis-
> solution into whiteness and snow?
> Birkin was frightened. He was tired, too, when he had reached this length
> of speculation. Suddenly his strange, strained attention gave way, he could
> not attend to these mysteries any more. There was another way, the way of
> freedom. There was the paradisal entry into pure, single being, the individ-
> ual soul taking precedence over love and desire for union, stronger than
> any pangs of emotion, a lovely state of free proud singleness, which accepted
> the obligation of the permanent connection with others, and with the other,
> submits to the yoke and leash of love, but never forfeits its own proud
> individual singleness, even while it loves and yields.

The relationships of the novel are founded on this opposition, on the
idea of death and life and death-in-life; and the characters move entirely
in terms of these two impulses, their conflicts and their embraces developing out of their allegiance to one or the other. Love is, of course, Lawrence's focus, since he wished to say that in modern life we use love for
death-purposes more frequently than we do for life-purposes. ("The point
about love is that we hate the word because we have vulgarised it. It ought
to be prescribed, tabooed from utterance, for many years, till we get a
new better idea.") Lawrence's theme, as we have suggested, is dramatized
in terms of a struggle between what he calls Will (which may be either
sensual or "spiritual," a death impulse in either case) and Being, that
integration of the total self which is life. Will is the integration of the
drive of ego toward power, toward domination; it has its inverse in the
desire to be overpowered, to be dominated, to yield everything to dissolution. Will is mechanical, and its symbol is therefore the machine; its
historical and social embodiment is an industrial society that lives by
war. Being is the integration of life forces in total and complete self-
responsibility. Its historical embodiment lives in the future.

Lawrence had, of course a conviction that the novel can still do what
it has never done in the past. It is a conviction that follows upon his generally prophetic purpose. In the famous ninth chapter of *Lady Chatterley's Lover*, he says that the novel "can inform and lead into new places
the flow of our sympathetic consciousness, and it can lead our sympathy
away in recoil from things gone dead." The two elements here point to
the two major technical developments in this novel: the concern with the
future, with the smashing of dead patterns and the release of life into
new ones, has a direct effect in the concept of structure and the use of
structure that we have examined; the attempt to make a direct approach

to our "sympathetic consciousness" has an immediate effect in Lawrence's sense of language and his use of language. The fourth difference, then, is in the style of *Women in Love,* and particularly in the visionary quality that is generated by the style.

An appeal to our "sympathetic consciousness" must be absolutely direct —as direct as music or dance. We must be made to *feel* this conflict not in our intellects but in our nerves, as it were, if it is to mean anything at all. Lawrence argues throughout, of course, but the only effective argument is in the direct presentation, which comes to us, if it does, through the style. This Lawrence seemed to know, since he deliberately attempts, first of all, a kind of incantatory prose through the use of repetition, a kind of drugged choral quality, which is perhaps what E. M. Forster had in mind when he said that Lawrence was the only modern novelist "in whom song predominates, who has the rapt bardic quality." It is Forster, too, who speaks of the achievement of Lawrence's style as the "irradiation of the universe and the objects that compose it." This would have to do with diction and figure rather than with rhythm, and we can perhaps see the intention in the high use of color, and in the resulting spectacular quality of the images and of the flitting scenes: ". . . through the man in the closed wagon Gudrun could see the whole scene spectacularly, isolated and momentary, like a vision isolated in eternity." This is a description of the best moments in the novel—scenes such as that where the whole party goes bathing:

> . . . The first to run across the lawn was the little Italian, small and like a cat, her white legs twinkling as she went, ducking slightly her head, that was tied in a gold silk kerchief. She tripped through the gate and down the grass, and stood, like a tiny figure of ivory and bronze, at the water's edge, having dropped off her towelling, watching the swans, which came up in surprise. Then out ran Miss Bradley, like a large, soft plum in her dark-blue suit. Then Gerald came, a scarlet silk kerchief round his loins, his towels over his arms. He seemed to flaunt himself a little in the sun, lingering and laughing, strolling easily, looking white but natural in his nakedness. Then came Sir Joshua, in an overcoat, and lastly Hermione, striking with stiff grace from out of a great mantle of purple silk, her head tied up in purple and gold. Handsome was her stiff, long body, her straight-stepping white legs, there was a static magnificence about her as she let the cloak float loosely away from her striding. She crossed the lawn like some strange memory, and passed slowly towards the water.

Attempts at this quality of the spectacular, of the hallucinated, are not always successful; certainly the three women dancing in Oriental costumes conveniently provided do not quite get into the convention that Lawrence is trying to develop, and the scene of Gudrun, doing her Dalcroze rhythms in the presence of the livestock, does not quite escape the ridiculous. Yet we must recognize, all through the novel, this attempt at the spectacular, the eternally isolated, which leads to the hallucinated effects, and throughout to the strangely irritating compulsive qualities of dreams:

> . . . She put her hand on the arm of her care-worn, sallow father and froth-ing her light draperies, proceeded over the eternal red carpet. Her father, mute and yellowish, his black beard making him look more care-worn, mounted the steps stiffly, as if his spirit were absent; but the laughing mist of the bride went along with him undiminished.

> And no bridegroom had arrived! It was intolerable for her. Ursula, her heart strained with anxiety, was watching the hill beyond; the white, de-scending road, that should give sight of him. There was a carriage. It was running. It had just come into sight. Yes, it was he. Ursula turned towards the bride and the people, and, from her place of vantage, gave an inarticu-late cry. She wanted to warn them that he was coming. But her cry was inarticulate and inaudible, and she flushed deeply, between her desire and her wincing confusion.

To this development of style we should add the insistent contrast of the diction between the mechanical and the organic, and the attempt of the style to persuade us of the *force* inhering in all life. A third development of style is mentioned in Lawrence's own preface. "In point of style, fault is often found with the continual, slightly modified repetition. The only answer is that it is natural to the author; and that every natural crisis in emotion or passion or understanding comes from this pulsing, frictional to-and-fro which works up to culmination." The attempt to duplicate, in syntactical movement itself, the dialectical flow of the theme is perhaps a mistaken aesthetic ambition, but we should observe it as part of Law-rence's particular kind of integrity as an artist.

The intention of *Women in Love* is so tremendous, so central to our lives, that we must for our own sakes make an effort to tolerate it. I say tolerate for the reason that I have known almost no readers who, on *first* reading, did not find it either opaque beyond endurance, or tiresome, or revolting. This has been the response even of readers who can agree with Lawrence when he in effect equates plot as we have known it with a morality that has lost its relevance, even its reality. Yet is it not the fact that the reason the novel is difficult to judge is that it will not accept the disciplines of plot but does not quite find some new limitation that will *contain* this material, so that we are repeatedly asked to love Lawrence the man in order to accept Lawrence the novelist? Scenes like that in which Birkin invites Gerald to be his blood brother, repulsive to our social sense, grotesque before our literary taste, simply say, "Take me at my own level of sincerity, of seriousness, and not at yours, and you will see that this is exactly right." And the question is whether a novelist has the right to impose himself to this extent on his reader, even when his reader is eager to accept as much as he can, even when his reader, like the present writer, cannot, after eight or ten readings of this novel, imagine being without it. It is possible that *Women in Love* attempts to do more than the novel as we know it and even as Lawrence developed it itself knows how to do. This does not for a moment mean that the attempt must not be made. No novelist speaks more directly to us than Lawrence, and if we can't hear him, we are, I quite believe, lost. But he has not, in this book, found the whole way to speak. His attempt to move into the realm of psychic drama we can take seriously in a way that we cannot take the diluted attempt of Virginia Woolf; but can we always hear what Lawrence wants us to hear? The question is not whether he is *right;* the question is: What is a novel?

Judging *Women in Love* in its own terms as a single work, I should say that its success is partial; judging it as a step in a career, I should remove the qualification. It is perhaps the most important single work in Lawrence's formal education. If we follow him on from *Women in Love,* through the next really shattered books, and to the end, we will see that he took, finally, two ways: in his last two books, *Lady Chatterley's Lover* and *The Man Who Died*—both, in my view, very great books—he divided the intention that in *Women in Love* is one. In *Lady Chatterley,* he retrenches his claims a little—it is a novel in a solid and sustained social context, and it is a novel with a clear and happily developed plot, in which characters function fully and the author lets them speak for themselves; in *The Man Who Died,* he made an absolutely unqualified claim for the sanctity of the purely self-responsible individual human being, society not more than a shadowy threat outside the novel, and he gives us a real image of what he does not give us in Birkin, the wholly integrated man; but he writes in the form of the fable. And this is, perhaps, as far as we have gone with the novel.

For the novel always drags us back into the world, into circumstance. Conrad says that "the energy of evil is so much more forcible than the energy of good," and perhaps this is because in novels, at least, pure evil does not exist whereas there are those novelists who attempt to make pure good prevail. Those who read—those who can stay to read *Women in Love* to the last fifty pages—the death of Gerald in the snow and the grievous pathos of Birkin without him—those readers come, I think, upon fifty pages that have more power of a particular kind than any other fifty pages in any other English or American novel. It is what we might call the real Russian bang. But Gerald is not the saint, he is the sinner; he is—us; and as we can see in reading novels in some ways so different as *Middlemarch* and *The Wings of the Dove,* sinners—for the very reason that the novel as we have so far known it is a genre that deals with individuals in a social context—sinners it can save for art, but its saints are damned.

The Plumed Serpent: Vision and Language

by Harry T. Moore

The Plumed Serpent is at once Lawrence's most ambitious attempt in the area of the novel and his most notable failure—and yet it has some good qualities, particularly in the descriptive elements of the writing. But *The Plumed Serpent* remains Lawrence's *Pierre*, his *Romola*, his *Kreutzer Sonata*, though comparatively a poorer novel than any of these (except maybe *Pierre*) and perhaps more nearly a prophetic fable, like *Sartor Resartus* and *Thus Spake Zarathustra*, than a novel per se. When *The Plumed Serpent* came out in 1926, its American publisher, Alfred Knopf, listed it under Lawrence's novels; then, recognizing its generic difficulties, Knopf later classified it officially as *belles-lettres*.

In placing the book among Lawrence's imaginative works, one must put it with *Aaron's Rod* (1922) and *Kangaroo* (1923). *The Plumed Serpent* and these two earlier volumes constitute Lawrence's trilogy on the theme of leadership, an important concern in the 1920's. Mussolini and Hitler were then rising to power in Italy and Germany, two countries which Lawrence frequently visited.

During World War I he had completed the two books regarded by most critics as his finest: *The Rainbow*, which came out in 1915, and *Women in Love*, which was published in 1920 after about four years of delay. In these two novels dealing with men and women from various social groups in his native Midlands, Lawrence had put forth his message to mankind. Their art was of such high quality that the preachment in them, unlike that in *The Plumed Serpent*, was not ruinous; in them, Lawrence's message was integrated with plot and character in such a way as to make the theme not distortingly intrusive. Those two novels dramatically express Lawrence's deepest vision as man and as artist.

But after finishing *Women in Love* in the winter of 1916-17, Lawrence went through a creatively barren time; for several years he produced only bits of poetry and fiction, giving most of his writing energy to hortatory essays such as the "Education of the People" series which went unpublished in his lifetime, or to critical expositions such as the articles which were later collected in *Studies in Classic American Litera-*

"*The Plumed Serpent*: Vision and Language" by Harry T. Moore was written expressly for this anthology and is printed by permission of the author.

61

ture. These last represent the beginnings of Lawrence's definite interest in the New World, an interest that reached its apotheosis in *The Plumed Serpent*. As a child, Lawrence had read Cooper and his stories of the Red Indians; later, in recognizing the greatness of *Moby Dick* and in speaking out in its behalf, he became one of the influential early voices in the Melville revival. And when the *Studies* were published in their final form in 1923, they showed that Lawrence had made a profound exploration of the New World spirit, as represented by Cooper and Melville, as well as by Poe, Hawthorne, Whitman, and the others whom he investigated. All of them helped influence *The Plumed Serpent* by giving Lawrence a sense of the New World's still unextinguished primitivism, by providing him with some understanding of a new community based on older forms and, in some cases, by deepening his own vision of "darkness."

Before turning to *The Plumed Serpent*, Lawrence also wrote *The Lost Girl* (1920), begun before the war but completed after it. Lawrence had returned to the Mediterranean at the end of 1919, after five years' confinement to an England that he had found increasingly dismal, ruined by its exultant and (to him) disgusting attitude toward the war. But in the sunlight of the green lands he felt a rebirth of his imaginative power. The Red Indians somehow crept into *The Lost Girl* in what seems almost a mockery of Cooper—the parody of a play staged by the theatrical troupe with whom the lost girl, Alvina, becomes involved.

There are no Red Indians in *Aaron's Rod*, which is a male version of *The Lost Girl*; Aaron Sisson, like Alvina, comes down to Italy; but unlike Alvina he has no earthy Ciccio to attract him there; rather he is lured by the influence of a bearded Lawrence-like man, Rawdon Lilly, who speaks to Aaron of power urges and of the necessity of yielding to "a greater soul," presumably Lilly, who—despite his disclaimer of Nietzsche-ism—is intrinsically Nietzschean in his vision of an *Übermensch* who will lead mankind across the abyss to a more splendid future. Lawrence, in *Movements in European History* (1921), had spoken well of Attila and Bismarck and had suggested that a strong man would save Europe; at the end of *Aaron's Rod*, it seems that Aaron will submit to Lilly, give him an allegiance which Lilly has fought for as Naphtha and Settembrini in Thomas Mann's *The Magic Mountain* fight for the discipleship of Hans Castorp, who like Aaron is an ordinary human being; but it is the ordinary human being—capable, like Hans Castorp, of becoming "a genius of experience"—whom prophetic men want to capture.

In *Kangaroo*, the procedure is almost entirely reversed. The Lawrence-like man in that story is prophetic enough, but he is weary of trying to save and to lead Europe. On his way to the New World, R. L. Somers, the visionary writer and working man's son, comes to Australia, a fresh country; in Sydney he meets a prophet, a leader, who tempts him to join his revolutionary movement, made up largely of war veterans and somewhat resembling the fascism whose beginnings Lawrence had witnessed in Italy (*Aaron's Rod* includes a vivid account of the *fascisti* in a street riot). The Australian leader, a Jewish lawyer named Ben Cooley who is known as "Kangaroo" for his resemblance to the nation's totemic animal, wants Somers to become a kind of Goebbels of his movement. Somers is also tempted in a similar way by the Australian socialists.

He rejects both groups because he realizes that "the only thing one can stick to is one's own isolate being and the God in whom it is rooted." Kangaroo, and to a lesser extent the socialist Willie Struthers, put Somers in somewhat the same position as Lilly had put Aaron; but Somers manifests his independence and moves on to America, where he will be "killed," according to Kangaroo, himself dying from wounds received in a riot and from his despair over Somers' rejection of him and his beliefs. It perhaps didn't occur to Lawrence, who was severely antidemocratic, that his own isolate position was possible only in a democracy; at least he doesn't give Somers such a realization. We know now that anarchism of Somers' type is possible only in a free society. Let Kangaroo or even Willie Struthers take over the State, and there are no more isolate beings.

In his thoughts on isolation and finding roots in the god of one's own being, Somers had proceeded to the idea that "the only thing to look to is the God who fulfills one from the dark. And the only thing to wait for is for men to find their aloneness and their God in the darkness. Then one can meet as worshippers, in a sacred contact in the dark." It almost sounds as if Lawrence were already writing *The Plumed Serpent*.

But before he began that book in Mexico early in 1923, he was exposed to parts of the United States, and even to some of the "dark gods" of the Indian dances of the Southwest, of which he wrote in several travel essays. And while composing *The Plumed Serpent*, between 1923 and 1925, Lawrence was working out some of its ideas in poems such as "The Red Wolf" and in stories such as "The Woman Who Rode Away." In the poem, Lawrence projects his own attraction toward the Indian way of life and his half-recognized incompatibility with it; in "The Woman Who Rode Away," a white woman in Mexico goes out as a voluntary sacrifice to a tribe of Indians who preserve the ancient Aztec blood-rituals in a lost community and believe that the white man's rule is waning—the woman's going down to them to have her heart cut out symbolizes the coming extinction of white power.

The protagonist of *The Plumed Serpent* is also a woman; and although she too goes out to submit to the dark forces and the dark men, it is not death toward which she goes. Yet, despite the bias of the book, it is not necessarily life either; at least it is not life as we have come to know it in Western communities. But the matter is really left unresolved.

Why did Lawrence select a woman as the reflector of the experience of *The Plumed Serpent*? John Middleton Murry, in that weirdly erroneous book, *Son of Woman*—which came out in 1931, the year after Lawrence's death—opened a false trail of speculation when he suggested that by the time Lawrence came to write *The Plumed Serpent,* his spokesman-character, such as Birkin in *Women in Love,* or Lilly, or Somers, was dead: "The Man disappears, the Woman remains. . . . Lawrence is not reborn, nor ever will be . . ."; presumably Lawrence had given up. This is wrong, because Lawrence did put himself into the novel—but in strange guise; in *The Plumed Serpent* he projects himself as a native Mexican, Don Cipriano, General Viedma. Here he is the avatar of those long-celebrated dark gods. Granted that it is not a successful embodiment, granted that the dark gods are not convincingly projected to the reader, Lawrence nevertheless does not envision himself as dead. Murry was probably influenced by the fact that Lawrence himself nearly died in Mexico just about the time he finished *The Plumed Serpent;* apparently this illness was the first serious manifestation of the tuberculosis that was to kill him just five years later. Perhaps the intensity of working on the final stages of *The Plumed Serpent* helped bring Lawrence near death; but in the book and in all his comments about it he certainly saw himself as Cipriano, representative not only of the dark gods of the story's religious revival, but as a somewhat Nietzschean *Übermensch,* a bridge toward a better future—in any event, a supremely vitalistic figure.

Kate Leslie, the woman in *The Plumed Serpent,* is the widow of an Irish politician who had worn himself out working for a cause. Such an idea was not new in Lawrence's work, for in *The Rainbow* Lydia Lensky had brought a new strain into the Brangwen family after her husband had worked himself to death as a Polish revolutionary. And Kate is in certain respects a later version of Ursula Brangwen of *The Rainbow* and *Women in Love,* the questing woman who seeks emancipation in union.

Lawrence was certainly right in not putting another Birkin-Lilly-Somers into *The Plumed Serpent*: he had done enough of that kind of self-projection. And he could successfully present a story from the woman's view, as he so often did, because he was concerned with it. *The Rainbow* and many of his later books deal with women as central characters, and with that problem of emancipation in union, the ideal expressed in *Kangaroo* in the chapter, "At Sea in Marriage." There Lawrence reflects that in too many marriages, two ships are lashed together and steered from a single helm; ideally, they should float side by side on the same course. In *Women in Love,* Birkin had expressed a similar thought to Ursula when he spoke of "two stars in balanced conjunction." This is the kind of relationship Lawrence celebrated, and it represents the relationship of Kate and Cipriano in *The Plumed Serpent.* The fault of the book does not lie in the presentation of its central human relationships, but rather in the direction of its community ideology. The leadership of the so-called white races might be wobbling—Lawrence disliked Wilson and Lenin and detested Lloyd George—but neither Western man nor the rest of humanity will find a solution to their problems in the revival of the pre-Columbian gods of Mexico.

Because Lawrence repeatedly showed a wise understanding of current political movements, Martin Jarrett-Kerr says (in *D. H. Lawrence and Human Existence*) that in considering *The Plumed Serpent* we must assume "either that Lawrence has had an almost unbelievable lapse from sanity; or that the theme of this is not, as it might appear at first sight, primarily 'political' at all." Admittedly, Lawrence was in *The Plumed Serpent* often speaking symbolically rather than literally; he was being religio-mystic. Applied to individual cases, all this might be interesting indeed, and on the religious side Lawrence often had much to say that was important; unfortunately, this novel concerns the taking over of a country and, by corollary, profound political problems are involved. Government by mysticism simply will not do.

In other books, Lawrence criticized civilization harshly, but he attempted melioration only in terms of a seemingly plausible social order. In *The Plumed Serpent* he carries his attack on civilization to the point of a comprehensive destructiveness, and then proceeds to set up a new order—really an ancient and entirely outmoded one—as the basis of future existence. But, as he himself says in various other books—and the figure is Lawrence's—we must not haul down the flag of our civilized consciousness; he noted, for example, that Melville fled from his Pacific paradise when he had a chance to do so. Yet in *The Plumed Serpent* Lawrence seems definitely to be recommending that we haul down the flag of our civilized consciousness; the primitivistic influences from which he had taken only partial nourishment for a while became too strong for him. Lawrence was usually a man seeking balance (what he called "polarity") between the instinctual and the overintellectual; in *The Plumed Serpent* he is too much on the purely destructive side of the unthinking primitive —or apparently wants to be.

The Plumed Serpent does not begin on the prophetic note of religious resurrection, but the opening effectively prepares the way for the main theme by showing the grime and depravity of present-day Mexico. The grime is in the place and people—the men in the bullfight crowd are crawling with lice—while the depravity, which is the cause and perpetuation of the grime, is found partly in the commercialized debasement of an ancient ritual into a modern bullfight. Kate "had always been afraid of bulls, fear tempered with reverence of the great Mithraic beast," and at the arena she pities the gored horses whose bowels are spilled out onto the sand. She cannot stand it; this Europa will not stay to be vicariously raped. On her way out she is assisted by Cipriano, General Viedma, whom she now meets for the first time; his very name, the Cyprian, has important connotations, since Cypress was the isle where the ancients worshiped the goddess of love. It must be added that this opening sequence—

with its city Mexicans and with its visiting Americans who consciously want to be made sick by the bullfight—is skillful narrative, with the hard, violent colors of Mexico and with all the force of Lawrence's social observation of that land where recent revolution had not blotted out ancestral memories of the blood-rites of the Aztecs or the brutality of the Conquistadores.

The whole story cannot be summarized here; it is enough to say that Kate leaves Mexico City to live in a village on the Lake of Chapala, on the shore of which she will be sexually regenerated; the very waters of the lake look, appropriately, like sperm. Almost without knowing it, Kate becomes a part of the religiously motivated revolution of Cipriano and his friend, the true leader of the movement, the charismatic Don Ramón Carrasco. Kate even marries Cipriano in the mystic rites of the ancient religion of Quetzalcoatl, the feathered serpent of the pre-Columbian Mexicans; Kate becomes a vegetation goddess of the new regime which removes the Catholic images from the churches. But Kate never quite believes in the symbols that replace them; and certainly Lawrence never convincingly shows how Ramón and Cipriano will really improve the lot of the peons they inspire. As for Kate, at the end of the book she tells herself: "What a fraud I am! I know all the time it is I who don't altogether want them. I want myself to myself. But I can fool them so they shan't find out." Aloud she says to Cipriano: "You won't let me go!"

Lawrence was a specialist at the indefinite ending. *Sons and Lovers, Women in Love, Lady Chatterley's Lover,* and stories such as *The Fox* and *St. Mawr* all have the inconclusive conclusion—this is of course part of Lawrence's dynamism; his avoidance of the static. His lovers never quite find fulfillment, but only go in the general direction of it; life itself gives promise rather than perfection.

Lawrence once said that one can't lie in the novel, but much of *The Plumed Serpent* tries to lie. The hymns of Quetzacoatl, the people hypnotized into chanting in the plazas, the ceremonials of Don Ramón and Cipriano—all these have a partial effectiveness, but ultimately they are meaningless to the reader. They are in some ways reminiscent of the megalomaniac oration in Venice of the self-drunken superman, Stelio Effrena, in a far worse novel—D'Annunzio's *The Flame.* (Lawrence's book, for all its occasional silliness, lacks the swollen egoism of D'Annunzio's.) And those mass-hypnosis passages in *The Plumed Serpent* are further reminiscent of the torchlight parades, the rising banners, and the chanting crowds of Nazism; indeed, this book has caused some readers to think of Lawrence as a fascist. Despite those frenzied sections of *The Plumed Serpent,* however, and—as has been extensively shown elsewhere —Lawrence was not a fascist; this fiercely individualistic man, who knew fascism only as a tourist and didn't like it, would have fought every encroachment upon his freedom. As an outcast in his native England during the war, as a man who—together with his German wife—was wrongly suspected of spying, Lawrence had experienced mass bullying and a modified form of state control, and hated them. Admittedly, it is difficult to be indulgent toward some parts of *The Plumed Serpent,* such as Cipriano's legalized murders, and for a time Lawrence seems to have lost his good sense and, indeed, most of his gifts—except his magnificent descriptive and narrative powers.

One example of these will serve. Kate is sitting alone on her verandah near the lake:

> . . . Morning! Brilliant sun pouring into the patio, on the hibiscus flowers and the fluttering yellow and green rags of the banana trees. Birds swiftly coming and going, with tropical suddenness. In the dense shadow of the mango grove, white-clad Indians going like ghosts. The sense of fierce sun and, almost more impressive, of dark, intense shadow.

That is full of Lawrence's lavish carelessness—it is a series of phrases rather than complete sentences—but it captures the life and color and shape and movement of the place as few writers could; and when, a few sentences later, there "silently appears an old man with one egg held up mysteriously, like some symbol," the scene is sealed in with wonder. Throughout, Lawrence presents the physical Mexico in his bright and kinetic prose; as a travel book, *The Plumed Serpent* is almost self-contained, an outstanding example of that genre. Few modern novels can match its evocation of the Mexican landscape, the smashing rains, the attack by Ramón's enemies on the hacienda, or the bullfight. It is the philosophy of the book that is often objectionable; the book is somewhat like an opera with magnificent music and a ridiculous libretto.

This statement could lead to some digressive arguments. The question of literature and belief is valuably discussed in the book of that name by Martin Jarrett-Kerr; and there is a point of reference in T. S. Eliot's Dante essay, in which he says we can admire a man's poetry without necessarily going along with his beliefs. The issue is clouded, however, because of the empathy that at least partially accompanies most reading. So it goes; but the fact remains that the ideology of *The Plumed Serpent* is repugnant to many who nevertheless admire the prose-poetry of the book.

Many Lawrencean constants appear in the story. One of these is the woman powered by will, represented here by Ramón's first wife, Carlota, who in her frustration goes into a kind of insanity: the very name Carlota has in Mexico suggestions of madness. When Ramón is presiding over the Quetzalcoatl ceremonies, Carlota's shouted opposition hits upon another familiar Lawrencean theme: frenzy or violence in church; in *The Rainbow,* Ursula giggles hysterically when Skrebensky sings a hymn; in the story "Fannie and Annie," Mrs. Nixon, "a devil of a woman," screams accusations at Harry Goodall during the hymn-singing at a village chapel; in another story, "The Last Laugh," some kind of poltergeist wrecks the interior of a church; and in *The Plumed Serpent,* there is not only Carlota's hysteria but the violation of all the churches by Don Ramón's followers. Lawrence, who consistently attacked established religion, was, wishfully at least, a shatterer of the traditional churches.

Another recurring Lawrencean theme found in this book is the Sleeping Beauty motif which underlies so much of Lawrence's work. It began with Ursula in *The Rainbow* and *Women in Love,* and by the time of *Lady Chatterley's Lover* it had become, with its woodland scenes, virtually the Briar Rose variant of the Sleeping Beauty myth. In Lawrence's fiction, most of the women are either the will-driven type, like Mrs. Morel and Miriam in *Sons and Lovers* and Carlota in *The Plumed Serpent,* or they are unawakened, dreaming women, like Lady Daphne in "The Ladybird," who is aroused to life by Count Dionys. In *The Plumed Serpent,* Teresa, whom Don Ramón marries after Carlota's death, is already awakened, though Kate fits neatly into the Sleeping Beauty pattern.

But there are some Lawrencean constants which are missing in this book. Humor, for example, is one of Lawrence's gifts that is in abeyance here. Lawrence could write good comedy, as in the portrait of the father in *Sons and Lovers* coming home in the afternoon from the mine and taking out his frustrations on the parson he finds visiting for tea, or as in the marketplace scene in *Women in Love,* when Birkin and Ursula decide they don't want a chair they have bought and attempt to give it to a lower-class couple who immediately become suspicious; or in countless other stories, including the trim little satires of Lawrence's last period, such as those in *The Lovely Lady* (1933). But in *The Plumed Serpent,* Lawrence's sense of the comic and the satiric seems to have been asleep. While Don Ramón is delivering some of his pomposities, the reader might consider Lawrence's statement in his essay, "The Novel" (in *Reflections on the Death of a Porcupine*): "If, in Plato's *Dialogues,* somebody had suddenly stood on his head and given smooth Plato a kick in the wind, and set the whole school in an uproar, then Plato would have been put into a much truer relation to the universe." Don Ramón, too.

Yet, despite all the negative comments on *The Plumed Serpent* by critics from Leavis to Vivas, the book has defenders. To William York Tindall, it represents Lawrence's ultimate working out of an objective correlative. Mr. Tindall in his Introduction to the 1951 reprint of *The Plumed Serpent* finds "this glowing landscape, where flat figures move in ritual patterns," to be "one of the great creations of our time," and "at once design and vision." But the vision, even when it is—as Mr. Tindall skillfully shows—organically expressed through symbol and myth, is too distorted. That Kate reawakens sexually, as Mr. Tindall points out, is true; and it is also true that she undergoes a religious rebirth, though it is a rebirth into an outmoded and rather crazy evangelism. But the political rebirth he claims for her simply doesn't exist, for Kate takes no part in the political goings-on, sketchy as they are. Her messiahs are preachers who sway the masses for whom they have contempt—Don Ramón again and again calls the people monkeys, and Cipriano ("I am the red Huitzilopochtli of the knife") wants his storm troopers to take over the country by force, "meeting metal with metal." To this, however, Ramón says: "No! No! Let it spread itself"—precisely the strategy Hitler was to use a few years later when he won the chancellorship not by violence but through voting strength.

Myth and symbol are one thing; we have learned, in our time, that to have them incarnated in a government which will coerce those who don't submit to its myth and symbol, to its mass hypnosis, is quite another. But the critic Jascha Kessler, in "Descent in Darkness: The Myth of *The Plumed Serpent*" (in *A D. H. Lawrence Miscellany*, 1959), justifies the action of the novel since so much of it takes place at mythic and symbolic levels. He discerns in the story the anthropological formulas of separation and initiation. Kate hears the call to adventure, crosses the first threshold (to "a peculiar region"), is aware of seeking wholeness of being, takes the road of trials, and goes through the final phases of initiation. In regard to formula, all this may be true; but what does it mean? Kate is, let us grant, sexually attracted to the dashing Cipriano—and like Chekhov's "Darling," she enters empathetically into the activities of her man of the moment. But Lawrence never puts her into the trances such as Ramón and Cipriano fall into in their *Blutbrüderschaft* scene, that curious echo of the wrestling sequence in *Women in Love*. Kate is a woman, capable of loving, but like Harriet in *Kangaroo* she really distrusts all the male activity and participation in events, which she calls "all that other stuff"; she goes along merely because Cipriano attracts her. The rapture produced by the "Hymns of Quetzalcoatl" does not. How curiously like the Congregational hymns of Lawrence's childhood these Quetzalcoatl chants are, with Mexican-Aztec ornaments added; and the dark-faced Mexicans singing in the plaza are like the coal-masked miners singing as they walked home through the streets of Lawrence's childhood. The difference is that the colliers sang individual songs; the Quetzalcoatl hymns are somewhat elegant surrogates for the *Horst Wessel Lied*. Don Ramón is once again being the exact contemporary and spiritual associate of Hitler and of von Ludendorff when he says: "I wish the Teutonic world would once more think in terms of Thor and Wotan."

Lawrence in *Kangaroo* had seen the issues clearly, and rejected the temptations of "transports"; here, transports become contagious as they often do under the spell of evangelism and hymn-singing. But fortunately, Lawrence—as if in spite of himself—keeps that grain of skepticism in Kate, and although she accepts the blood-rituals and stays in Mexico, she is reluctant and at the end begs her lover to find some compulsion to keep her; at one point she seems to be staying largely because

Piccadilly might be muddy! In *Beyond the Mexique Bay* (1934), Aldous
Huxley quite rightly notes that, by the time he finished *The Plumed
Serpent*, Lawrence himself no longer believed in it. And, unlike Kate,
who at least hadn't left by the end of the story, Lawrence got out.

Years before *The Plumed Serpent*, in writing *Sons and Lovers*, *The
Rainbow*, and *Women in Love*, Lawrence had been aware that he was
producing masterpieces; he had a just pride in them. As he worked on
The Plumed Serpent he felt that it was a magnum opus, particularly
since it came after years of shorter works—poems, essays, and stories—and
slighter novels such as *Aaron's Rod* and *Kangaroo*, which are, as we have
seen, the earlier parts of the leadership trilogy. In his own experience
Lawrence had failed in leadership; his efforts to set up a pantisocracy in
New Mexico had collapsed as friends refused to join him and as the
wealthy and fiercely willful Mabel Dodge Luhan kept intruding upon his
life. Lawrence's long visits to Old Mexico were, as Mrs. Luhan has admitted, in part escapes from her; and the novel of Old Mexico is to a
great extent the channeling off of frustrations coming out of Lawrence's
own failures in New Mexico. This no doubt accounts to some extent for
the dichotomy between language and vision in *The Plumed Serpent*: Lawrence had matured in expressional power, so that he could write superbly
of the physical aspects of Mexico, but his beliefs were at the time uncertain, blurred, distorted.

Eventually his vision cleared, and in 1928, three years after he completed *The Plumed Serpent*, he made what amounted to a partial repudiation of the book in a letter:

> The leader of men is a back number. After all, at the back of the hero is
> the militant ideal: and the militant ideal or ideal militant seems to me also
> a cold egg. . . . The leader-cum-follower relationship is a bore. And the new
> sort of relationship will be some sort of tenderness, sensitive, between men
> and men and men and women, not the one up one down, lead on I follow,
> *ich dien* sort of business. So you see I'm becoming a lamb at last. . . .

Lawrence had by that time written *Lady Chatterley's Lover*, the story
of the reawakening and regeneration of a woman—not in a mass-hypnosis
group—but as an individual. And in 1929, four years after *The Plumed
Serpent*, Lawrence published *The Escaped Cock* (after his death the publishers timidly changed the title to *The Man Who Died*), the story of a
prophet who in his resurrection has abandoned prophecy.

Indeed, Lawrence after the aberration of *The Plumed Serpent* became
somewhat mellower ("a lamb at last"), and in an essay written in 1928,
"Insouciance," he humorously shows the value of detachment. On a hotel
balcony in Switzerland he is trying to enjoy the scene before him, but his
calm is shattered by a little old lady who "cares," who is one of those
modern people who

. . . simply are eaten up with caring. They are so busy caring about Fascism or Leagues of Nations or whether France is right or whether Marriage is threatened, that they never know where they are. They certainly never live on the spot where they are. They inhabit abstract space, the desert void of politics, principles, right and wrong, and so forth. They are doomed to be abstract. . . . There was a direct sensuous contact between me, the lake, mountains, cherry trees, mowers, and a certain invisible but noisy chaffinch in a clipped lime tree.

But the little old lady with her abstract shears "beheaded me, and flung my head into abstract space."

Lawrence's later work shows a recovery from *The Plumed Serpent;* after all, *Lady Chatterley* is his fourth-best novel, ranking behind *Women in Love, The Rainbow,* and *Sons and Lovers.* The remarkable novella of his last period, *The Escaped Cock,* has already been mentioned; and surely his last poems, particularly "Bavarian Gentians," are his finest. And yet, and yet—that tremendous volcano of a failure, *The Plumed Serpent,* somehow compels attention as it stands pouring out its bitter smoke above the valley of Mexico.

Lady Chatterley's Lover: The Deed of Life

by Julian Moynahan

"And here lies the vast importance of the novel, properly handled. It can inform and lead into new places the flow of our sympathetic consciousness, and it can lead our sympathy away in recoil from things gone dead."

I

Lady Chatterley's Lover[1] dramatizes two opposed orientations toward life, two distinct modes of human awareness: the one abstract, cerebral, and unvital; the other concrete, physical, and organic. A relatively clear statement of the distinction may be found in Lawrence's long essay, "Apropos of *Lady Chatterley's Lover*," written two years after he had published the Florence edition of his novel:

> There are many ways of knowing, there are many sorts of knowledge. But the two ways of knowing, for man, are knowing in terms of apartness, which is mental, rational, scientific, and knowing in terms of togetherness, which is religious and poetic. . . .
> But relationship is threefold. First there is the relationship to the living universe. Then comes the relationship of man to woman. Then comes the relationship of man to man. And each is a blood-relationship, not mere spirit or mind. We have abstracted the universe into Matter and Force, we have abstracted men and women into separate personalities—personalities being isolated units, incapable of togetherness—so that all great relationships are bodiless, dead.

The novel's structural method involves a simple juxtaposition of the two modes; its narrative method combines explicit interpretative comment

"*Lady Chatterley's Lover*: The Deed of Life" by Julian Moynahan. From *ELH*, XXVI (March 1959), 66-90. Copyright © 1959 by *ELH*. Reprinted by permission of the author and The Johns Hopkins Press.

[1] Page numbers following direct quotations from the text refer to *Lady Chatterley's Lover* (Paris, privately printed, 1929) but accord closely, often exactly, with the Grove Press hardbound edition of 1959. The Paris edition carries the subtitle "The Author's Unabridged Popular Edition." It was issued by Lawrence in May 1929 in an attempt to combat piracy of the expensive Florence edition of 1928.

by a narrator who from the beginning makes clear his sympathy for the vitalist viewpoint together with lucid and objective renderings of characters, situations, and settings. Furthermore, there is a sort of synecdochic method employed in the narration. Wragby Hall and the industrial village of Tevershall are realized in themselves but come also to stand for entire industrial, social, and even spiritual orders dominant in the modern world, more especially in twentieth century England. Sir Clifford Chatterley sums up a modern habit of mind as well as a ruling class in transition from one type of economic proprietorship to another. In contrast, the gamekeeper, Oliver Mellors, not only follows but represents the organic way of life, and the wood in which he lurks is a spatial metaphor of the natural order, or what Lawrence frequently called "the living universe." These are but a few of the simple and necessarily rigid equations the novel sets up between particular and general conditions. Of course very few novels have been written which fully resist the regular habit of readers to discover general truths mirrored in particularized and historically limited episodes. But few novels are so explicit and so demanding in the control they impose on the reader's moral imagination as *Lady Chatterley's Lover*.

Among the leading characters only the heroine, Connie Chatterley, plays no rigid representative role; and it is her freedom of action which creates the possibility of drama. As she shuttles from one realm to another —both in space and in terms of inner awareness—from Wragby Hall to the gamekeeper's hunt in the woods, her experiences project the energies of the two modes in conflict with one another. She is both booty and battleground in the ensuing struggle between vital and unvital ways of apprehending experience. If it is not too scandalous a suggestion, Lady Chatterley may be said to stand for ourselves, for all those puzzled modern people who have not yet resolved the question of whether they wish to be domiciled at Wragby Hall or in Wragby wood, of whether to live among powerful abstractions or growing things. If the alternatives appear rigidly posed, then that is a limitation which the novel fully accepts. Life can be mapped according to other patterns as even Lawrence knew. But in this story the idea emerges clearly that Lady Chatterley—we—cannot have it both ways. There is no possibility of compromise between vitality and its opposite.

Although the heroine possesses a freedom of role and action unknown to such representative figures as the lord and the gamekeeper, this does not mean that dramatic interest ever depends upon suspense of outcome. From the beginning Connie is no more free to choose the realm of "death-in-life" than Alvina Houghton in *The Lost Girl* was free to continue living alone beside her father's shop in Woodhouse. Freedom in the novel is merely relative. In Lawrence's last novel it extends only to questions of means. The heroine must escape her husband and what he stands for; but for a time she is free to entertain various alternatives: to hesitate, to become confused, to relapse, but never finally to make the great refusal. This is all very much like *The Lost Girl*, but for various reasons much better than that novel. For one thing, the later book brings fully into the light ideas and values which in *The Lost Girl* were distorted by equivocal descriptions. In *Lady Chatterley's Lover* only things mysterious in themselves—for example, the sensations of a woman during an orgasm —are described mysteriously. The novel is explicit to the point of pedantry about matters which *The Lost Girl* only managed to treat by indirection. Whereas Cicio possessed "the sensual secrets," Mellors possesses a highly specific sexual technique, a lengthily reported sexual biography, and a prophetic program for his contemporaries which he has worked out in occasionally bizarre detail. If some of Mellors' self-revelations seem absurd, his willingness to take a firm stand on issues crucial to the novel's meaning seems all to the good. Lawrence's descriptions of his dark heroes in such novels as *The Lost Girl* and *The Plumed Serpent* are more often picturesque than significant. These posturing and strutting males seem cheaply glamorous by comparison with the gamekeeper.

There are other reasons why *Lady Chatterley's Lover* is a much better novel than *The Lost Girl*. First, the realm of the vital is not created as a terminus toward which the heroine moves instinctively, following without thought various obscure hints and signs. Instead it is richly embodied early in the novel and sustained as a genuine meaning to the end. There is no collapse, and the reader is given the fullest opportunity to appraise the significance of the vital career as it not only is defined through the explicit comments of the narrator and by leading characters like Connie, Mellors, and Dukes, but also realized in imaginative terms of description and dramatization. The heroine is not raped into fulfillment but must use her head as well as her body to escape unwholesome circumstances.

Secondly, the unvital mode is boldly and subtly defined. Woodhouse was a puny and obvious metaphor of death-in-life. Lawrence was by no means the first to flog the dead horse of provincial and small-town mores. But Wragby Hall is something else again. It represents domination not only in the sphere of ideas and sensibility but also in the sphere of economics. Clifford's change of vocation from a writer of ultramodern stories whose essence is nothingness to that of ultramodern engineer-industrialist developing techniques to exploit further the exhausted mineral soils of his region and to increase the alienation of his workmen from wholesome living conditions is hardly a trivial incident in this connection. The manor house rests on a foundation of abstractions the greatest of which is money. In the struggle between the vital and the antivital Sir Clifford holds most if not all the cards. The gamekeeper has no following; he is beset on all sides, and even at the end his victory is by no means clearcut.

A third point of superiority over many of Lawrence's earlier novels can be developed from the previous point. Within the limitations of a particular interpretation of history, culture, and humanity, *Lady Chatterley's*

Lover appraises the human situation realistically. Abstraction looms large, and vital mysteries shine with but a diminished glimmer in the modern world and in the novel. As Mellors writes to his mistress at the end he mentions "the little glow there is between you and me" (p. 363) and remarks, "all the bad times that ever have been, haven't been able to blow the crocus out" (p. 363). In this novel the value of vitality is embodied in tender and vulnerable things, while insentience has the sanction of powerful institutions, individuals, and movements. The story has a poignant quality. After reading it we may find the guarantees of extraordinary developments imperfectly realized in such books as *The Rainbow* and *Women in Love* almost glib, a mere whistling in the dark. One might say that in Lawrence's last novel his prophetic vision returns to earth after failing to sustain itself on the lofty heights occupied in novels like *The Rainbow* and *The Plumed Serpent. Lady Chatterley's Lover* opens with these observations:

> Ours is essentially a tragic age, so we refuse to take it tragically. The cataclysm has happened, we are among the ruins, we start to build up new little habitats, to have new little hopes. It is rather hard work: there is now no smooth road into the future. (p. 12)

In the context of the whole novel tragedy refers to a great deal more than a world war. The ruins are perhaps the abstracted spirit of the age itself. The new habitats and hopes are fixed in such images as that of a little clearing in the midst of a remnant of forest, and in the scrupulously designed description of a man working with his hands to repair a broken pheasant coop. The incommensurability of the little hope and the enormous negation which is modern life is assumed in the novel and does not, I believe, ever become the object of pathetic reflection. After yielding ourselves to the viewpoint dramatized, and after reflecting upon what the last quarter-century has contributed to the realization of Lawrence's prophetic hopes, we might indeed weep—except that the novel teaches us that the power in life which sustains the crocus is, strictly speaking, unconquerable. Or have we finally reached an intensity of negation where this is no longer true?

A final reason for the superiority of *Lady Chatterley's Lover* is the rich simplicity of its structural design. This design is realized most powerfully and significantly in spatial terms, in terms of setting. The most enduring meanings the novel projects are inextricably bound up with the arrangement of three locations—the manor house, the industrial village, the wood—and their spatial relations with one another under a fume-laden atmosphere which seems to be no better and no worse than Pittsburgh's or northern New Jersey's. Many of Lawrence's novels are built around a central contrast: in *The Rainbow* the contrast is between things as they are and a promised transformation of being; in *The Plumed Serpent*

it is between a Europeanized and an aboriginal Mexico; in *The Lost Girl*
it is between "higher" and "lower" selves, or, spatially, between Woodhouse and southern Italy. All these contrasts from one point of view
come to the same thing. They express the opposition between "two ways
of knowing." In *Lady Chatterley's Lover* the same contrast is represented
through settings which impinge on one another, which coexist at the
same time, in the same district. There is no appeal to the strange and
far to fix either side of the contrast and no appeal to the future. The
novel concentrates its drama within the space of a few square miles, and
Lawrence summons all his powers of description to present this space as
it is: a portion of English soil in transition from a semi-rural, semi-
industrial condition to one of total industrialization. If the novel demands that we regard these few miles as an epitome of the larger world of
Western civilization itself, we may find it easy to assent because in so
many ways Lawrence's microcosm looks and smells like the world we
know.

The wood is the vital center of Lawrence's panorama. It is menaced
on one side by the ugly houses and mining installations of the colliery
village; on the other it is owned but not valued by the occupants of the
dreary manor house. There is social and economic hostility between village and manor, but both workers and owner unite in opposition to
everything the wood represents. Both worship the abstractions of money,
power and property, and both are devoted to the mechanistic organization of human affairs. The wood stands approximately in between two
forces of negation. It is Lawrence's sacred wood within which life-
mysteries are enacted. These are of birth, budding, and growth, embodied
in the annual cycle of fertility in tree, flower, and animal, humanly embodied also in the sexual encounters between the gamekeeper and the
lady; for out of these encounters proceed a rebirth of feeling in both
people, the possibility of a new life together, and finally the promise of a
child. The love affair moves in phase with the organic burgeoning of the
wood during a wet but beautiful spring. It extends from the time of the
first flowers to a time when the trees and flowers are in full bloom.

For no character in the novel is the wood a natural and inevitable
habitat. Connie and Mellors are both somewhat battered products of unwholesome civilization who, as it were, stumble onto sacred ground while
following paths leading from opposite sides. Mellors arrives first from the
direction of Tevershall; the lady comes trailing down some months later
from the "eminence" on which Wragby sits. In the not wholly adequate
shelter of a remnant of Sherwood Forest they create through the sex act
that condition of interconnection which is the *sine qua non* of escape
from the "tragic" world but which certainly does not guarantee that escape. For the wood symbolizes not only a way of life but also the
beleaguered and vulnerable status to which the vital career has been
reduced. The vastness of the original forest has declined under the steady

attrition of civilization to a thin wood which barely conceals the lovers from prying eyes and barely provides cover for the pheasants and rabbits which are its only wildlife. Mellors grimly tracks down the colliers who poach on his preserves, but there are other kinds of invasion that he is powerless to resist. From Tevershall comes the obscene Bertha Coutts to fill the sensitive glade with domestic uproar, and from Wragby comes Clifford in his motorized chair to ride down the wild flowers while musing on the felicities and responsibilities of being a property owner. For reasons of family pride the Chatterleys have been interested in preserving the remaining forest. But we are told that this interest can yield to "higher" claims. During the late war, Clifford's father, Sir Geoffrey, in an excess of patriotic zeal had cut hundreds of trees to provide trench timber for the troops in Belgium and France:

> . . . On the crown of the knoll where the oaks had stood, now was bareness; and from there you could look over the trees to the colliery railway, and the new works at Stacks Gate. Connie had stood and had looked, it was a breach in the pure seclusion of the wood. It let in the world. (p. 47)

Throughout the novel we are made aware of this process of attrition, as though in a short time the trees and glades will disappear, leaving village and hall locked—like the aristocratic Sir Clifford and the plebeian Mrs. Bolton at the end of the story—in monstrous, unvital embrace. Finally, not only is the wood surrounded, but also it is being attacked from beneath. The vertical shafts of the local mines lead to horizontal corridors fanning out in all directions. The rich soil of Wragby wood is undermined by coal diggings, while its flora and fauna are being reduced at ground level. Simultaneously from the skies come poisonous fumes and "smuts" to sicken the vegetation and reduce the vigor of the animals. All in all it is through his power to project a crisis of industrial civilization in these concrete terms that Lawrence is able to make his point compelling.

II

Since from one point of view the theme of *Lady Chatterley's Lover* is concreteness *versus* abstraction, it is appropriate that the success of Lawrence's representative method should depend largely on richly concrete realizations of persons, settings, and situations, that the power of his prophecy should depend on the power of his art to particularize meanings which may be extended toward broader conditions and widely applicable truths of experience. Here I want to examine some features of the two opposed modes or realms of experience as they are fictionally embodied and to raise some questions both about the artistic success of these representations and about the ideas to which they may be referred. Although the story proceeds in a kind of dialectical movement, usually alternating scenes at Wragby with scenes in the gamekeeper's domain, there is no reason why we cannot examine each realm in turn.

DEATH-IN-LIFE

An abiding impression of Sir Clifford and of most of the intellectuals who foregather at Wragby Hall during the early part of the story is that they are not very real. But this hardly supplies a ground for criticism of the portrayal of Sir Clifford since his unreality is precisely the point the novel makes. He is a "hurt thing" (p. 14), a "lost thing" (p. 15) whose capacity to be involved in life has been destroyed by the war. He is able to think and to experience egoistic feeling but cannot get in touch. It seems to his wife, and nothing happens in the story to contradict her view, that at the core of him there is only "a negation of human contact" (p. 15). His is not a problem of war neurosis or of the psychology of invalidism. Perhaps the best way to regard him is in the nature of an experimental hypothesis: given such and such conditions, then what other conditions will result? Looked at in this way, the character remains interesting throughout the novel and vibrates with a queer kind of mechanical energy, like those incredibly energetic yet two-dimensional characters one finds in Dickens and in the novels of Smollett and Fielding.

The hypothesis may be stated as follows: what will a man do with himself and with others when his physical attachment to experience has been violently and permanently severed? The novel's answer is that such a man will create a "simulacrum of reality" (p. 18), a complex pattern of abstract relationships to substitute for felt connections between himself and others. Within this pattern or web he will enjoy the illusion of life, but all the time he will not be alive at all. Here one might remark that the "adjustment" is harmless enough, but this ignores the problem of others. Actually, Clifford's first great crime is that he draws his wife into his orbit of nonexistence. The abstracted man who cannot live in himself leans with crushing weight on his partner. He slowly draws from her those vital energies which sustain her in being, but can only waste what he absorbs since nothing can restore him to life.

In this depiction of Clifford's parasitism Lawrence is working once again with an assumption which is basic to all his work. It is that there is life in the vital sense and death in the sense of the unvital but no third thing, no possibility of an attitude of non-attachment—one which neither preys on the vitality of others nor is based on the capacity of physical self-realization. In Lawrence generally the ground of all value is physical experience. This is both his characteristic limitation and the theme that unifies all his works—fiction, poetry, essays, and treatises. The only reality and the only marvel is to be alive in the flesh. At the same time an individual can only experience his aliveness through direct relationship with another living thing. He can fuse himself in contemplation with the life of trees, flowers, or animals, but the crucial experience of relatedness is, appropriately enough, a sexual experience with a woman: appropriate because it conforms to the order of nature, because for Lawrence touch is a more powerful mode of connectedness than sight, because sex is, in sensory and emotional terms, a stronger experience of connection than any other. All this can be put into a single doctrinal statement: to know and possess onself is to have experienced a unity with live things and persons outside oneself. These Lawrencean convictions are essentially a product of intuition, but they receive some reinforcement in the speculations of at least one major modern philosopher. A. N. Whitehead has presented similar conclusions about men's relations to a "living universe" in his essay, "Nature Alive" (in *Modes of Thought,* New York, 1938), although needless to say he does not concern himself with the sexual relation. But Whitehead argues that all mental experience is derived from bodily functioning and that strictly speaking no one can determine where our bodies end and where the surrounding physical environment begins. A man is alive in nature and nature is alive in him; his sense of self is included in his sense of otherness, and *vice versa.* Therefore, "togetherness" is not only a way of knowing but the fundamental mode of being.

Clifford's first pattern of abstraction is created with words. As a writer he spins verbal cobwebs, and in his daily association with Connie he invariably tries to reduce concrete experience to formulae. He attempts to fill the void between his wife and himself with phrases like "the habit of intimacy" (p. 57) and "our steadily-lived life" (p. 51). But within his orbit the only reality for Connie is "nothingness, and over it a hypocrisy of words" (p. 57). Because he accepts words as a facsimile of reality, verbal connections as a substitute for felt connections, he comes to worship success. He wishes to be talked about, written about, recognized as something, because he is nothing. And, although wealthy and not avaricious, he seeks money as the visible yet abstract emblem of success.

In midcareer Clifford orients himself in a new pattern of abstraction. This time it is economic and industrial power that gives him the illusion of life. He is brilliantly successful at developing new methods of mining organization because he cannot see human beings as flesh-and-blood realities, only as functions of an abstractly formulated process. His social views are summed up in his slogan, "the function determines the individual" (p. 220)—a man *is* no more than what he does. Now Clifford is in a position to commit far greater crimes than before. As an industrialist he draws men and women by the thousands into his orbit of nonexistence. He becomes a leader in a civilized society described at one point by the word *insane* (p. 113) and gains new confidence and toughness from his success in manipulating men and machines. He is described as becoming "almost a *creature,* with a hard, efficient shell of an exterior and a pulpy

interior, one of the amazing crabs and lobsters of the modern industrial
and financial world, invertebrates of the crustacean order, with shells of
steel, like machines, and inner bodies of soft pulp" (p. 129). From the
pulp of his inner life emanate just two vibrations—an impulse of self-
assertion and a contradictory impulse of terrified dependency. When
Connie casts him off he transfers this dependency to Mrs. Bolton, and at
the end is left in a strange state of equilibrium:

> After this, Clifford became like a child with Mrs. Bolton. He would hold
> her hand, and rest his head on her breast, and when she once lightly kissed
> him, he said "Yes! Do kiss me! Do kiss me!" And when she sponged his
> great blond body, he would say the same: "Do kiss me!" and she would
> lightly kiss his body, anywhere, half in mockery.
>   And he lay with a queer, blank face like a child, with a bit of the wonder-
> ment of a child. And he would gaze on her with wide, childish eyes, in a
> relaxation of madonna-worship. . . .
>   Mrs. Bolton was both thrilled and ashamed, she both loved and hated it.
> Yet she never rebuffed or rebuked him. And they drew into a closer physical
> intimacy, an intimacy of perversity, when he was a child stricken with an
> apparent candour and an apparent wonderment, that looked almost like a
> religious exaltation: the perverse and literal rendering of "except ye become
> again as a little child."—While she was the Magna Mater, full of power and
> potency, having the great blond child-man under her will and her stroke
> entirely.
>   The curious thing was that when this child-man, which Clifford was now
> and which he had been becoming for years, emerged into the world, it was
> much sharper and keener than the real man used to be. . . . It was as if
> his very passivity and prostitution to the Magna Mater gave him insight
> into material business affairs, and lent him a certain remarkable inhuman
> force. The wallowing in private emotion, the utter abasement of his manly
> self, seemed to lend him a second nature, cold, almost visionary, business-
> clever. In business he was quite inhuman. (pp. 352-53)

As a portrait of the modern business man Clifford is surely no better
than a monstrous caricature. It would be incorrect to regard him as the
imaginative representation of some such cliché of popular psychology as
"Men who succeed in business are often emotionally underdeveloped and
infantile." I think it would be more appropriate to see him as a kind of
imagined limit toward which certain tendencies in modern life might be
moving. Real people fall somewhere between the limits defined at one
extreme by Sir Clifford Chatterley and at the other by the gamekeeper.

The narrative presentation of Clifford is carefully handled so as to
prevent the reader ever coming at the character directly. His utterances
are invariably hedged round with interpretative comment by the narrator
or by Connie which draws out the depraved implications of what he says
and does. He is always an illustration of disconnectedness; never for a
moment does he emerge as a man who has suffered a terrible wound and

is to be pitied for it. If even briefly the reader could feel with him as a human being, then his whole characterization would seem terribly cruel, and Lawrence's demonstration would be fatally flawed. But the truth is that Clifford in this novel is himself a man entirely defined by his functions. There is nothing left over to pity. Riding about the estate in his motorized chair he is a kind of mechanical centaur who, because he is only half human, is not human at all. Voidness cannot be villainous, nor can it become an object of sympathy.

Clifford is essential to the novel, but the same cannot be said for those characters who sit about in the drawing room at Wragby discussing the superiority of mind over matter and revealing their diseased attitudes toward love, working people, and the sex act. Insofar as many of these people—Lady Bennerley, Charles May, Hammond, and Tommy Dukes —are devitalized, two-dimensional creatures, they are no more than tautological variations on Clifford himself. Their discussions seem hopelessly dated. These characters do not appear in the first version of the novel (published as *The First Lady Chatterley* by Dial Press in 1944) and add little to the final version. Dukes, of course, is a spokesman for the vital and "phallic" consciousness: "Real knowledge comes out of the whole corpus of the consciousness; out of your belly and your penis as much as out of your brain and mind" (p. 41). In saying this he anticipates the views of Mellors, but it is hard to see why such press agentry should be necessary. When Mellors enters the story, it soon turns out that he can speak for himself, sometimes to the point of tediousness. Dukes in his own words is a "mental-lifer" (p. 44) who holds the right ideas but cannot act upon them. He is the Hamlet, or rather the Prufrock, of *Lady Chatterley's Lover.*

The novel's second powerful representation of "death-in-life" is concentrated in a set passage of description occurring about midway in the story. It is a genuine tour de force running on for eleven pages and covering in meticulous detail the physical appearance of three industrial villages and the many miles of semi-industrial countryside which lie around them. Things seen are richly rendered as fact and simultaneously judged and analyzed by the newly awakened heroine, Connie Chatterley. It is dramatically appropriate that she should interpret her impressions as she does. At the same time the entire description may easily stand as Lawrence's own last indignant comment on the crimes perpetrated by an industrial civilization against essential human needs and capacities.

Connie drives from Wragby through Tevershall, the new village of Stacks Gate, and on to Uthwaite, an old Midland village where the Chatterley family are still looked upon as county gentry. In and around the villages she observes coal miners and other workmen, working-class homes and shopping districts, schools, churches, factories, pubs, and hotels. Her perspective is constantly shifting as the car mounts hills and drops down into valleys, crawls through narrow streets crowded with traffic, o'

runs swiftly through open country. In the end this moving panorama
of an entire district creates a striking and large image of human disorder
spread out upon a portion of the earth's surface scarred and ravaged by
man himself.

To the heroine the hideousness of these raw villages expresses much the
same meaning as Wragby and its master. Ugliness is seen as evidence of
"the utter absence of the instinct for shapely beauty which every bird and
beast has, the utter death of the human intuitive faculty" (p. 180). As
she hears school children bawling out a song in one of the new school
buildings she asks, "what could possibly become of such people, a people
in whom the living intuitive faculty was dead as nails, and only queer
mechanical yells and uncanny will-power remained?" (p. 181). These
observations are not sentimental, nor are they validated by any program
of social or economic reform she has in mind for the improvement of
the lives of the industrial masses. Instead the natural grace and vigor
of human beings left free to express themselves in physical and instinctive
ways is the assumption from which criticism follows. No social or economic class is assigned full blame for producing the "half-corpses" of the
"new race of mankind" (p. 182), although there is a vague distinction
between leaders and led in the questions: "Ah God, what has man done
to man? What have the leaders of men been doing to their fellow man?"
(p. 182).

Actually, the description embodies a mordant irony. Connie observes
that the new mining villages and industrial installations are crowding
in upon the parks and manors of the rich, cultivated people of the district.
These magnates had set the industrial process in motion when they first
began to exploit the mineral resources of their hitherto rural properties.
Their desire for profits had created the conditions which produced the
dehumanization of the workers and the denaturing of soil and atmosphere. Now the miners, "elemental creatures, weird and distorted, of the
mineral world" (p. 190), build their houses at the very gates of the manor
parks. The owners are being shoved out of their places by the inhuman
pressure of the industrial masses for living room:

> This is history. One England blots out another. The mines had made the
> halls wealthy. Now they were blotting them out, as they had already blotted
> out the cottages. The industrial England blots out the agricultural England.
> One meaning blots out another. . . . And the continuity is not organic,
> but mechanical. (p. 186)

The description as a whole does not protest change as such, or rest its
case on an imagined superiority of past to present. The essential protest
is against a change which seems to be altogether uncontrolled by human
beings. Men have made a machine—civilization—and now the machine
proceeds to make men—in its own image. In the end there can be no

distinction between victim and victimizer because the machine, manned by dehumanized creatures like Sir Clifford and the half-corpses whom he employs, victimizes all alike. This pessimistic conclusion is most poignantly expressed by the gamekeeper as he looks out at night from his leafy shelter toward the nearby industrial area:

> . . . The fault lay there, out there, in those evil electric lights and diabolical rattlings of engines. There, in the world of the mechanical greedy, greedy mechanism and mechanized greed, sparkling with lights and gushing hot metal and roaring with traffic, there lay the vast evil thing, ready to destroy whatever did not conform. Soon it would destroy the wood, and the bluebells would spring no more. All vulnerable things must perish under the rolling and running of iron. (p. 140)

The profound sense of crisis communicated by the description I have been discussing depends partly on the patience and skill with which closely observed facts of daily experience have been grouped to make a unified, overwhelming impression, partly on the validity of the idea that underlies the description. The idea is that men, because they are alive, cannot without fatal injury to themselves be subordinated to that which is not alive. Living is not a matter of functions but of the organic wholeness and health of a physical species. Industrialism, insofar as it maims the human organism, or forces it to form a shell of insentience to protect its vulnerable substance, defeats the great human ends for which it was designed. Lawrence's attack on industrialism is not conducted on idealistic grounds. It stems from his keen sense that men and women, like tree, bird, and flower, are physically alive and growing. This is the basic human reality, and all higher possibilities depend upon the healthy condition of the physical man and woman.

Perhaps we are so used to the demands civilization makes upon us to regard our bodies merely as serviceable instruments that we cannot respond to Lawrence's insistence that *our bodies are our selves* and that the only way to be alive is in the flesh. But it seems to me he has discovered the perfect place to rest a case against an industrial civilization. For no one pretends that such a civilization offers spiritual rewards to its supporters. It offers merely the promise of a richer material existence, and Lawrence suggests that the offer is a swindle. What is given by one hand is taken away by the other, since dead men cannot appreciate, except in a simulated way, the benefits of life. On this view all wars are lost, all five-year plans fail, because men cannot wage military battles or battles of production without dying "vitally." This is because vulnerability and tenderness are of the essence of the human, and these qualities cannot be preserved in large, difficult enterprises requiring the subordination of individuals to impersonal processes. A man must live in the now; if he does not, he will find himself dead in the hereafter.

To cope with the argument on its own terms one might grant the
tendency of the "insentient iron world" (p. 140) to maim and destroy
the vital essence of human beings, but argue that Lawrence overplays
vulnerability and tenderness. It is possible that the "human intuitive
faculty," anchored as it is in the powerful surges of the body's life, can
survive the ugliness and disintegration of ugly towns and the inhuman
efficiency of assembly lines? Does it not seem true that toughness alike
with sensitiveness is demonstrated in the power of most growing things
to maintain themselves in being? Granted that the basis of endurance is
the same in man and crocus, is the man less hardy than the crocus? Perhaps the Lawrencean answer would be that the crocus knows when it is
time to die, but many human beings, who ought to accept the fact that
they are already dead, fashion for themselves a simulacrum and continue
during some years to spread death among the living in the manner of
Clifford Chatterley.

THE VITAL REALM

Constance Chatterley's trip into Wragby Wood is, in the prophetic
terms the novel establishes, a journey from death into life and from the
profoundly unreal into reality. Wragby is dominated by the word, and,
as Lawrence remarks in a passage of "Apropos of *Lady Chatterley's
Lover*," the word is insufficient to establish that "vivid and nourishing
relation to the cosmos and the universe" which is man's only hope of
sustaining himself fulfilled in the midst of life:

> . . . It is no use asking for a Word to fulfil such a need. No Word, no
> Logos, no Utterance will ever do it. The Word is uttered, most of it: we
> need only pay true attention. But who will call us to the Deed, the great
> Deed of the Seasons and the year, the Deed of the soul's cycle, the Deed of
> a woman's life at one with a man's. . . . It is the *Deed* of life we have now
> to learn: we are supposed to have learnt the Word, but, alas, look at us.
> Word-perfect we may be, but Deed-demented. Let us prepare now for the
> death of our present "little" life, and the re-emergence in a bigger life, in
> touch with the moving cosmos.

This is the prophetic dimension in which the reader must view the
heroine's quest. At the same time, it would be foolish to deny that from
another perspective Constance Chatterley is merely a bored society woman
of rather low moral character who is swept forward into fulfillment in
spite of herself. Her personal background, her girlish sexual adventures
with German students in the Black Forest, her nerve-wracking affair with
the careerist, Michaelis, contain nothing to admire. Her only qualification
for the role of heroine is a capacity to come alive in the body, to become
awakened instinctually, and to be "at one with a man's life." But of

course this is the only qualification demanded. Connie's lack of distinction is all to the good if we agree that her reorientation in life is enacted convincingly, since then her success holds out a promise to all. To confer on an ordinary woman an extraordinary fate and to suggest that there is no other fate worth seeking is what *Lady Chatterley's Lover*, like *The Lost Girl* before it, tries to do. The earlier novel fails because it presents no experience embodying the "vivid relation," no setting where that relation is convincingly enacted. The sexual episodes in the "sacred" wood are dramatic experiences embodying such a relation in *Lady Chatterley's Lover*. Less ambiguously than in any earlier novel Lawrence completes his prophetic mission here by balancing rejection against affirmation, the attack on an insensate civilization against a celebration of creative possibilities in warmly physical, interpersonal human experience. When the sexual scenes are looked at in this way, the importance of their function in the total action becomes evident. Union in sexual experience demands as concrete expression as disconnectedness at Wragby and in the industrial environs.

The only serious argument that can be raised against these scenes has to do with the inadequacy of words—any words—to set forth the meaning and drama of intimate physical and emotional experiences in which consciousness, on the narrator's own admission, surges in a dimension of reality inaccessible to language. For example, let us consider the following passage from a scene in which Connie and the gamekeeper come to a sexual climax together:

> And it seemed she was like the sea, nothing but dark waves rising and heaving, heaving with a great swell, so that slowly her whole darkness was in motion, and she was ocean rolling its dark, dumb mass. Oh, and far down inside her the deeps parted and rolled asunder, in long, far-travelling billows, and ever, at the quick of her, the depths parted and rolled asunder from the center of soft plunging, as the plunger went deeper and deeper, touching lower, and she was deeper and deeper and deeper disclosed, and heavier the billows of her rolled away to some shore, uncovering her, and closer and closer plunged the palpable unknown, and further and further rolled the waves of herself away from herself, leaving her, till suddenly, in a soft, shuddering convulsion, the quick of all her plasm was touched, she knew herself touched, the consummation was upon her, and she was gone. She was gone, she was not, and she was born: a woman. (p. 208)

This is beautiful enough in its way, but somehow these heavy rhythms and overlapping repetitions of word and phrase seem verbose. The narrator cannot adequately synthesize this sort of experience in words any more than one might adequately describe the circulation of the blood from an "inside" viewpoint. The description has some good features. It avoids the grey vocabulary of sexual science; it is ingenious in its attempt to match up verbal rhythms with the mounting neural tensions of sexual excitation. But ingenuity is hardly enough to do the job here. The reader fails to achieve any deep realization of the sexual mystery and instead is liable to find himself stopping to ask questions about the plain prose meaning of such things as "the quick of the plasm," the statement that this woman has now become a woman (what was she a few moments earlier?), or the statement that at the height of the experience "she was not." In a piece of music like Wagner's *Liebestod* sequence in *Tristan und Isolde,* which is orgasmic if you like, such questions do not arise. Given the kind of materials he works with, any composer may conceivably create in a structure of pure sound a perfect analogue of the feminine sexual climax. Words, however, ordinarily cannot do this, unless they are wrenched from normal grammatical relationship and purified of their ordinary signific meanings. Here the narrator does not choose to withdraw from the scene; Lawrence does not choose to develop some version of the stream of consciousness technique which might render the kind of pure suggestiveness music is capable of rendering. The ocean-swimmer woman-man analogy on which the passage is built remains curiously formal, not quite an argument but too much like an argument to overwhelm and flood the reader's awareness with emotive meanings.

The problem of language is less intense when less central features of sexual relations are described or dramatized, but it is still there. The gamekeeper's use of the dialect and of the Anglo-Saxon four-letter words possesses the sort of charm that cloys in repetition. Perhaps the slurs, elisions, and crooning sounds of Midland vernacular are more appropriate to tender, erotic conversations than the tight-lipped accents of Received Standard British, but this is something difficult for an untravelled American reader to judge. Also, the four-letter words will or will not have their effect depending on a reader's personal background. They may seem fresh, honest, and direct to someone who has never heard them used eight or ten times to a sentence by ordinary, unvital men in discussions of the news, politics, baseball, and movies. For this reader most of their magic had been rubbed off before he was out of grammar school.

I would suggest that after a certain point the sexual scenes simply are not available for the kind of critical analysis one might perform on scenes of a less provocative subject matter. Most criticism bases itself on the assumption that a community of devoted and intelligent readers will make somewhat similar responses to the same material. Criticism seeks to articulate those responses and to discover their ground in the reading material itself. But here if there is anything in Lawrence's belief that modern civilization corrupts or disorganizes man's sexual nature, it becomes clear that every reader must go his own way, giving his impressions without expecting much support from other readers. Objectivity becomes impossible. My own impression is that some of the renderings of sexual intimacy are beautiful and convincing. More often there is too much solemnity in the speeches and attitudes of both man and woman.

Certain scenes strike me as downright silly: Mellors' address to his penis (p. 252); the scene in which Connie and Mellors wreathe flowers about each other's bodies with particular attention to the pubic zone (pp. 265-76).

It is easier to understand why we should be given so much nakedness and so many descriptions of the sexual experience than to make fine distinctions between degrees of effectiveness in particular scenes. The insentient outer world denies the primary value of the body's physical life and aspires toward an ideal condition of disembodiment. But in the wood, where this value is asserted, naked contact between the physical man and woman is more important than anything else. Furthermore, the closest possible contact comes in sexual intercourse, an experience defined by the novel as a fusion into a temporary unity of man with woman, woman with man, the two together with the secret heart of life. The possibility of a rebirth of wholesome feeling is grounded in the sex act because only at the moment of orgasm does the individual escape his self-obsession into identification with the "living universe." When he or she returns from his blind mystical illumination—one which is not separable from the powerful sensual feelings which momentarily overwhelm ordinary awareness—he discovers himself to be *changed*, as if he had looked into the face of God Himself. This is mysticism. I do not assume in making use of the term that such experience is "unreal," only that, like more orthodox varieties of the experience, it will never yield up its meaning to the nonmystic. As Connie Chatterley lies with her lover in a condition described as "one perfect concentric fluid of feeling" (p. 158), she utters inarticulate little cries. The narrator's reverent comment is that here we have "the voice out of the uttermost night, the life!" (p. 158). It is easier to believe in this miracle—a miracle because it is not the woman crying out but the voice of the universe itself—than to comprehend it.

The reader may more easily come to terms with that part of the redemptory pattern of action which leads up to the sexual scenes. The first sexual encounter between gamekeeper and heroine actually completes rather than begins the drama of her passing over from one life-orientation to another. For Connie this process of transition is painful, and it is poignantly realized in some of the most moving descriptive-dramatic passages in the novel. The sexual scenes succeeding the first really add nothing new. Connie has her moments of resistance. She has to undergo a sort of basic training in the arts of the vital career, and later chapters take up the practical problem of how the lovers are to translate their adulterous connection into a permanent, workable living arrangement. But when the heroine first enters the hut to give herself to her husband's servant, she has crossed the gulf between the unliving and the living. The central section is substantially complete.

This action of passing over is presented as a series of definable moments of realization. The process is not wholly internalized or reflective, for each hesitant step forward follows an occasion of experience in which Connie comes into contact with some form of the vital outside herself. The mode of contact is at first visual. Later other modes of perception come into play, and finally it is a touch which gently presses her forward into fulfillment. . . .

A point of departure is established during a walk in the woods with Sir Clifford. Connie is bored with life, entangled in a shoddy love affair with Michaelis, entangled in the web of Clifford's phrases about the steadily lived life. Suddenly, the new gamekeeper, whom Connie has never met, emerges from a sidepath in the wood "like the sudden rush of a threat out of nowhere" (p. 52):

> She was watching a brown spaniel that had run out of a side-path, and was looking towards them with lifted nose, making a soft, fluffy bark. A man with a gun strode swiftly, softly out after the dog, facing their way as if about to attack them; then stopped instead, saluted, and was turning down hill. It was only the new game-keeper, but he had frightened Connie, he seemed to emerge with such a swift menace. (p. 52)

The description simultaneously expresses the heroine's alienation from what is real and suggests that, unlike Clifford, she is not beyond cure. Although frightened she is not indifferent. The threat conceals a promise which she is not yet capable of realizing, but when she turns her attention back to Clifford and Wragby, her sense of the profound meaninglessness of her existence has become intensified.

For a time after this encounter Connie makes no progress out of her condition of alienation. As a man the gamekeeper seems to her to be aloof, surly, even hostile. She continues her affair with the writer and goes on accepting "the great nothingness of life" as "the one end of living" (p. 63). She does, however, get into the habit of taking long walks in the woods alone, but it is wintertime and even the trees seem to her to express only "depth within depth of grey, hopeless inertia, silence, nothingness" (p. 75).

Connie is shocked into awareness for the second time when by accident she observes the gamekeeper washing himself in the open air behind his cottage. A commonplace experience becomes "visionary" when for some moments this woman who has devoted her life to nothingness recognizes that she is in the presence of something. Her conscious mind rejects the vision, but "in her womb" (p. 77) she knows she has been exposed to a reality which is fundamental and concrete: "the warm, white flame of a single life, revealing itself in contours that one might touch: a body" (p. 77). When she returns home she strips off her clothing before a mirror and examines her own body inch by inch. Painfully, she recognizes that it is becoming meaningless and ugly. She has been swindled out of her first youth by what she calls "the mental life" (p. 81), with its abstractness and its neglect of the body as an essential human reality.

From here on she is in covert rebellion against her husband's world. At the same time Mellors remains withdrawn and suspicious. She increases the frequency of her walks in the woods during the month of March and experiences a whole series of recognitions which can be turned back as perspectives on her own dynamic state of being. On a cold, brilliant March day she enters the woods while certain phrases sweep through her consciousness:

> . . . Ye must be born again! I believe in the resurrection of the body! Except a grain of wheat fall into the earth and die, it shall by no means bring forth. When the crocus cometh forth I too will emerge and see the sun! (pp. 98-99)

The wind, described as the breath of Persephone, who is "out of hell on a cold morning" (p. 99), and as though it were trying to break itself free of the branches in which it has become entangled, excites her. An identification between the woman and the wind is established through the emphasis on the idea of escape and release. She sits with her back against a young pine tree and becomes excited as it sways against her "elastic and powerful, rising up" (p. 100). The description, of course, has phallic overtones and foreshadows some of the phallic rituals which take place in later sexual scenes. But what makes these descriptions beautiful and exciting for the reader is the imaginative power with which the idea is communicated that there is a real connection between the life springing in the reawakened woods and the changing, revitalized feeling of the woman.

To be at one with the life of the woods is a great deal in itself. Nevertheless the heroine's change of awareness cannot be arrested at this Thoreauvian point of vital realization. She is now "loose and adrift" (p. 100) between the old life and the new, and must exert herself to find new moorings. From this point on it is only the reluctance of the gamekeeper to become himself reawakened under the pathetically inadequate auspices of the beleaguered wood which delays fate. Day after day Connie comes to the little clearing to watch Mellors at work performing the wholesome tasks of pheasant husbandry and then returns home alone to Wragby where Mrs. Bolton has already begun to replace her as Clifford's companion and nurse. The gamekeeper remains wary until the beautiful scene in which Connie takes up a newly born pheasant chick in her hand, then bows herself down and weeps:

> Connie crouched in front of the last coop. The three chicks had run in. But still their cheeky heads came poking sharply through the yellow feathers, then withdrawing, then only one beady little head eyeing forth from the vast mother-body.

"I'd love to touch them," she said, putting her fingers gingerly through the bars of the coop. But the mother-hen pecked at her hand fiercely, and Connie drew back startled and frightened.

"How she pecks at me! She hates me!" she said in a wondering voice. "But I wouldn't hurt them!"

The man standing above her laughed, and crouched down beside her, knees apart, and put his hand with quiet confidence slowly into the coop. The old hen pecked at him, but not so savagely. And slowly, softly, with sure gentle fingers, he felt among the old bird's feathers and drew out a faintly-peeping chick in his closed hand.

"There!" he said, holding out his hand to her. She took the little drab thing between her hands, and there it stood, on its impossible little stalks of legs, its atom of balancing life trembling through its almost weightless feet into Connie's hands. But it lifted its handsome, clean-shaped little head boldly, and looked sharply round, and gave a little "peep." "So adorable! So cheeky!" she said softly.

The keeper, squatting beside her, was also watching with an amused face the bold little bird in her hands. Suddenly he saw a tear fall on to her wrist. (p. 135)

She has been moved by the touch of new life in the tiny bird who stands so boldly on her outstretched hands. She weeps because her own maternal instincts have been frustrated, because her life is emotionally barren, because she is a woman without a warm physical connection with anybody or anything. Perhaps also she weeps because the direct physical apprehension of this "atom of balancing life" is painful, as though Lawrence were saying here that to know the world in the way of naked contact is painful at first for those who have been "ravished by dead words become obscene, and dead ideas become obsessions" (p. 109).

In the climax of this scene there is a reversal. Now it is the gamekeeper who is "touched," who experiences a moment of overwhelming realization which leads him, despite misgivings, to begin life anew, to become once again tender and vulnerable and open in a world full of the sharp edges and points of antivital abstractions and grim, uncontrollable machines.

In the hut to which the couple retire the woman asks herself over and over again, "Was it real?" and "Why was this necessary?" (p. 137), but then, deciding to lay down the burden of herself, she reflects that she is "to be had for the taking" (p. 137). This phrase, so often employed cynically, expresses here a change which is in the final analysis deeply spiritual and even religious in implication. A lady yields her favors to a surly gamekeeper: a woman yields up herself to life and is saved. This is an equation the novel as a whole insists upon and which Lawrence's art attempts to sustain. The common experience becomes charged with the most extraordinary significance and the highest value life holds. This balance is perilous. To hold experience in this radiant and ennobling perspective is not an easy thing to do. Here, I think, the balance is maintained, and the reader can believe in what he sees.

III

Lawrence's last novel bears detailed and striking resemblances to his first, *The White Peacock*. Each has a gamekeeper, a wood, a lady who must choose between an industrial magnate and a "natural" man. But the two books contrast sharply in the way they turn out. In the earlier novel the lady chooses the magnate while the vital man sickens and dies. As a matter of fact, this pessimistic conclusion is doubled since no less than two men identified with the woods and fields, the farmer George Saxton and the gamekeeper Frank Annable, come to unhappy ends. But Mellors at the end of *Lady Chatterley's Lover* is still on his feet and, although gloomy enough about the future, can find the energy to set about planning a new life for himself and his mistress. Even in the letter that closes Lawrence's last novel, Mellors, despite his predictions of doom for modern industrial man, greets Connie hopefully and sets out his absurd program of salvation for the masses with conviction, if not with any idea that people are going to do what he suggests:

> . . . If only they were educated to *live* instead of earn and spend, they could manage very happily on twenty-five shillings. If the men wore scarlet trousers as I said, they wouldn't think so much of money; if they could dance and hop and skip, and sing and swagger and be handsome, they could do with very little cash. And amuse the women themselves, and be amused by the women. They ought to learn to be naked and handsome, and to sing in a mass and dance the old group dances, and carve the stools they sit on, and embroider their own emblems. Then they wouldn't need money. (p. 362)

This boyish and anarchic dream of peace on an earth magically transformed from the cold, crowded, and raw place that it by and large is— and was when people still danced group dances and hopped and skipped —into an innocent and sensual Garden rejects tragic knowledge of man's difficult position in the world. It flies in the face of facts. It is immature. Nevertheless, Lawrence was well aware that no one but a Lawrencean gamekeeper could believe in such a program. He did not want men of the twentieth century to don white jackets and scarlet trousers pulled tight across the buttocks. But he did want men and women of the "tragic" age to look at themselves and to raise the question of whether the tragic view of man's plight took full account of creative human possibilities. He wanted us to look at our maturity and to consider whether it did not become for some people a mask concealing deadness.

The genuine yet carefully restrained optimism of *Lady Chatterley's*

Lover is founded on a belief that the world is alive and that aliveness is the only thing worth cherishing. Men and societies denying this fundamental fact will sicken and die. In *The White Peacock* the gamekeeper had remarked, "Tell a woman not to come in a wood till she can look at natural things—she might see something." Connie Chatterley, unlike the heroine of *The White Peacock*, does come into the woods and lingers there until she sees something. More clearly and more persuasively than in any previous novel, Lawrence brings the reader into touch with that vision, the mystery which, as one suspected from the beginning, was only of life itself.

The Continuity of Lawrence's Short Novels

by Monroe Engel

Lawrence's short novels are a special and sustained achievement belonging roughly to the last decade of his life. It is of course not clear at precisely what point the long story becomes the short novel, but with *The Fox* (1918-19; revised and lengthened in 1921), not only does Lawrence write a story that is appreciably longer than his earlier stories (about three times the length of "The Prussian Officer," for example), but he establishes certain themes—and, more peculiarly, certain patterns and devices for vivifying these themes—that become generic for his longer stories.

The Fox is written in a markedly objective style verging on irony, or a kind of satire with only the mutest comedy. The elastic fluency of the style also allows direct seriousness, even earnestness. The opening pages describe a peculiar state of disorder suggested by the facts that the two girls in the story are known by their surnames; that March, who had "learned carpentry and joinery at the evening classes in Islington," was "the man about the place"; and that on the farm, nothing prospers: the heifer gets through the fences, and the girls sell the cow—not insignificantly—just before it is to calf, "afraid of the coming event." The fowls are drowsy in the morning, but stay up half the night; and the fox carries them off at will. All in all, the girls "were living on their losses, as Banford said," and they acquired a "low opinion of Nature altogether."

This detailing of disorder is perhaps overdone, labored, and some other elements in the story seem too insisted on also—a kind of heaviness from which the subsequent short novels do not suffer. For March—who is obviously from the first the more restive and savable of the two girls—the fox represents an escape from her present deadening life, an escape conceived in increasingly sexual terms. "Her heart beats to the fox," she is "possessed by him." Then, when the young man appears, he is at once seen in foxy terms. He has "a ruddy, roundish face, with fairish hair,

"The Continuity of Lawrence's Short Novels" by Monroe Engel. From *The Hudson Review*, XI (Summer, 1958), 201-10. Copyright © 1958 by *The Hudson Review*. Reprinted by permission of the author and *The Hudson Review*. Minor changes have been made with the author's permission.

rather long, flattened to his forehead with sweat. His eyes were blue, and very bright and sharp. On his cheeks, on the fresh ruddy skin, were fine, fair hairs, like a down but sharper. It gave him a slightly glistening look." And he is the fabulous fox as well as the natural one, the sly predatory Reynard, for "Having his heavy sack on his shoulders, he stooped, thrusting his head forward. His hat was loose in one hand."

Most of the time, though, the analogy is to the natural fox. The analogy is intentionally overt from the beginning. Lawrence says of the boy that "to March he was the fox"; and once March says to him: "I thought you were the fox." The effect then comes not from a hidden analogy suddenly bursting on the reader's consciousness with the force of discovery, but from the detailed accumulation of the analogy, supported by Lawrence's genius for the description of nature and animals.

The analogy, and March's sexual dream of the fox, are such that we quite accept the remark, late in the story, that March's upper lip lifts "away from her two white, front teeth, with a curious, almost rabbit-look. . . . that helpless fascinated rabbit-look." And accept too the serious weight of sexual implication when she examines the dead fox, and to her hand "his wonderful black glinted brush was full and frictional, wonderful."

The boy's fox-likeness matters—given Lawrence's beliefs—in ways other than simply his vital quickness, or his sexual splendor. There is also "always . . . the same ruddy, self-contained look on his face, as though he were keeping himself to himself." The essential concerns in this story are more nearly simply sexual than in the later ones, but even here this self-contained boy says: "If I marry, I want to feel it's for all my life." And part of his claim to March is that there can be more permanence for her in a relationship with him than in one with Banford. The permanent marriage of two self-contained people is close to Lawrence's ideal.

For of course here as elsewhere, Lawrence is trying to render imaginatively what the relationship between the sexes is and might be, and the contest—between the boy and Banford—for March, is a contest that appears repeatedly, though in various guises, in Lawrence's work: a contest in which the new kind of lover must win the still neutral beloved from the claims of the old kind of love. Banford and March are held together by the old kind of love. Whether that love is also abnormal is largely beside the point. It is not simply that March encases her soft flesh in manly dress for Banford, and shows it in female dress for the boy Henry—though this simple device has enormous and, once more, overt effect in the story. It is rather that March feels responsible for Banford's health and happiness and well-being, and feels safe and sane with her. Sanity and over-responsibility are the marks, in all the short novels, of the old love. It was from these self-destroying feelings that March "wanted the boy to save her."

With Henry—who kills Banford to free March for himself—she feels something else. The story is at its weakest in these final pages, expanded in Lawrence's 1921 revision, which attempt to get at what the nature of the new kind of relationship between man and woman will be. Lawrence, who wished to write social and prescriptive fiction, felt a responsibility to substantiate the better world he preached. A similar impulse and failure can be found in the final act of *Prometheus Unbound*. Each of Lawrence's short novels has this kind of visionary finale, but they become increasingly successful.

The Captain's Doll (1921) is in a similarly objective style, with the author detached even from the proponents of his thesis. But there is less bent of irony this time than of wonder, for *The Captain's Doll* is peculiarly a story about beauty. Again, the meaningful working of the story depends on an overt analogy—between Captain Hepburn and the doll portrait that Hannele makes of him, but doesn't make him into. For this time the analogy is a kind of anti-analogy—the doll is what Captain Hepburn must not become: "any *woman*, today," the Captain says, "no matter *how* much she loves her man—she could start any minute and make a doll of him. And the doll would be her hero; and her hero would be no more than her doll."

All the short novels make heavy use of analogy. This is the only one, however, in which the analogy is to an inanimate object, and the inanimate fixedness of the doll limits its range of usefulness. The use it has, though, is exact and startling, and is at least inherent in the first unseemly appearance of the doll, flourishing head downwards.

Again, as in *The Fox*, the story starts with disordered relationships, and the action concerns the choice a neutral person, Hannele, must make between conventional love and a new kind of relationship. But the choice as posed here is more complicated and rich than in *The Fox*. For one thing, conventional love is given formidable and deeply attractive proponents in Mitchka, the Regierungsrat, and Mrs. Hepburn, who has, in her husband's account of her at least, a quality of out-of-the-world or primitive magic that will recur in the subsequent short novels as a quality reserved for certain adherents of the new order only. Also, the new kind of relationship is suggested more exactly and coherently in *The Captain's Doll* than it was in *The Fox*, and is less simply sexual.

The dramatic acceptability of the doctrine in this story depends on its being given dramatic validity, rather than being merely sermonized as at the end of *The Fox*. It comes too from the substantial impressiveness of Hepburn as a character, and from his and the author's nearly painful sense of the pull and attractions of the old ways, and particularly of the mortal painfulness of beauty (as in the bathing scene in Section xiii). And on the lake, at the very end of the story, we even get a flash of what the life of Hepburn and Hannele may be together, united in this new kind of marriage.

In *The Ladybird* (1921-22), Lawrence told Middleton Murry he had "the quick of a new thing." The "quick" lies chiefly in the character of the Bohemian Count Dionys, who is a resurrected man in a more intellectual, varied, and charming way than Hepburn. Dionys, of course, is purposefully named; but he is the magic Pan, not the vulgar Bacchus.

Again the objective style verges on irony, but this time it is a grave kind of irony, as seen in the opening description of Lady Beveridge. The style is subtle, the exact weight of meaning unfixed. Nothing but such complex fluency of style could make the scenes between Daphne and Count Dionys—and particularly the climactic scene in Count Dionys' bedroom—convincing, and free from any air of the ludicrous.

Again—as in the two previous stories—there is a contest for the neutral soul: the soul of Lady Daphne. But the forces in this contest are not in each case single figures. Lady Beveridge and Basil are a team—the fully civilized or naturally repressed characters, bound to the old civilized kind of selfless love. This is in contrast to Lord Beveridge and Lady Daphne, who are *un*naturally repressed—repressed, that is, in opposition to their own natures. With Lord Beveridge, the repression is nearly final, despite his choleric intransigence and personal integrity. But with Daphne it is not yet final. Even her body cannot accept it, is in disorder, as shown by the tendency to tuberculosis from which she suffers when under stress —a tendency, of course, that Lawrence also had, and which he seems often to have attributed to social causes, to his inability to find a healthy moral atmosphere in which to live. The character who has thrown off civilized repression, the other principal in the contest, is of course Count Dionys.

Perhaps the most remarkable scene in the active contest is the long debate on love between Count Dionys and Basil, the champion of conventional love, who has told Daphne that his love for her now is a sacrament, and that he considers himself an eager sacrifice to her, and could happily die on her altar. These champions of different attitudes toward love carry on their debate with Daphne sitting between them, finding it "curious that while her sympathy . . . was with the Count, it was her husband whose words she believed to be true." So the schism between her mind, educated to repression, and that other part of her which suffers under this repression, is made dramatically clear. It is an indication of the energy of the ideas and the fluency of the style, that this almost formal debate is always dramatic, never abstracted from the situation, and never tedious—even as is the nobly ludicrous debate between Hepburn and Hannele on the bus in *The Captain's Doll*.

Again animal analogy is important in the story—principally the ladybird analogy from which it gets its title. The ladybird, on the crest of Count Dionys' family, is, he thinks, a descendant of the Egyptian scarab. This leads to a deceptively casual and not quite open exchange:

"Do you know Fabre?" put in Lord Beveridge. "He suggests that the beetle rolling a little ball of dung before him, in a dry old field, must have suggested to the Egyptians the First Principle that set the globe rolling. And so the scarab became the creative principle—or something like that."

"That the earth is a tiny ball of dry dung is good," said Basil.

"Between the claws of a ladybird," added Daphne.

"That is what it is, to go back to one's origin," said Lady Beveridge.

"Perhaps they meant that it was the principle of decomposition which first set the ball rolling," said the Count.

"The ball would have to be *there* first," said Basil.

"Certainly. But it hadn't started to roll. Then the principle of decomposition started it." The Count smiled as if it were a joke.

"I am no Egyptologist," said Lady Beveridge, "so I can't judge."

The analogy between Count Dionys and this usefully destructive ladybird is admirably clear.

The place of magic—slight and off to one side in *The Captain's Doll,* and to the wrong side at that—is very important in *The Ladybird.* Not the occult theorizing about light and dark—recurrent in so much of Lawrence's fiction—but rather the magic that is conveyed by the songs in the story, the magic of personal power. When Daphne uses the Count's thimble, a German song occurs to her:

> *Wenn ich ein Vöglein wär*
> *Und auch zwei Flüglein hätt'*
> *Flög ich zu dir—*

This is obviously a song of the ladybird, though in her conscious mind Daphne labels it a song of longing for her absent husband. And Daphne is finally brought to the Count—resolving the schism between her conscious and unconscious will—by the "old songs of his childhood" that he sings, an "intense peeping . . . like a witchcraft . . . a ventriloquist sound or a bat's uncanny peeping . . . inaudible to any one but herself. . . . It was like a thread which she followed out of the world."

Again the resurrection to a new way is not easy, not a trick, but a painful, chastening separation of the self from the accustomed world and —most painfully, and for Daphne particularly—from its surface beauties. Yet at the end of *The Ladybird,* the reader is convinced that he has glimpsed in Daphne and Dionys some special capacity possessed neither by the other characters in the story, nor by himself.

In *St. Mawr* (1924) the objective style is at times a style of high comedy, and particularly when Mrs. Witt is on scene. Again, of course, the story depends on a central analogy—stressed by the title—between a human being and an animal. But the horse St. Mawr defines Rico not by similarity but by contrast. In this way, the analogy is something like that in

The Captain's Doll. Once more the analogy is entirely overt, and is suggested or anticipated well before the horse even appears, in a horsey description of Rico in the second paragraph. Rico is all fraudulent play, never the real thing (Mr. Leavis has pointed to the significance of his playing at being an artist). Even his sexuality is bogus. His marriage with Lou is "a marriage . . . without sex"; and so there is brutal irony in the circumstance that he wears a ring, sent him by a female admirer, bearing a "lovely intaglio of Priapus under an apple bough." What Lou requires —and Rico is not at all—is a Dionys, the Pan of the dinner table conversation with the painter Cartwright.

The only men in the story who are at all Pan-like are Phoenix and Lewis, the two grooms, and Phoenix doesn't quite make it either. Lewis, however, is the real thing. He and St. Mawr both avoid physical contact with women because—presumably, and as he says—modern women are incapable of the proper and necessary respect for their husbands. Again part of the real creative accomplishment of the story is that it can make ideas and notions that we might resist or find absurd out of context, convincing and moving in context. This is particularly true of the long conversation between Lewis and Mrs. Witt during the crosscountry ride they take together to save St. Mawr. The ride culminates with Lewis's refusal of Mrs. Witt's offer of marriage; but before this offer, which ends all exchanges between them, Lewis has shown himself another of the Lawrence characters endowed with other-worldly magic. Mrs. Witt, who in her relations with every other man she ever knew had "conquered his country," feels that Lewis looks "at her as if from out of another country, a country of which he was an inhabitant, and where she had never been." And this magic property is given simpler demonstration by Lewis's naive, stubborn, but only partially credulous talk about falling-stars and ash-tree seeds and the people of the moon. When he sees a falling-star, Lewis thinks to himself: *"There's movement in the sky. The world is going to change again. They're throwing something to us from the distance, and we've got to have it, whether we want it or not."*

St. Mawr is an ambitious story. In the disaster in which St. Mawr is disgraced, he is the figure of unrepressed man ridden by repressed man, Rico. The accident occurs, not fortuitously, when the horse shies at a dead snake. And—supporting the same suggestions—this precipitates for Lou an overwhelming vision of evil.[1]

The magic and visionary qualities emerging through all the preceding

---

[1] It might, incidentally, be interesting to compare Lou's vision on the expedition to the Devil's Chair, and Mrs. Witt's related lassitude toward the end of the story, with the enervating vision of Mrs. Moore in *A Passage to India,* after her visit to the Marabar caves. In a letter to Middleton Murry written just after he had completed *St. Mawr,* Lawrence says: ". . . the *Passage to India* interested me very much . . . the repudiation of our white bunk is genuine, sincere, and pretty thorough, it seems to me. Negative, yes. But King Charles must have his head off. Homage to the headsman."

short novels, dominate the middle and end of *St. Mawr*. The very end—
the description of the deserted mountain ranch in the American Southwest—is a vision of the potential and possibility that Lawrence in his
more optimistic thoughts about America considered it to possess. Lou
Witt is not saved here, but is to be brought—possibly—to the condition
that precedes any radically new life, a kind of exalted waiting, without
sexuality or, really, any connection with other human beings. Lewis and
St. Mawr—who has finally found his mate in a long-legged Texas mare:
a touch that surely fails to add to the seriousness of the story—drop out
before the end, and Phoenix, too, is in effect disposed of. The final pages
—marred only at times by Lawrence's preachy vein—give an affecting
picture of the beauty and effort of man's attempt to bring order into
chaos. And we have here again the Shelleyan attempt to envision with
some concreteness the condition abstractly prescribed.

The Man Who Died (1927) is entirely visionary and miraculous. Here
the objective style is more formal, to help convey the quality of myth,
and again analogy is important. At first Lawrence had called the story
"The Escaped Cock"—a title that accentuates the analogy, as do the
titles of the other short novels. As usual, the overt import of the analogy
requires no expounding.

The theme of the resurrected man (and the Pan-Christ) had occurred in
several of the other short novels, in different degrees of importance.
Dionys is a resurrected man, coming back to life after being near death,
and after considering himself dead and wishing his death. So too is Captain Hepburn in *The Captain's Doll*. In *St. Mawr*, Lou Witt—writing to
her mother—says she wishes no more marriages, and understands "why
Jesus said: *Noli me tangere*. Touch me not, I am not yet ascended unto
the Father. . . . That is all my cry to all the world." And this, of course,
is the repeated cry of the man who had died.

It is unnecessary, here, to outline Lawrence's sexual prescriptions. But
clearly of great moment in this story are the reverential and respecting
wonder between the man and the priestess, and that they know and need
to know so little about each other, thus retaining a kind of inviolate
personal integrity. Nor is anything like mere sexuality being invoked—
not, for example, the slavish sexuality of the slaves. And once more, the
extraordinary beauty of the narrative, often gratuitous to its immediate
intent, prevents import from becoming anything so meagre as doctrine.

These stories have a richness and intricacy—purposeful, and also nearly
accidental virtues—that summary cannot suggest. What should be suggested is the achievement not only of form—which often appears to be
lacking in the long novels of the same period—but of something very
close to formula. There is a bold repetition—often with increasing evidence of intention—of certain elements, principally: the objective and
fluent style; analogy—generally animal analogy; disordered relationships;
the opposition of traditional love and a new kind of relationship between

the sexes, dramatized by a contest between these forces for a neutral beloved; the use of magic; and the visionary ending, associated with the emergent theme of resurrection, and given final importance in *The Man Who Died*. Altogether, these short novels constitute an extraordinary body of imaginatively realized thesis fiction.

In the short novels, Lawrence puts into practice some of the objectives he sets himself in the letter to Edward Garnett defending the early draft of *The Rainbow*, and objecting to the practice of the great traditional novelists of fitting all their characters into a moral scheme. This moral scheme is, he says, "whatever the extraordinariness of the characters themselves, dull, old, dead." For himself, he wants to get away from "the old stable ego of the character," and make the characters, instead, fall into "some other rhythmic form, as when one draws a fiddlebow across a fine tray delicately sanded, the sand takes lines unknown."

For reasons having to do largely with the implications of length, these more formal principles of characterization may be more peculiarly suited to the short novel than to the long. In *The Fox*, the attempt to break the tyranny of the moral scheme is still flagrant and crude. But in the short novels that follow—particularly beginning with *The Ladybird* and its "quick of a new thing"—ego in any conventional sense is no longer the spring of action. Characters act instead in an intricate formal pattern, vivifying and responding to a central concern. The extremity of Lawrence's views required highly formal expression to be in any way acceptable, and the artifice of these short novels is nearly as formal as ballet or ritual dance.

Lawrence's Quarrel with Christianity:
The Man Who Died

by Graham Hough

After innumerable attempts at defining the basis of his objection to democracy, scattered through his work from *Women in Love* onwards, Lawrence gets it out most clearly at the eleventh hour in *Apocalypse*:

> The mass of men have only the tiniest touch of individuality, if any. The mass of men live and move, think and feel collectively, and have practically no individual emotions, feelings or thoughts at all. They are fragments of the collective or social consciousness. It has always been so, and it always will be so.

Which has not prevented him saying earlier that the end of all education and social life is the development of the individual. So it is—but only so far as the individual exists. And in most men the individual exists very little, the rest of them being realized in their share of the collectivity.

Most men are largely citizens, members of the community, collective men. And "as a citizen, as a collective being, man has his fulfillment in the gratification of his power sense." A man may wish to be a unit of pure altruistic love, but since he is inescapably a member of the political community, he is also inescapably a unit of worldly power. A man must be both a unit of love and a unit of power; he must satisfy himself both in the love-mode and the power-mode. This theme, appearing in almost the last words Lawrence wrote, goes back to a far earlier period of his career. It is expressed in almost similar terms in the last chapter of *Aaron's Rod*:

> I told you there were two urges—two great life-urges, didn't I? There may be more. But it comes on me so strongly, now, that there are two: love and power. And we've been trying to work ourselves, at least as individuals, from

the love-urge exclusively, hating the power-urge and repressing it. And now
I find we've got to accept the very thing we've hated.

We've exhausted our love-urge, for the moment. And yet we try to force
it to continue working. So we get inevitably anarchy and murder. It's no
good. We've got to accept the power motive, accept it in deep responsibility.

And this is as good a point as any to enter Lawrence's long quarrel
with Christianity. For Christianity as Lawrence always sees it is the
attempt to live from the love-motive alone—to make love, *caritas,* pure
altruism the only motive in life: "The essence of Christianity is a love of
mankind." Of course this takes no account whatever of historic and
doctrinal Christianity in all its developed complexity; still worse, from
the Christian point of view, it takes no account of the *source* of that love,
which should be the motive of all faith and all action. Still, in a thousand
places in his fiction and expository writing Lawrence makes the identification between Christianity and the doctrine of pure, universal, altruistic
love. It is against this doctrine of Kangaroo's that Somers revolts, exalts
his own dark god and preserves his integrity. It is against this doctrine
that Don Ramón revolts and triumphs over in the person of Doña
Carlota. It is against this doctrine that the Ursula of *The Rainbow* revolts when she shakes the little sister who has slapped her face, and feels
the better for it—"unchristian but clean." On every level from the
prophetic to the trivial Lawrence sees Christianity as the love-ideal and
rejects it.

Two thousand years ago Western man embarked on the attempt to
live from the love-motive alone. Sometimes Lawrence puts it a few hundred years earlier, with Platonism and the rise of the higher religions.
He refers to this momentous step in the history of humanity in at least
two different ways. Sometimes he sees it as a great rejection, a failure of
courage, a refusal of the responsibility of life, sometimes as a necessary
development, living and valid for its time and for centuries to come, but
now at an end. Perhaps the second judgment represents his steadiest and
most central belief:

> I know the greatness of Christianity: it is a past greatness. I know that,
> but for those early Christians, we should never have emerged from the chaos
> and hopeless disaster of the Dark Ages. If I had lived in the year 400, pray
> God, I should have been a true and passionate Christian. The adventurer.
> But now I live in 1924, and the Christian venture is done. The adventure
> is gone out of Christianity. We must start on a new venture towards God.

In either case, the love-mode is exhausted. Christianity is kept going by
a barren effort of will, it has no longer any connection with the deep
sources of life; and the consequences of this continuing will-driven autom-
atism of love is to be seen everywhere in the modern world.

The psychological and personal consequences have been touched on sufficiently often already. The withered and fluttering figure of Doña Carlota is supposed to represent the etiolation of spiritual love; and the unsleeping will behind it has strained her relation to Don Ramón beyond the breaking point. When Kangaroo proposes to love Somers, Somers reflects: "He doesn't love *me,* he just turns a great general emotion on me, like a tap. . . . Damn his love, he wants to *force* me." Hermione wants to love Birkin spiritually, and when Birkin, to preserve his integrity, has to reject her, she tries to knock his brains out. Farther back still, the unhappy Paul of *Sons and Lovers* is in the toils of a "spiritual" love which should have been a happy physical relation, but can never become so because of Miriam's fixed spiritual will; and his situation is complicated because there is another woman, his mother, who also wants to possess his soul. The common element in all these admittedly complex and varying situations is a love which is cut off from the natural carnal roots of love, and continues to exist simply as a function of the will. It is sterile in itself and becomes life-exhausting to whoever exercises it. Since it is something imposed on the object of love, not a reciprocal relation, it becomes inevitably a kind of spiritual bullying, and must inevitably be rejected by anyone who wishes to preserve his individual being. And all this in Lawrence's eyes is an inevitable consequence in personal relations of the Christian love-doctrine, the Christian discipline of the heart.

There is an analogous development in public life. The universal sentiment of love for mankind is similarly cut off from the natural roots of human comradeship, the warm, carnal physical community; known, for instance, by men working together in a common manual task or playing together in a ritual dance. These are communities of power, and have behind them the inexhaustible vitality of a common physical life. The love of mankind offers only a community of sentiment, and can be maintained only as a fixed direction of the will. So, like private spiritual love, it becomes a kind of bullying. *Sois mon frère ou je te tue.* Hence the devastating wars by which Christendom has been riven. Further, this kind of love is not a true communal feeling at all; it is a product of the individual will, of the ego, of all that is most personal and least deeply rooted in man. It demands that each man shall be an individual power-house of universal love. This has two consequences. The first, only clearly apparent late in the Christian cycle, but its inevitable and logical development, is democracy. Each individual must love all others, equally and impartially —the Whitmanesque universal brotherhood. The mysteries of power and lordship are denied—for they would be a break in the uniformity of universal love. So that universal love becomes a forcing of the same ideal sentiment on all alike; or looked at in reverse, a claim by each individual alike for the same universal consideration. And this claim is false, for all men do not possess individuality in the same measure. And this brings us to the second consequence of the demand for universal love—the demand that all men shall be fully individuals, and that each shall be a separate individual source of universal spiritual love. It is a demand for the impossible, and it falsifies the whole relation of man to man:

> In democracy, bullying inevitably takes the place of power. Bullying is the negative form of power. The modern Christian state is a soul-destroying force, for it is made up of fragments which have no organic whole, only a collective whole. In a hierarchy each part is organic and vital, as my finger is an organic and vital part of me. But a democracy is bound in the end to be obscene, for it is composed of myriads of dis-united fragments, each fragment assuming to itself a false wholeness, a false individuality. Modern democracy is made up of millions of fractional parts all asserting their own wholeness.

Christianity, in fact, is designed for a world of free, pure, bodiless individuals, not for a world of men—men, who exist largely in their undifferentiated physical community, most of whom are capable of very little individual spiritual development. "Christianity, then, is the ideal, but it is impossible." Lawrence agrees with Dostoevsky's Grand Inquisitor, as he makes plain in an introduction that he wrote to that dialogue. Christ loved man, but loved him in the wrong way. The following words of the Inquisitor might almost have been written by Lawrence himself: "By showing him so much respect, thou didst, as it were, cease to feel for him—thou who hast loved him more than thyself. Respecting him less, thou wouldst have asked less of him. That would have been more like love, for his burden would have been lighter." Or, as Lawrence paraphrases it: "To be able to live at all, mankind must be loved more tolerantly and more contemptuously than Jesus loved it, loved for all that, more truly, since it is loved for itself, for what it is, not for what it ought to be, free and limitless."

But man is not free and limitless. He needs earthly bread, the satisfaction of his physical appetites, and he needs to acknowledge that satisfaction as a divine gift. And he needs authority, someone to bow down to, the acknowledgment of power—not the spiritual power of an unseen god, but embodied power in the flesh. To restore health to the community of men it is first necessary to accept the power-motive again, to acknowledge the legitimacy of both individual authority and collective power. The mass of undeveloped mankind will find their vicarious fulfilment in this acknowledgment. Lawrence worries constantly over this problem of power from *Aaron's Rod* to *The Plumed Serpent*; and never successfully. His negative analyses of the corruptions of "white" love and democratic humanitarianism are piercing and profound; yet the dark god of power who is to be not destructive but life-giving is never successfully evoked. The attempts to embody him in fiction produce fascist leaders or posturing mountebanks. It might be said that this is exactly what such attempts produce in life—these are the only practical embodiments of the dark god. History since Lawrence's death might well seem to confirm the accusation. I think Lawrence could still reply that this is not so; it is precisely because the reality of power is shirked by the general "democratic" presuppositions that, like all realities that have been denied and suppressed, it reasserts itself in violent and terrible explosions. If the reality had always been admitted to its rightful place, the explosions would not have been necessary.

He would in part be right. The most committed liberal democrat would be free to admit that the calamities of the last thirty years are in part a result of the decadence of his own ideals, a decadence evident in the general loss of all sense both of the proper mode of exercising authority and the proper mode of submitting to it. This decay is not yet arrested, and Lawrence is one of its sharpest analysts. He was asking a real question, though he never found an answer.

It may be that Lawrence had himself too many relics of Christianity in his heart ever to be able to cope with the problem of earthly power, or even thoroughly to accept the necessity he asserted. Certainly he knew too little of how it works and how it is obtained. What could a man who had never had an ordinary job, never had a place in a community of men, never exercised or submitted to authority, know of political reality? His characters become steadily less convincing the nearer they come to exercising political power. The only way Lawrence can realize power and convey the sense of it, unhampered by ignorance or an inner resistance, is when it is displayed in nature. Lou Carrington submits to the "wild spirit" she finds in the mountains of Taos, but it is hard to see her submitting to any human embodiment of it. Lawrence becomes aware of this failure himself, for after *The Plumed Serpent* we hear less of the power-mode. He is still equally concerned with the failure of "Christian" love, but he is now inclined to find the alternative in "a new tenderness," a fleshly tenderness. *Lady Chatterley* is supposed to be the illustration of this tenderness, and the story which explores its relation to Christianity is *The Man Who Died.*

As Lawrence's attention shifts from power to sensual tenderness as the alternative to Christian love, the opposition becomes less intense; and it becomes easier for him to represent his doctrine as a completion of Christianity rather than a contradiction. Spiritual love and sensual love are, after all, both forms of love: and the Christian depreciation of sexuality[1] is an accident rather than the essence of its doctrine. *The Man Who Died,* therefore, comes nearer to being a reconciliation with Christianity than anything else Lawrence wrote. In other places sensual

---

[1] I take it for granted that Christianity does depreciate sexuality, or at most make reluctant concessions to it; and that Lawrence was right in believing this, wherever else he was wrong; and that the Chestertonian (and post-Chestertonian) trick of representing Christianity as a robustly Rabelaisian sort of faith is a vulgar propagandist perversion.

love is seen as the negation of "white" love, *agape,* Christian love. Here
we come near to seeing it as a transcendence, reached by death and
rebirth. And this means that it represents, not the climax of his art, which
it certainly is not, but a climactic point in the development of his thought.

This story of the rejected prophet, almost killed, left for dead, returning
painfully to life, and finding it, not in the resumption of his mission, but
in the knowledge of a woman—this story of the resurrection is certainly
Lawrence's most audacious enterprise. Many readers have found in it the
final evidence of the arrogance, the ignorant presumption of which Lawrence has often been accused. To take a story so tremendous, so profoundly interwoven with the life of our civilization, and "to try to improve on it," as I have heard it said, may well seem to suggest something
of the kind. I think the charge can be dismissed if we are careful enough
to see what Lawrence was trying to do. Although the prophet is unnamed,
the identification with Jesus is not disguised. The Crucifixion, the En-
tombment, St. Mary Magdalen, the journey to Emmaus are all explicitly
referred to. Yet what is the Jesus to whom the story refers? The "historical Jesus," the Lamb of God who takes away the sins of the world,
the Christ who shall come again with glory to judge the living and the
dead? Surely none of these. Lawrence had believed since he was twenty
that Jesus was "as human as we are"; but he is not trying to provide a
demythologized historical version of his end, more acceptable to positivists
than a supernatural resurrection. George Moore attempts something of
the kind in *The Brook Kerith*; but not Lawrence. And the cosmic and
eschatological bearings of the Gospel story concern him even less. There
is no suggestion anywhere in his tale that the death and resurrection of
Jesus is a mystery of redemption or that it affects the destiny of mankind.
Lawrence is concerned with two aspects of the Christian myth, and two
only: one, the value of Christian love; the other, the personal destiny of
Jesus the teacher. What he has done is not to vulgarize or reduce the
splendors and mysteries of traditional Christology; he simply leaves them
on one side. He has taken Jesus as what he believed him to be; a human
teacher; he sees what he believes to be the consequences of his teaching,
and tries according to his own lights to push beyond it. Certainly an
audacious attempt, possibly a misguided one, but to anyone who cares
to read what Lawrence wrote, not to rest on a conceptual summary, it
will not, I think, appear as an attempt made without due reverence.

The story was originally called *The Escaped Cock* and ended at Part I,
with the prophet setting out alone to walk through the world, vividly
aware of life in the flesh, but as yet without any active participation in it.
The central symbol of this part of the story is the cock itself, tied by the
leg by the vulgar peasant, released by the prophet. The first act of his
reborn existence is to let it fly free; and its newfound freedom is a symbol
of his own sensuous faculties, imprisoned during the years of his mission
and almost extinguished during his passion and death. For it has been a

real death. With great discretion Lawrence avoids the question of a miraculous resurrection. What does it matter? One who has suffered, as the prophet has done, the extremity of physical and spiritual torment has in effect died; and if his vital powers should, miraculously or unmiraculously, return, it is a real rebirth. In the concentration-camp world that we have produced after twenty centuries of Christian civilization there are many people who know this. At first the prophet walks in the world like one who is still not of it:

> He felt the cool silkiness of the young wheat under his feet that had been dead, and the roughishness of its separate life was apparent to him. At the edges of rocks, he saw the silky, silvery-haired buds of the scarlet anemone bending downwards. And they too were in another world. In his own world he was alone, utterly alone.

He can feel no kinship with the tender life of the young spring; and this may serve to remind us how different Lawrence's nature religion is from the Wordsworthianism of the nineteenth century. Lawrence is more aware of the tormenting complexity of human experience, of the indirectness, even the contrariety of the relation between man and external nature. Man cannot learn of man by passively receiving impulses from a vernal wood, but only by adventures in the world of men. The prophet awakens to the new life of the body only when he realizes that the peasant woman desires him. He does not desire her; he has died and does not desire anything; anyway, he knows that she is hard, short-sighted and greedy. But the knowledge of her desire awakens in him a new realization:

> Risen from the dead, he had realised at last that the body, too, has its little life; and beyond that, the greater life. He was virgin, in recoil from the little, greedy life of the body. But now he knew that virginity is a form of greed; and that the body rises again to give and to take, to take and to give, ungreedily.

So he does not reject her harshly—"he spoke a quiet pleasant word to her and turned away."

But he has another and a sterner rejection to make, the rejection of his own former mission, and of Madeleine, the woman who had believed in him. They meet, and she wishes him to come back to her and the disciples. But he only replies that the day of his interference with others is done, the teacher and the savior are dead in him. In a sense he accepts this death: betrayal and death are the natural end of such a mission. "I wanted to be greater than the limits of my own hands and feet, so I brought betrayal on myself." This is what happens to the man who would embrace multitudes when he has never truly embraced even one. On his second meeting with Madeleine he again rejects her entreaties, saying that he must ascend to the Father. She does not understand, and he does not explain; but the reader will remember that in Lawrence's mythology the Father was also the Flesh.

Madeleine, who wants to devote everything to him, is also under the spell of a hard necessity. In her life as a carnal sinner she had taken more than she gave. Now she wants to give without taking, and that is denied her. The prophet prefers the society of the peasants, for their earthy inert companionship "would put no compulsion on him." He dreads the love of which he had once been the preacher, the love that compels.

The central symbol of the second part of the story is the priestess. She is a priestess of Isis, Isis in search of the dead Osiris, and like the prophet she is virgin. She had known many men in her youth, Caesar and Antony among them, but had remained always cool and untouched; and an old philosopher had told her that women such as she must reject the splendid and the assertive and wait for the reborn man.

The lovely description of her temple and its setting is a delicate Mediterranean landscape, nature at its most humane, friendly and responsive. At the moment when the stranger lands on her shores—the stranger who is the prophet on his travels—she is idly watching two slaves, a boy and a girl. The boy beats the girl, and in a moment of half-frightened excitement copulates with her, scared and shamefaced. The priestess turns away indifferently. These are the loves of slaves; whatever fulfillment she is to find has no more in common with these vulgar couplings than with the loves of Caesars. When the stranger-prophet asks for shelter he is given it, indifferently and impersonally. A slave suspects that he is an escaped malefactor, and the priestess goes to look at him as he sleeps:

> She had no interest in men, particularly in the servile class. Yet she looked at the sleeping face. It was worn, hollow, and rather ugly. But, a true priestess, she saw the other kind of beauty in it, the sheer stillness of the deeper life.
> . . . There was a beauty of much suffering, and the strange calm candour of finer life in the whole delicate ugliness of the face. For the first time, she was touched on the quick at the sight of a man, as if the tip of a fine flame of living had touched her. It was the first time.

Both the prophet and the priestess are separate, cut off from the common life around them. She is surrounded only by slaves, and she found slaves repellent. "They were so embedded in their lesser life, and their appetites and their small consciousness were a little disgusting." And as for the prophet—"He had come back to life, but not the same life that he had left, the life of the little people and the little day. Reborn, he was in the other life, the greater day of the human consciousness." Both are aristocrats of the spirit and both are incomplete—she because she is the living representative of Isis in search of Osiris; and he because he has died and come back to the world and still dreads its contact. She realizes that she has not yet found her Osiris, and he realizes that there is the whole vista of a new life before him that he has not yet been able to touch.

And when she becomes Isis to his Osiris (for there are no surprises in this story), we are to see it not only as the satisfaction of a long-denied bodily hunger (it is that, too), but as the consummation for each of them of a solitary life of spiritual exploration—a spiritual journey that can never be complete until it has reached carnal fruition that will alter its whole meaning. She who has played out her life as a drama of search has now found. "And she said to herself, 'He is Osiris. I wish to know no more.'" And he who has died, returned to the world, but not yet felt himself to be living again, knows that he is risen from the dead when he feels desire for the woman and the power to satisfy it. When the life of the little world, in the shape of the slaves and the Roman soldiers, breaks in upon these Christian-Osirian mysteries, the prophet takes a boat and slips away, healed, whole, risen in the body, content to take what may come on another day.

Aesthetically, no doubt, the story was more satisfying in its first form, when it ended with the prophet's rejection of his old mission and his yet unfulfilled knowledge that a new life awaits him. The temptation to be explicit about what cannot properly be explained is always the *ignis fatuus* for which Lawrence is content to lose his way. The attempt to *present* the experience of one who has stepped inside the gates of death and come out again seems foredoomed to failure. As it turns out, the failure is of a different kind from that which might have been expected. It is a breakdown of continuity, not a breakdown of expression. The idyll of the stranger and the priestess is beautifully done; the balance between fabulous remoteness and concrete sensuous realization is delicately held; and Lawrence convinces us as he rarely does that the conjunction he describes is that of two rare beings, each with an exquisitely specialized individual life, yet satisfying each other completely by meeting on a ground which is beyond the personal life of either. And over it all is shed like sunshine the warm tolerant beauty of the ancient Mediterranean world—a beauty which may be partly the product of Arcadian fantasy, but still forms a real and living part of European experience.

All this is true. But it is also true that it is hard to accept the stranger of the second part of the book as identical with the prophet of the first. In the first part the broad, unspecific outlines of fable are filled out with what we know of the Gospel narrative, which is still very close to us. The invented myth is given density and immediacy by its dependence on the great public myth. In the second part the invented myth stands alone, and like all products of the pure personal imagination, it is thinner than what history or the mythopoeic faculty of a whole culture supplies. The stranger in the second part is not so much a different person as a person out of a different story; the change is a change in the mode of conception. For the tale has two kinds of significance, unequally distributed—the one more prominent in the first part, the other in the later addition.

It can be interpreted synchronically or diachronically, to borrow terms from the linguists. Synchronically, it is simply what Lawrence first called it—a story of the Resurrection, deriving much of its strength from its background of the Gospel narrative, passing over into a more rootless fantasy as this recedes into the distance. Its theme is the necessity of rejecting the Christian love-ideal for a man who has really risen in the flesh. And right or wrong, we recognize this as an integral part of the Lawrencean thesis. The second part of the story is a more arbitrary invention, and as such abides our question. Should the fulfillment of the flesh, the obvious natural destiny of mortal creatures, be discovered so late and after such long wandering? Should it, for the sake of Lawrence's thesis, be a healer for creatures who have been so long estranged from the roots of life? Could it be so, for beings who have been so long specialized in other directions, one of whom has suffered to death? It would be absurd to press these questions too hard, but they do at least begin to obtrude themselves. They can be answered by seeing the tale in the second way, diachronically; not as the story of a particular man at a particular time, but as an allegory of the course of Christian civilization. The death of the prophet is also a symbol of the death of the Christian dispensation. Christian civilization is dying after two thousand years. But the story of man is a continuity, and no culture ever really dies: it comes to life again, to a new life, which it is at first incapable of realizing and is unable to face. The passion and death of the prophet are the death-agonies of Christian culture ("Ours is a tragic age," as Lawrence said at the beginning of *Lady Chatterley*), and the second part of the story is a foreshadowing of the new dispensation that is to come. But it is a new dispensation only reached by death and rebirth. The fleshly tenderness that is to replace Christian love in the new order can never be the pristine, unembarrassed pagan delectation. The one thing a post-Christian can never be is a pagan, C. S. Lewis has remarked; and Lawrence is showing his sense of this. Christianity may be brought into touch again with the old nature-mysteries of death and rebirth, as it is in this tale; but they will be changed in the process. The fleshly healing is painfully, almost fearfully accepted by the priestess and the prophet, after years of deprivation and a season of anguish; and so it must be in the history of Western man. It will not be among *hommes moyens sensuels* that the new apprehension of life is born. Theirs is the "little day," as it always has been, under any dispensation. But to encompass this in the greater day will be the task precisely of those who have most completely submitted to the old spiritual disciplines. True, the mission of Christianity has to be rejected, but it has been lived through before it has been rejected, and nothing can ever be the same again. If a new order is to come into being, it will in all its splendor and joy be the inheritor of the Christian abnegation and suffering.

I believe that this, or something like it, is what Lawrence is saying in *The Man Who Died,* and that this is the most developed state of his relation to Christianity. The hostility had, after all, never been unmitigated. "Give me the mystery and let the world live for me"—Kate's cry in *The Plumed Serpent* was Lawrence's own. And Christianity, at any rate Catholic Christianity, was at least a guardian of the mystery in the midst of the desert of mechanized civilization. As Lawrence sees it, Catholicism had even preserved some of the old earthy pagan consciousness, and through the cycle of the liturgical year had kept in touch with the rhythm of the seasons, the essential rhythm of man's life on earth. As the inheritor of the sense of vital mystery which was the essence of religion, the Catholic Church seemed at times to him a vehicle of hope. It was a sympathy of sentiment only, not at all of dogma, intermittently awakened in Lawrence by his love for the Mediterranean world. Far stronger was the perpetual intellectual and moral preoccupation with Christian civilization and Christian ethics; a preoccupation so intense that he is able to orientate himself only by taking bearings on the Christian position he had abandoned.

For of course he had abandoned it; and the Christians (there are some) who would use Lawrence's stream to turn their own mills have need of caution. He often looks at Christianity with sympathy, but to do so he always has to turn it upside down. A choice had to be made, and Lawrence, in fact, made it in early life. However he may use Christian language, he uses it to a different end. For Christianity the life of the flesh receives its sanction and purpose from a life of the spirit which is eternal and transcendent. For Lawrence the life of the spirit has its justification in enriching and glorifying the life of the flesh of which it is in any case an epiphenomenon. It is at once an older and a newer religion that he is celebrating with what were almost his last words.

> For man, the vast marvel is to be alive. For man, as for flower, beast and bird, the supreme triumph is to be most vividly, most perfectly alive. Whatever the unborn and the dead may know, they cannot know the beauty, the marvel of being alive in the flesh. The dead may look after the afterwards. But the magnificent here and now of life in the flesh is ours, and ours alone, and ours only for a time. We ought to dance with rapture that we should be alive and in the flesh, and part of the living, incarnate cosmos. I am part of the sun as my eye is part of me. That I am part of the earth my feet know perfectly, and my blood is part of the sea. My soul knows that I am part of the human race, my soul is an organic part of the great human soul, as my spirit is part of my nation. In my own very self I am part of my family. There is nothing of me that is alone and absolute except my mind, and we shall find that the mind has no existence by itself, it is only the glitter of the sun on the surface of the waters.

Ritual Form in "The Blind Man"

by Mark Spilka

Lawrence was not an incredible mystic; his grasp of human exchange was impressively sound; his sense of the quick and the dead uniquely strong. Indeed, the resurrection or destruction of the human soul, within the living body, was central to his work; and by resurrection Lawrence meant no more—and, in all fairness, no less—than emergence into greater fullness of being: hence the struggle to transcend mere "blood-intimacy" with the life-force in *The Rainbow;* or the struggle to regain that lost vitality in *Lady Chatterley's Lover,* after the long trek around the world had convinced Lawrence of the general sterility of modern life. So he had often preached the need to waken the phallic or bodily forms of consciousness in man; but more than this, he had always preached the "Holy Ghost" life, or the life of the self in its wholeness: "the individual in his pure singleness, in his totality of consciousness, in his oneness of being: the Holy Ghost which is with us after our Pentecost, and which we may not deny."

The resurrection, then, is to greater fullness of being, and with this in mind, we can begin to understand the curious ritual pattern of Lawrence's work: those daily rites with the sun, for example, in the strange short story, "Sun"; or the pledge to life-destruction in the rabbit scene from *Women in Love;* or the floral rites in *Sons and Lovers,* where the living relationship between men, women, and flowers is used to push the story along: and for this, take Mrs. Morel's garden swoon, before Paul's birth; or the whole attempt by Paul and Miriam to commune over flowers, à la Wordsworth; or the extraordinary flower-picking scene between Paul, Miriam, and Clara; the floral benediction as Paul and Clara make love; and finally, the spontaneous gift of flowers to Miriam as the novel ends. But this is not the place for structural explication. For the moment, I simply want to emphasize that most of Lawrence's works move forward through ritual scenes, toward ritualistic ends. For just as the essence of religious ritual is communion, so Lawrence saw all deeply significant contacts between human beings—or even between man and the living universe—as spontaneous forms of communion, either sacred or debased, either nourishing or reductive; and just as the old primitive "rites of passage" always center on basic events like birth, rebirth into manhood, death, and resurrection to the greater life beyond, so Lawrence's stories always center on rebirth and death—the emergence into greater or lesser forms of being. But if this is true, then the sexual scenes in *Lady Chatterley's Lover* can only be understood as "dramatic" rites of communion. And even the famous moon scenes in both *Women in Love* and *The Rainbow* can only be understood in terms of actual rapport, pro and con, between the protagonists and the moon-as-living-force: these men and women participate, that is to say, in ritualistic situations which fall within the larger flow of the novels. And so, as the novels move along, these figures rise up toward organic being as certain statues by Rodin rise up out of a raw rough marble base—still rooted in the vague unknown, but nonetheless organic in themselves.

The pattern suggested here is a complicated one, but a typical short story, "The Blind Man," may help to clarify its nature. The central characters of the story are Maurice Pervin, who comes home blind and badly disfigured from World War I; his wife Isabel, a woman with intellectual tastes who luxuriates, nonetheless, in passionate love; and Bertie Reid, her second or third cousin, a sort of intellectual neuter with whom she once enjoyed some cultural rapport. Bertie's visit to the Pervin farm, after a long absence, gives the story its impetus, but the emotional context of that visit demands some attention here.

In the year since Maurice's return, the Pervins have enjoyed complete and deeply satisfying love; they have isolated themselves from society and have built a rich, dark world together, in keeping with Maurice's blindness: he tends to menial tasks about the farm, she reviews books for a Scottish newspaper, and they talk, sing, and read together "in a wonderful and unspeakable intimacy." Pervin himself has always been a sensual man, but now, feeling his way about the farm, drenched always in darkness, his whole sensual apparatus is aroused and transformed, as it were, into a new center of consciousness:

> Pervin moved about almost unconsciously in his familiar surroundings, dark though everything was. He seemed to know the presence of objects before he touched them. It was a pleasure to him to rock thus through a world of things, carried on the flood in a sort of blood-prescience. He did not think much or trouble much. So long as he kept this sheer immediacy of blood-contact with the substantial world he was happy, he wanted no intervention of visual consciousness. In this state there was a certain rich positivity, bordering sometimes on rapture. Life seemed to move in him like a tide lapping, lapping and advancing, enveloping all things darkly. It was a pleasure to stretch forth the hand and meet the unseen object, clasp it, and

possess it in pure contact. He did not try to remember, to visualize. He did not want to. The new way of consciousness substituted itself in him.

This new way of consciousness is the famous "phallic" or bodily form of consciousness, and Pervin's sense of the life-flow can easily be traced to its awakening. His blindness has resulted, then, in a change of being, and this change has led in turn to closer contact with primitive forces. This is the nature of his emotional state, and a moment later Lawrence reveals its direction:

> The rich suffusion of this state generally kept him happy, reaching its culmination in the consuming passion for his wife. But at times the flow would seem to be checked and thrown back. Then it would beat inside him like a tangled sea, and he was tortured in the shattered chaos of his own blood. He grew to dread this arrest, this throw-back, this chaos inside himself, when he seemed merely at the mercy of his own powerful and conflicting elements. How to get some measure of control or surety, this was the question. And when the question rose maddening in him, he would clench his fists as if he would *compel* the whole universe to submit to him. But it was in vain. He could not even compel himself.

So Pervin, like the Brangwen men in *The Rainbow,* is caught and held within a state of blood-prescience. And the potential danger of that state is kept in focus by a series of ritual scenes. He moves forward toward his wife, for example, out of the fecund darkness of the barn. His wife can actually *feel* him coming toward her, and the darkness itself seems like "a strange swirl of violent life . . . upon her." She feels giddy, and afraid even of her husband as she meets him in his own rich world of unresolved blood-intimacy. So that the scene can only be described, in ritualistic terms, as a communion of fear.

Then Bertie Reid arrives at the farm, and a second dramatic scene occurs as husband and wife take dinner with their special guest. And here, in the safety of the house, the scar on Pervin's face suggests some form of limitation or arrest to Isabel. The scar strikes Bertie this way too. He looks away from it with difficulty, and "without knowing what he [does]," he picks up "a little crystal bowl of violets" and sniffs at them. The flowers, of course, are alive and organic, while Pervin remains fixed within a single form of consciousness. Thus an awkward moment occurs when Reid places them in Maurice's hands, so that he may smell them too, and the blind man's "large, warm-looking fingers" close for a moment "over the thin white fingers of the barrister." Both Isabel and Reid are afraid and deeply disturbed at this point, and again we have, in ritualistic terms, a mounting communion of fear.

The emotional threat dissolves, however, with the final ritual scene. Later that evening, Bertie looks for Maurice and finds him in the barn, pulping turnips. The two begin to chat about Isabel's happiness, Mau-

rice's scar, and the casual nature of their own acquaintanceship. Then
Maurice suddenly asks if he may touch him. Bertie complies, reluctantly,
and Maurice gathers his head in his sensitive fingers, shifts and adjusts his
grasp until he has covered the whole face, then grasps the shoulder, arm,
and hand before him. The bachelor lawyer feels annihilated by all this;
he quivers with revulsion as Maurice asks him now to touch his own
blind eyes. But again he complies:

> . . . He lifted his hand, and laid the fingers on the scar, on the scarred eyes.
> Maurice suddenly covered them with his own hand, pressed the fingers of
> the other man upon his disfigured eye-sockets, trembling in every fibre, and
> rocking slightly, slowly, from side to side. He remained thus for a minute
> or more, whilst Bertie stood as if in a swoon, unconscious, imprisoned.
>
> Then suddenly Maurice removed the hand of the other man from his
> brow, and stood holding it in his own.
>
> "Oh, my God," he said, "we shall know each other now, shan't we? We
> shall know each other now."

A writer like James Joyce might see an "epiphany" in such an experience—a static, timeless manifestation of some spiritual essence; but Lawrence sees instead a kinetic transformation of being, in both Pervin and
Reid: for when the two return to Isabel, Maurice stands "with his feet
apart, like a strange colossus," while Bertie is now "like a mollusc whose
shell is broken." Through the friendship rite, one man moves toward
greater fullness of being; his blindness is transcended, his unresolved
blood-intimacy released, and the limited circle of marriage itself is broken
by "the new delicate fulfillment of mortal friendship"; but the other man
is destroyed by the experience; his outer bulwark against life is smashed,
his inner vacuum thoroughly exposed. Thus the ritual pattern of the
story is complete. There are ironies, of course, and resonant implications,
as in more static and symbolic forms. The path, the way out of darkness
which opens for the Pervins is quickly closed by Bertie's fear of passionate
friendship. Yet the change of being in Maurice, as in Bertie, is real and
valid. The ritual form conveys a new life-possibility: a step beyond marriage which makes marriage possible, a breakthrough to that fuller life
which Lawrence tried to project in all his work, in strongly dramatic
terms, and with a strong *dramatic* sense of the odds against it.

This general pattern, this ritualistic movement toward organic being,
or away from it, would seem to vitiate the usual charges against Lawrence: that he had no operative sense of form; that his work was merely
impressionistic; or that he kept remarkable faith with the living moment,
yet never produced a complete work of art. Thus Frederick Hoffman
argues:

> Form for Lawrence was unimportant—though he was capable of writing
> aptly finished short tales and novelettes, his longer novels are held to-

gether by a succession of moments of crucial experience; its continuity is fitful, the *modus vivendi* a series of revitalized crises of bodily relationship.

This criticism is sound, in part: the tales and novelettes are often "aptly finished" and the novels often "fitful": but Hoffman falsely assumes that emotional life in Lawrence's fiction is formless in itself. As tales like "The Blind Man" show us, Lawrence felt otherwise. His faith in the living moment was uniquely counterbalanced by his faith in the human soul, whose death and resurrection within the living body was his chief concern. And so, to accommodate his concept of the soul as a stable but ever-changing element, a kind of second ego which moves along within the flux of life, waxing and waning in accord with man's emotional experience, he discovered and employed emotional form; he learned to deal directly and obliquely with specific states of being: in other words, he learned to chronicle the movements of the soul—and learned this primarily in the novels, from which most of the shorter tales evolve. Thus, in the better part of his works, long or short, the "crucial moments" always mount or flow toward definite ends, and Hoffman— among others—fails to account for this fact. Granted, the emotional form breaks down or backs against itself, like Pervin's sensual flow, whenever Lawrence wrestles with those problems which he cannot solve. But significantly enough, this breakdown coincides with the troubled middle period of his life—the period stretching from *The Lost Girl* through *Aaron's Rod, Kangaroo, The Boy in the Bush,* and *The Plumed Serpent.* But the four greatest novels—those which express his finest psychological and moral insights—are all well-organized along ritualistic lines. It seems scarcely accidental, then, that a man is born (incipiently) at the end of *Sons and Lovers;* a woman is born (again incipiently) as *The Rainbow* ends; while in *Women in Love* a man and a woman meet and marry— and conceive a child some eight years later, in *Lady Chatterley's Lover.* For these four novels represent an impressive and decidedly artistic attempt on Lawrence's part to set forth the conditions of manhood, womanhood, and marriage, as he felt and understood them in his own life. These novels coincide, that is, with his own "rites of passage"—with the early years of elopement and self-discovery, and with the later years of maturity and self-adjustment, when he was able to synthesize his material and to give new order to the experience of love.

A Rocking-Horse: The Symbol,
the Pattern, the Way to Live

by W. D. Snodgrass

> "Daddy! Daddy!" he cried to his father. "Daddy, look what they
> are doing! Daddy, they're beating the poor little horse!"
> —*Crime and Punishment*

"The Rocking-Horse Winner" seems the perfect story by the least
meticulous of serious writers. It has been anthologized, analyzed by New
Critics and force-fed to innumerable undergraduates. J. Arthur Rank has
filmed it. Yet no one has seriously investigated the story's chief structural
feature, the symbolic extensions of the rocking-horse itself, and I feel that
in ignoring several meaning-areas of this story we ignore some of Lawrence's most stimulating thought.

Though the reach of the symbol is overwhelming, in some sense the
story is "about" its literal, narrative level: the life of the family that
chooses money instead of some more stable value, that takes money as its
nexus of affection. The first fault apparently lay with the mother. The
story opens:

> There was a woman who was beautiful, who started with all the advan-
> tages, yet she had no luck. She married for love, and the love turned to
> dust. She had bonny children, yet she felt they had been thrust upon her,
> and she could not love them . . . at the center of her heart was a hard
> little place that could not feel love, not for anybody.

We never learn much more about her problems, about *why* her love
turned to dust. But the rhyming verb *thrust* is shrewdly chosen and placed;
knowing Lawrence, we may well guess that Hester's dissatisfaction is, at
least in large part, sexual. We needn't say that the sexual factor is the sole
or even primary cause of her frigidity, but it is usually a major expression

"A Rocking-Horse: The Symbol, the Pattern, the Way to Live" by W. D. Snodgrass.
From *The Hudson Review*, XI (Summer, 1958), 191-200. Copyright © 1958 by *The
Hudson Review*. Reprinted by permission of the author and *The Hudson Review*.
Footnotes have been added by the editor.

and index of it, and becomes causal. Lawrence wrote in an amazing letter to John Middleton Murry:

> A woman unsatisfied must have luxuries. But a woman who loves a man would sleep on a board. . . . You've tried to satisfy Katherine with what you could earn for her, give her: and she will only be satisfied with what you *are*.

There could scarcely be a more apt description of Hester's situation. As for her husband, we cannot even guess what he *is;* he gives too few clues. Failing to supply the luxuries that both he and his wife demand, he has withdrawn, ceased to exist. The one thing he could always give—himself, the person he is—seems part of a discarded currency. The mother, the father, finally the boy—each in turn has withdrawn his vital emotions and affections from commitment in and to the family. Withdrawing, they have denied their own needs, the one thing that could be "known" and "sure." They have, instead, committed their lives to an external, money, and so to "luck," since all externals are finally beyond control and cannot be really known. Thus, it is Paul's attempt to bring an external into his control by knowledge which destroys him. It is a failure of definition.

The father's withdrawal, of course, leaves a gap which encourages Paul in a natural Oedipal urge to replace him. And money becomes the medium of that replacement. So the money in the story must be taken literally, but is also a symbolic substitute for love and affection (since it has that meaning to the characters themselves), and ultimately for sperm. We know that money is not, to Paul, a good in itself—it is only a way to win his mother's affection, "compel her attention," show her that *he* is lucky though his father is not. That money has no real use for Hester either becomes only too clear in that crucial scene where Paul sends her the birthday present of five thousand pounds hoping to alleviate her problems, relax the household, and so release her affections. His present only makes her colder, harder, more luxurious, and:

> . . . the voices in the house, behind the sprays of mimosa and almond blossom, and from under the piles of iridescent cushions, simply trilled and screamed in a sort of ecstasy: "There *must* be more money! Oh-h-h; there *must* be more money. Oh, now, now-w! Now-w-w—there must be more money;—more than ever!"

The mother and father have driven themselves to provide the mother with what she, actually, needs least. And she has squandered it, one would guess, precisely to show her scorn for it and for the husband who provides it. Money as a symbolic substitute has only sharpened the craving it was meant to satisfy; the family has set up a vicious circle which will finally close upon Paul.

As several critics have noted, the story resembles many well-known fairy tales or magical stories in which the hero bargains with evil powers for personal advantages or forbidden knowledge. These bargains are always "rigged" so that the hero, after his apparent triumphs, will lose in the end—this being, in itself, the standard "moral." Gordon and Tate sum up their interpretation: "the boy, Paul, has invoked strange gods and pays the penalty with his death." Robert Gorham Davis goes on to point out that many witches supposedly rode hobby-horses of one sort or another (*e.g.*, the witch's broom) to rock themselves into a magical and prophetic trance. When he rides, Paul's eyes glare blue and strange, he will speak to no one, his sisters fear him. He stares into the horse's wooden face: "Its red mouth was slightly open, its big eye was wide and glassy-bright." More and more engrossed in his doom as the story progresses, he becomes "wild-eyed and strange . . . his big blue eyes blazing with a sort of madness." We hear again and again of the uncanny blaze of his eyes until finally, at his collapse, they are "like blue stones." Clearly enough, he is held in some self-induced prophetic frenzy, a line of meaning carefully developed by the story. When Paul first asserts to his mother that he is "lucky," he claims that God told him so. This seems pure invention, yet may well be a kind of *hubris,* considering the conversation that had just passed with his mother:

> "Nobody ever knows why one person is lucky and another unlucky."
> "Don't they? Nobody at all? Does nobody know?"
> "Perhaps God. But He never tells."

Whether Paul really believes that Gold told him so, he certainly does become lucky. And others come to believe that superhuman powers are involved. Bassett thinks of "Master Paul" as a seer and takes an explicitly worshipful tone towards him. He grows "serious as a church" and twice tells Uncle Oscar in a "secret, religious voice. . . . 'It's as if he had it from heaven.'" These hints of occultism culminate in Uncle Oscar's benediction:

> "My God, Hester, you're eighty-odd thousand to the good, and a poor devil of a son to the bad. But poor devil, poor devil, he's best gone out of a life where he rides his rocking-horse to find a winner."

So, in some sense, Paul *is* demonic, yet a poor devil; though he has compacted with evil, his intentions were good and he has destroyed only himself. At first metaphorically, in the end literally, he has committed suicide. But that may be, finally, the essence of evil.

It is clear, then, that the story is talking about some sort of religious perversion. But *what* sort? Who are the strange gods: how does Paul serve them and receive their information? We must return here, I think, to the problem of knowledge and intellection. Paul is destroyed, we have said, by his desire to "know." It is not only that he has chosen wrong ways of knowing or wrong things to know. The evil is that he *has* chosen to know, to live by intellection. Lawrence wrote, in a letter to Ernest Collings:

> My great religion is a belief in the blood, the flesh, as being wiser than the intellect. We can go wrong in our minds. But what our blood feels and believes and says, is always true. *The intellect is only a bit and bridle.* What do I care about knowledge. . . . I conceive a man's body as a kind of flame . . . and the intellect is just the light that is shed on to the things around. . . . A flame isn't a flame because it lights up two, or twenty objects on a table. It's a flame because it is itself. And we have forgotten ourselves. . . . The real way of living is to answer to one's wants. Not "I want to light up with my intelligence as many things as possible" but ". . . I want that liberty, I want that woman, I want that pound of peaches, I want to go to sleep, I want to go to the pub and have a good time, I want to look a beastly swell today, I want to kiss that girl, I want to insult that man."

(I have italicized the bit and bridle metaphor to underscore an immediate relationship to the rocking-horse of the story.)

Not one member of this family really knows his wants. Like most idealists, they have ignored the most important part of the command *Know thyself,* and so cannot deal with their most important problem, their own needs. To know one's needs is really to know one's own limits, hence one's definition. Lawrence's notion of living by "feeling" or "blood" (as opposed to "knowledge," "mind" or "personality") may be most easily understood, perhaps, as living according to what you *are,* not what you think you should be made over into; knowing yourself, not external standards. Thus, what Lawrence calls "feeling" could well be glossed as "knowing one's wants." Paul's family, lacking true knowledge of themselves, have turned their light, their intellect, outward, hoping to control the external world. The mother, refusing to clarify what her emotions really *are,* hopes to control herself and her world by acting "gentle and anxious for her children." She tries to be or act what she thinks she should be, not taking adequate notice of what she is and needs. She acts from precepts about motherhood, not from recognition of her own will, self-respect for her own motherhood. Thus, the apparent contradiction between Hester's coldness, the "hard . . . center of her heart," and, on the other hand, "all her tormented motherhood flooding upon her" when Paul collapses near the end of the story. Some deep source of affection has apparently lain hidden (and so tormented) in her, all along; it was her business to find and release it sooner. Similarly, Paul has a need for affection which he does not, and perhaps cannot, understand or manage: Like his mother, he is trying to cover this lack of self-knowledge with knowledge about the external world, which he hopes will bring him a fortune, and so affection.

Paul is, so, a symbol of civilized man, whipping himself on in a nervous endless "mechanical gallop," an "arrested prance," in chase of something which will destroy him if he ever catches it, and which he never really wanted anyway. He is the scientist, teacher, theorist, who must always know about the outside world so that he can manipulate it to what he believes is his advantage. Paradoxically, such knowledge comes to him only in isolation, in withdrawal from the physical world, so that his intellect may operate upon it unimpeded. And such control of the world as he can gain is useless because he has lost the knowledge of what he wants, what he is.

This, then, is another aspect of the general problem treated by the story. A still more specific form of withdrawal and domination is suggested by the names of the horses on which Paul bets. Those names—like the names of the characters—are a terrible temptation to ingenuity. One should certainly be wary of them. Yet two of them seem related to each other and strongly suggest another area into which the story's basic pattern extends. Paul's first winner, Singhalese, and his last, Malabar, have names which refer to British colonial regions of India. (A third name, Mirza, suggests "Mirzapur"—still another colonial region. But that is surely stretching things.) India is obviously one of the focal points of the modern disease of colonial empire; for years Malabar and Singhalese were winners for British stockholders and for the British people in general. The British, like any colonial power or large government or corporation, have gambled upon and tried to control peoples and materials which they never see and with which they never have any vital physical contacts. (Lawrence's essay "Men must Work and Women as Well" is significant here.)[1] They have lived by the work of others, one of the chief evils of which is that their own physical energies have no outlet and are turned into dissatisfactions and pseudo-needs which must be filled with more and more luxuries. And so long as they "knew," placed their bets right, they were rich, were able to afford more and more dissatisfactions. A similar process destroyed Spain: a similar process destroyed Paul.

Though these last several areas of discussion are only tenuously present, most readers would agree, I think, that the rocking-horse reaches symbolically toward such meanings: into family economy and relations, into the occult, into the modern intellectual spirit, into the financial and imperial manipulations of the modern State. But surely the sexual area is more basic to the story—is, indeed, the basic area in which begins the pattern of living which the rocking-horse symbolizes. It is precisely this

[1] See also Lawrence's interest in E. M. Forster's novel of British colonial conflict, *A Passage to India* (1924), with its suggestive use of the "Marabar" caves, as reported by Monroe Engel (see p. 98n). "The Rocking-Horse Winner" appeared in 1926 [Ed.].

area of the story and its interpretation which has been ignored, perhaps intentionally, by other commentators. Oddly enough, Lawrence himself has left an almost complete gloss of this aspect of the story in his amazing, infuriating, and brilliant article, "Pornography and Obscenity." There, Lawrence defines pornography not as art which stimulates sexual desire, but rather as art which contrives to make sex ugly (if only by excluding it) and so leads the observer away from sexual intercourse and toward masturbation. He continues:

> When the grey ones wail that the young man and young woman went and had sexual intercourse, they are bewailing the fact that the young man and the young woman didn't go separately and masturbate. Sex must go somewhere, especially in young people. So, in our glorious civilisation, it goes in masturbation. And the mass of our popular literature, the bulk of our popular amusements just exists to provoke masturbation. . . . The moral guardians who are prepared to censor all open and plain portrayal of sex must now be made to give their only justification: We prefer that the people shall masturbate.

Even a brief reading of the essay should convince one that Paul's mysterious ecstasy is not only religious, but sexual and onanistic. That is Paul's "secret of secrets." Just as the riding of a horse is an obvious symbol for the sex act, and "riding" was once the common sexual verb, so the rocking-horse stands for the child's imitation of the sex act, for the riding which goes nowhere.

We note in the passage quoted above that Lawrence thinks of masturbation chiefly as a substitute for some sort of intercourse. Similarly in the story:

> "Surely, you're too big for a rocking-horse!" his mother had remonstrated.
> "Well, you see, mother, till I can have a *real* horse, I like to have some sort of animal about," had been his quaint answer.

This is one of several doctrinal points where the reader will likely disagree with Lawrence. Nonetheless, the idea was prevalent at the time of writing and is common enough today that most men probably still think of masturbation chiefly as a sex substitute. And like the money substitute mentioned before, it can only famish the craving it is thought to ease. So we find another area in which the characters of the story don't know what they need; another and narrower vicious circle.

The tightening of that circle, the destruction of Paul, is carefully defined; here, one feels both agreement with Lawrence's thought and a strong admiration for his delineation of the process:

> . . . He went off by himself, vaguely, in a childish way, seeking for the clue to "luck." Absorbed, taking no heed of other people, he went about with a sort of stealth, seeking inwardly for luck.

Stealth becomes more and more a part of Paul. We hear again and again of his secret, his "secret within a secret," we hear his talk with Uncle Oscar:

> "I shouldn't like mother to know I was lucky," said the boy.
> "Why not, son?"
> "She'd stop me."
> "I don't think she would."
> "Oh!"—and the boy writhed in an odd way—"I *don't* want her to know, uncle."

We may quote here a passage from "Pornography and Obscenity":

> Masturbation is the one thoroughly secret act of the human being, more secret even than excrementation.

Naturally, any act accompanied by such stealth is damaging to the personality and to its view of itself. It involves an explicit denial of the self, a refusal to affirm the self and its acts (an imaginative suicide) and consequently a partial divorce from reality. But this is only part of that same general process of isolation. In the essay, Lawrence says:

> Most of the responses are dead, most of the awareness is dead, nearly all the constructive activity is dead, and all that remains is a sort of a shell, a half empty creature fatally self-preoccupied and incapable of either giving or taking. . . . And this is masturbation's result. Enclosed within the vicious circle of the self, with no vital contacts outside, the self becomes emptier and emptier, till it is almost a nullus, a nothingness.

And this is the process dramatized by the story. Paul draws back from his family, bit by bit, until he becomes strange and fearful to his sisters and will speak to no one, has grown beyond the nurse and has no real contact with his parents. Even Uncle Oscar feels uncomfortable around him. Finally he has moved his rocking-horse away from the family and taken it with him "to his own bedroom at the top of the house."

Lawrence believes that man's isolation is an unavoidable part of his definition as a human being—yet he needs all the contact he can possibly find. In his essay on Poe, Lawrence writes:

> Love is the mysterious vital attraction which draws things together, closer, closer together. For this reason sex is the actual crisis of love. For in sex the two blood-systems, in the male and female, concentrate and come into contact, the merest film intervening. Yet if the intervening film breaks down, it is death. . . .
>
> In sensual love, it is the two blood-systems, the man's and the woman's, which sweep up into pure contact, and almost *fuse*. Almost mingle. Never

quite. There is always the finest imaginable wall between the two blood waves, through which pass unknown vibrations, forces, but through which the blood itself must never break, or it means bleeding.

Sex, then, is man's closest link to other human beings and to the "unknown," his surest link into humanity, and it is this that Paul and his family have foresworn in their wilful isolation. And this isolation is more than physical. Again in "Pornography and Obscenity," we find:

> The great danger of masturbation lies in its merely exhaustive nature. In sexual intercourse, there is a give and take. A new stimulus enters as the native stimulus departs. Something quite new is added as the old surcharge is removed. And this is so in all sexual intercourse where two creatures are concerned, even in the homosexual intercourse. But in masturbation there is nothing but loss. There is no reciprocity. There is merely the spending away of a certain force, and no return. The body remains, in a sense, a corpse, after the act of self-abuse.

To what extent Lawrence thinks this reciprocity, this give and take, to be physical, I am not sure; I *am* sure it could easily be exaggerated. Lawrence makes a sharp distinction between the physical and the material. At any rate, it seems to me that the most important aspect of this sexual give-and-take is certainly emotional and psychological and that the stimulus which enters in sexual intercourse lies in coming to terms with an actual sexual partner who is real and in no wise "ideal." Thus, such a partner will afford both unexpectable pleasures and very real difficulties which must be recognized and overcome. But in masturbation these problems can be avoided. Most psychologists would agree that the most damaging thing about masturbation is that it is almost always accompanied by fantasy about intercourse with some "ideal" partner. Thus, one is led away from reality with its difficulties and unpredictable joys, into the self and its repetitive fantasies. This may seem rather far from the story, but I suggest that this explains the namelessness of the rocking-horse. (It also, of course, suggests shame and is valuable in manipulating the plot.) The real partner has a name which is always the same and stands for a certain configuration of personality with its quirks and glories; the fantasy partner, having no personality, has no name of his or her own but is given the name of such "real" partners as one might wish from week to week.

These, then, are the gods which Paul has invoked. This sexual problem gives, also, a startling range of irony to the religious texture of the story. The "secret within a secret . . . that which had no name" comes to be not only the shame of Paul's masturbation, but also a vicious and astounding parody of the "word within a word"—that which cannot be named. It should be clear from the material already quoted, and even more so from a reading of "Pornography and Obscenity," that it is popular religion—Christian idealism—that Lawrence is attacking, for it sup-

ports the "purity lie" and leaves masturbation as the only sexual expression, even at times openly condoning it. The strange gods are the familiar
ones; the occult heresy is popular Christian piety.

It is not clear, however, how Paul receives knowledge from his onanistic gods. Lawrence himself does not pretend to know *how* this comes
about, he only knows that it does exist:

> The only positive effect of masturbation is that it seems to release a cer-
> tain mental energy, in some people. But it is mental energy which manifests
> itself always in the same way, in a vicious circle of analysis and impotent
> criticism, or else a vicious circle of false and easy sympathy, sentimentalities.
> This sentimentalism and the niggling analysis, often self-analysis, of most
> of our modern literature, is a sign of self-abuse.

This momentary release of energy is, I take it, equivalent to finding the
name of the "winner" in the story. Thus the two great meaning-streams
of the story, intellection and masturbation, relate. Masturbation stands as
the primary area: the withdrawal and stealth, the intellectual participation in the physical, the need to know and magically control the external,
the driving of the self into a rigid, "mechanical gallop," the displacement
of motive, the whole rejection of self, all begins here. And the pattern,
once established, spreads, gradually infecting all the areas of life, familial,
economic, political, religious. Here, again, the reader may feel a doctrinal
disagreement, suspecting that masturbation is more symptomatic than
causal. Such disagreement scarcely touches the story, however, whose business is not to diagnose or cure, but to create a vision of life, which it does
with both scope and courage.[2]

I want to quote finally, one more passage from the essay "Pornography
and Obscenity" to round off the argument and tie up some loose ends,
and also simply because of its value, its sincerity. It is a kind of summa-
tion of the story's meaning and opens with a sentence roughly equivalent
to Uncle Oscar's judgment: "he's best gone out of a life where he rides a
rocking-horse to find a winner":

> If my life is merely to go on in a vicious circle of self-enclosure, mas-
> turbating self-consciousness, it is worth nothing to me. If my individual
> life is to be enclosed within the huge corrupt lie of society today, purity
> and the dirty little secret, then it is worth not much to me. Freedom is
> a very great reality. But it means, above all things, freedom from lies.
> It is, first, freedom from myself; from the lie of my all-importance, even

It should be noted that the tale is more profoundly integrated, psychologically and
socially, than the essay: the tale concerns a preadolescent child deprived of normal
maternal affection and exposed to monetary "whispers" who takes to "riding"; the
essay deals with young adults deprived of sexual love and exposed to pornographic
"whispers" which somehow foster the money-lie—it deals disjointedly with a *later* stage
of the conflict which the tale presents integrally (and *causally*) at inception [Ed.].

to myself; it is freedom from the self-conscious masturbating thing I am, self-enclosed. And second, freedom from the vast lie of the social world, the lie of purity and the dirty little secret. All the other monstrous lies lurk under the cloak of this one primary lie. The monstrous lie of money lurks under the cloak of purity. Kill the purity-lie and the money-lie will be defenseless.

We have to be sufficiently conscious, and self-conscious, to know our own limits and to be aware of the greater urge within us and beyond us. Then we cease to be primarily interested in ourselves. Then we learn to leave ourselves alone, in all the affective centres: not to force our feelings in any way, and never to force our sex. Then we make the great onslaught on the outside lie, the inside lie being settled. And that is freedom and the fight for freedom.

There are few more courageous statements in our literature.

Poet Without a Mask

by V. de S. Pinto

Samuel Palmer in a well-known passage called William Blake "a man without a mask." D. H. Lawrence might well be described as a poet without a mask. Nearly all the famous poets of the past have worn a mask of some sort. It may be a very grand and dignified one like Milton's, a gentlemanly one like Tennyson's, one with an ironic smile like the mask of Pope or a grotesque like that of Burns or Skelton. Of course all poets drop the mask occasionally, for a line or two or perhaps a whole poem. Shakespeare dropped it altogether in the best of his sonnets and gave us a glimpse of the most enigmatic personality in the whole of literature.

R. P. Blackmur in his essay on "Lawrence and Expressive Form" in his book *Language as Gesture* (1954) makes a carefully reasoned attack on Lawrence's poetry exactly because it is poetry without a mask. Although he does not use this image, his argument is in effect that the use of the mask is necessary for the production of good poetry. He quotes the following passage from Lawrence's Note prefixed to the two-volume edition of his *Collected Poems* (1928): "a young man is afraid of his demon and puts his hand over the demon's mouth sometimes. And the things the young man says are very rarely poetry." [1] Commenting on this passage, Blackmur writes: "I take the young man in the quotation to be just what Lawrence thought he was not, the poet as craftsman, and the demon was exactly that outburst of personal feeling which needed the discipline of craft to become a poem." [2] This seems to me to be a travesty of Lawrence's meaning. By the "demon" Lawrence certainly did not mean a mere "outburst of personal feeling." He meant what he calls in the Foreword to *The Fantasia of the Unconscious* "pure passionate experience," [3] or experience at a deeper level than the personal. In the original Intro-

"Poet Without a Mask" by V. de S. Pinto. From *The Critical Quarterly*, III (Spring, 1961), 5-18. Copyright © 1961 by *The Critical Quarterly*. Reprinted by permission of the author and *The Critical Quarterly*.

[1] *The Complete Poems of D. H. Lawrence*, 3 vols. (London: William Heinemann, Phoenix Edition, 1957), I, xxxvi.

[2] R. P. Blackmur, *Language as Gesture, Essays in Poetry* (London: Allen and Unwin, 1954), pp. 287, 288.

[3] *Fantasia of the Unconscious* (1933), p. 11.

duction to the *Collected Poems* he tells us that "the demon is timeless." [4]
He is what Blake calls the fourfold vision and what the Greeks called the
Muse. The interpretation of "the young man" as "the poet as craftsman"
is equally misleading. By "the young man" Lawrence means the immature writer who wants to make himself a mask to appear before the public
by means of the imitation of fashionable verse forms.

Blackmur's essay, however, is an important piece of criticism; like
Johnson's criticism of Milton, it is one of those important wrongheaded
pieces of criticism that contain valuable elements of truth. Blackmur's
main contention is that Lawrence's poetry, in spite of certain great qualities, which he admits that it possesses, is vitiated by what he calls "the
fallacy of the faith in expressive form," which he defines as the belief
"that if a thing is only intensely enough felt its mere expression in words
will give it satisfactory form, the dogma, in short, that once material becomes words it is its own best form." [5] Now I do not believe any English
writer of note held this dogma in the crude form as stated by Blackmur,
though Wordsworth in some passages in his Preface of 1800 came danger-
ously near to it and was rightly castigated for those passages by Coleridge
in the seventeenth chapter of *Biographia Literaria*. Some of Lawrence's
own statements about his poetry, which Blackmur does not quote, are
relevant here. In an early letter to Edward Marsh, who had objected to
the rhythms of some of his poems, he wrote: "I think, don't you know,
that my rhythms fit my mood pretty well, in the verse. And if the mood
is out of joint the rhythm often is. I have always tried to get an emotion
out in its course without altering it. It needs the finest instinct imaginable, much finer than the skill of craftsmen. That Japanese Yone Noguche
tried it. He doesn't quite bring it off. Often I don't—sometimes I do.
Sometimes Whitman is perfect. Remember skilled verse is dead in fifty
years." [6] It is a pity that Lawrence used the word "craftsman" in this
passage. What he is really pleading for is not a rejection of craftsmanship
but a different kind of craftsmanship from that of the user of traditional
forms. This is not, to use Blackmur's phrase, a matter of "mere expression
in words." Lawrence realizes it is something very difficult which "needs
the finest instinct imaginable, much finer than the skill of the craftsman."
He means "finer than the skill of the craftsman in traditional forms." Of
course his sweeping statement that "skilled verse is dead in fifty years"
needs a great deal of qualification. If he meant "carefully wrought verse
in traditional forms," hundreds of examples from Horace to Pope give
him the lie. What he probably meant was skilled mechanical imitations of
traditional verse forms.

Lawrence's Introduction to the American edition of his *New Poems*,

---

[4] *Phoenix: The Posthumous Papers of D. H. Lawrence,* edited by E. D. McDonald.
(London: William Heinemann, 1936), p. 254.

[5] Blackmur, *op. cit.,* p. 289.

[6] *The Letters of D. H. Lawrence,* p. 135.

though written in a rather florid style, is a much clearer and more mature statement of his poetic theory than the rather crudely phrased letter to Marsh. In this important essay he distinguishes between two kinds of poetry. One kind he describes as "the poetry of the beginning and the poetry of the end":

> It is of the nature of all that is complete and consummate. This complete-ness, this consummateness, the finality and the perfection are conveyed in exquisite form: the perfect symmetry, the rhythm which returns upon itself like a dance where the hands link and loosen and link for the supreme moment of the end. Perfected bygone moments, perfected mo-ments in the glimmering futurity, these are the treasured gem-like lyrics of Shelley and Keats.

Here Lawrence is recognizing the validity of the best sort of "skilled verse," all of which he had too hastily condemned in his letter to Marsh. His second kind of poetry he calls:

> . . . poetry of that which is at hand: the immediate present. In the im-mediate present there is no perfection, no consummation, nothing finished. The strands are all flying, quivering, intermingling into the web, the waters are shaking the moon. There is no round consummate moon on the face of running water, nor on the face of the unfinished tide. There are no gems of the living plasm. The living plasm vibrates unspeakably, it inhales the future, it exhales the past. It is the quick of both and yet it is neither.[7]

Lawrence is here distinguishing between traditional form on the one hand and expressive or organic form on the other. "Expressive form" is what Coleridge called "organic form." He contrasted "organic form" with "mechanical regularity" and wrote that it "is innate; it shapes, as it devel-ops, itself from within, and the fulness of its development is one and the same with the perfection of its outward form."[8] To use Lawrence's image, it attempts to reproduce "the unspeakable vibrations of the living plasm." Blackmur is surely wrong in his wholesale condemnation of organic or "expressive form." It is true that there are great dangers in this kind of writing, and, as Lawrence wrote, it needs the finest instinct imaginable, or it can easily lapse into empty rhetoric or mere disorder. I believe, however, that it is the only kind of poetic form which is really alive in the modern world. The real contrast is not, as Coleridge said, with me-chanical form but with what I would call traditional form. When tradi-tional form is alive, it expresses the poetic sensibility which the poet shares with his audience, in the great ages of poetry with the whole of his nation or linguistic group. In such periods traditional form is a mask

[7] *Phoenix: The Posthumous Papers of D. H. Lawrence*, pp. 218, 219.
[8] *Coleridge's Literary Criticism*, edited by Mackail, p 186.

which fits the poet's face perfectly; indeed, like the mask of Lord George Hell in Max Beerbohm's parable, it may be said to become identical with the face. Ever since the Renaissance it has been increasingly difficult to use traditional poetic forms successfully. The mask no longer fits the face. Hence in all European languages in the last three hundred years we can trace the progressive loosening of poetic rhythms and the mingling or abandonment of the traditional "kinds" of poetry, the movements towards free verse, the production of epic dramas and dramatic lyrics and forms that fall under none of the ancient classifications. In the twentieth century the poet is more isolated, perhaps, than he has ever been in the whole of human history. The use of traditional forms in such an age becomes more and more of a pretense, the pretense that there is a living society that shares the poetic sensibility embodied in traditional forms. Such a pretense is legitimate enough in minor poetry like that of the "decadents" of the Nineties, the Georgians, or today of Mr. Betjeman; and it may produce work of real charm in the hands of a sensitive craftsman. It is the use of the mask as a parlor game and not as a serious artistic activity like the use of the mask in Greek drama. A major prophetic poet like Blake or Lawrence cannot use the mask in this way. He has to create an organic or expressive form to express his naked, passionate experience in a world where no one shares his poetic sensibility, and this is a task of enormous difficulty.

It may be argued that the only possible form for great poetry in this age of science and realism is the novel or prose story, and there can be no question that Lawrence's poetic genius finds its fullest expression in prose works like *The Rainbow, Women in Love, St. Mawr* and *The Man Who Died.* Nevertheless I believe his work in verse is a very important part of his literary achievement. He said something in his verse that he could never have said in prose and his best poems, in my opinion, are among the most valuable and significant of the twentieth century. Indeed I would say that they are examples of the only kind of great poetry that can be written in the world in which we live. The Blake of *Songs of Experience* and the Wordsworth of "Resolution and Independence" are the prophets of this kind of poetry, which Lawrence has well described as

> Poetry of this immediate present, instant poetry . . . the unrestful, ungraspable poetry of the sheer present, poetry whose very permanency lies in its windlike transit.[9]

Lawrence's early poems are mostly autobiographical and are written in the form that was fashionable in the England of the second decade of the twentieth century—the short "nature poem" in rhyming verse, which the Georgians inherited from Hardy and Wordsworth. Lawrence uses this form clumsily enough and much of the experience that lies behind these

---

[9] *Phoenix: The Posthumous Papers of D. H. Lawrence,* p. 220.

early poems is expressed more successfully in the early novels and stories. He himself was quite aware of the inadequacy of his early verse. In the Introduction to his *Collected Poems* he writes with a modesty that recalls that of the young Keats that these poems were "struggling to say something which it takes a man twenty years to be able to say." [10] This, by the way, is not the kind of remark that is made by a young man who, in the words of Blackmur, was "wilfully careless of craftsmanship." Nevertheless, in spite of their shortcomings, these early poems are full of interest to the student of English poetry. They show us a young poet of genius struggling with an inadequate mode of expression like the Blake of *Poetical Sketches* and the Wordsworth of "The Evening Walk." In them, however, we can already see the notable qualities which Blackmur admits that Lawrence's poetry possesses; and which he describes admirably. The first is "a kind of furious underlying honesty of observation," [11] and the second a religious quality, for, as Blackmur rightly argues, Lawrence is a religious poet and his poetry is an attempt "to declare and rehearse symbolically his pious recognition of the substance of life." I would add to these a third quality, a mixture of tenderness and reverence, a sort of cosmic piety.

The first two qualities are well-illustrated in the poem called "Love on the Farm." This might be described as a "nature poem" and it certainly arises out of a keen-sighted observation of the "life of nature" on a Midland farm. Nature here is not the quiet landscape vision which found elegant expression in numerous Georgian poems. It is compounded of terror, beauty, and cruelty, full of contradictions, something at once disturbing and mysterious, lying behind the commonplace facts of English country life. The opening of the poem shows us a man going to kill a rabbit caught in a snare:

> Oh, water-hen, beside the rushes
> Hide your quaintly scarlet blushes,
> Still your quick tail, lie still as dead
> Till the distance folds over his ominous tread!
>
> The rabbit presses back her ears
> Turns back her liquid, anguished eyes
> And crouches low; then with wild spring
> Spurts from the terror of *his* oncoming.

When the rabbit is killed the man with "fingers that still smell grim of the rabbit's fur" goes into the house to embrace a woman. We are made to feel the terror of the rabbit, the large. kindly presence of the man, and the woman's identification of herself with the trapped animal:

[10] *The Collected Poems of D. H. Lawrence*, I, xxxvi.
[11] Blackmur, *op. cit.*, p. 297.

> God, I am caught in a snare!
> I know not what fine wire is round my throat;
> I only know I let him finger there
> My pulse of life, and let him nose like a stoat
> Who sniffs with joy before he drinks the blood.[12]

Lawrence does not tell us in this poem that sex and death are close together in nature but he makes us feel the numinous quality of their
closeness, its terror and mystery. It cannot be said, however, that the
commonplace rhythms, the awkward rhymes and crudely melodramatic
language help Lawrence in this poem. Yet already he is making us feel,
to use his own phrase, "the living plasm vibrate unspeakably."

The best expression of the qualities of tenderness and reverence in
Lawrence's early poetry is, perhaps, the poem called "Piano":

> Softly, in the dusk, a woman is singing to me;
> Taking me back down the vista of years, till I see
> A child sitting under the piano, in the boom of the tingling strings
> And pressing the small, poised feet of a mother who smiles as she sings.
>
> In spite of myself, the insidious mastery of song
> Betrays me back, till the heart of me weeps to belong
> To the old Sunday evenings at home, with winter outside
> And hymns in the cosy parlour, the tinkling piano our guide.
>
> So now it is vain for the singer to burst into clamour
> With the great black piano appassionato. The glamour
> Of childish days is upon me, my manhood is cast
> Down in the flood of remembrance, I weep like a child for the past.[13]

This poem has found its way into a number of anthologies, probably
because the compilers think it an expression of sentimental nostalgia.
It is nothing of the kind; it is an honest record of emotion, which, it is
important to note, is *controlled* emotion. The feelings awakened by the
song that brings back the scenes of his childhood to the poet are recognized as "insidious" and, although he yields to them, he is aware that in
some sense they are a betrayal. This poem provides a complete refutation
of Blackmur's charge that Lawrence was careless of craftsmanship in his
poetry. The original draft of this poem called "The Piano" survives in a
manuscript now in Nottingham University Library.[14] This early version
is diffuse, nostalgic and overcrowded with detail. The words *insidious*

---

[12] *The Collected Poems of D. H. Lawrence*, I, 14, 15.

[13] *Ibid.*, I, 137, 138.

[14] See "D. H. Lawrence: Some Hitherto Unpublished Material" by V. de S. Pinto,
Renaissance and Modern Studies, Vol. I (Nottingham, 1957), pp. 26, 27.

and *betray* do not occur in it. It contains five stanzas as opposed to the three of the printed version and it describes the concert singer, whose song brought back to Lawrence the memory of his childhood, as a "full throated woman" "singing a wild Hungarian air" with "her arms and her bosom and the whole of her soul bare." All this is suppressed in the final version and the impression rendered in the concentrated phase:

> To burst into clamour
> With the great black piano appassionato.

The poem in its final form is an early example of Lawrence's use of the controlled imagination which Blackmur denies to him. It is something rare in modern poetry, a successful rendering of unsentimental tenderness, worthy to be placed by Cowper's "Lines on his Mother's Picture" and Wordsworth's "Poor Susan."

Lawrence wrote that many of his poems were "so personal that, in their fragmentary fashion, they make up a biography of an emotional and inner life." [15] Actually, like Byron, he was a poet who could only reach his full maturity when he had got rid of the autobiographical preoccupation. The last phase of his autobiographical poetry, the conclusion of the saga of the young Lawrence, is to be found in the famous sequence, *Look! We Have Come Through!*, which is at once a kind of poetical record of his early married life and something far more ambitious. It is an attempt to give expression to the drama of the psychological relationship between a newly married husband and wife, a kind of duel of sex, where, in Lawrence's own words "the conflict of love and hate goes on . . . till it reaches some sort of conclusion, they transcend into some condition of blessedness." [16] This is a great subject, and, whatever else it may be, the sequence is certainly a psychological and autobiographical record of the highest interest. Amy Lowell is said to have thought that the sequence "made up a great novel, greater even than *Sons and Lovers*." This, of course, is an exaggeration but there is a grain of truth in it. The sequence contains the material for a notable novel or autobiographical work and I believe Lawrence would have been well advised to take a hint from Dante's *Vita Nuova* and cast it into the form of a prose narrative with interspersed lyrics. At this stage of his development Lawrence was seeking an escape from the conventional rhythms of early twentieth century English poetry, which, he rightly felt, were hampering his poetic expression. The logical outcome of the search for expressive form as far as meter is concerned was some kind of free verse, but the difficulty was to find the right kind. His two immediate guides to freer rhythms at this time were

[15] *The Collected Poems of D. H. Lawrence*, I, xxxv.
[16] *Look! We Have Come Through!*, edited by Warren Roberts (University of Texas, 1957). The quotation is from the full version of Lawrence's foreword to the sequence, which was abbreviated in the collected editions of his poems.

the imagist group of Ezra Pound and Amy Lowell, with which he had a temporary connection, and Walt Whitman. At the back of his mind there was certainly a deeper and more vital influence in his memories of the magnificent rhythms of the poetic prose or near-verse of the King James Bible, in which he had been steeped as a child and which he never ceased to study. Lawrence was far too big a man to be absorbed by the imagists or any other literary clique, but he learnt something from them. They helped him to escape from the vague generalities of the Georgians, their excessively literary diction and their lush and saccharine rhythms. Whitman was another matter. Lawrence was both attracted and repelled by him. In his *Studies in Classic American Literature* he shows that he was well aware of Whitman's weaknesses: "this awful Whitman," he calls him, "this post-mortem poet. This poet with the private soul leaking out of him all the time." Yet he hails him as a master and a liberator: "Whitman, the great poet has meant so much to me. Whitman, the one man breaking a way ahead." [17] He was right; Whitman was a great liberating influence for Lawrence, but he had to absorb and digest that influence before he could derive real benefit from it. Whitman showed him how to use large, free rhythms based on those of common speech yet filled with a music which is not to be found in common speech, but he also encouraged Lawrence's tendency to preach and orate, to *talk* about experience rather than express experience. The famous culminating poems in *Look! We Have Come Through!*, "New Heaven and New Earth," "Elysium" and "Manifesto" contain many examples of the bad undigested influence of Whitman on Lawrence. No one can doubt that these poems record intense and moving experiences with complete honesty and integrity, but they fail to turn those experiences into aesthetic experience for the reader. As Sir Herbert Read has written, in these poems, "Lawrence is expressing a wish for a wonder to happen, a wonder that is not intrinsically present in the verse itself." [18]

The best poetry in *Look! We Have Come Through!* is certainly in the lyrics. Such a poem as "A Doe at Evening" shows how the Imagists had helped him to "strip off the tinsel," to adapt a phrase of Byron's:

> As I went through the marshes
> a doe sprang out of the corn
> and flashed up the hill-side
> leaving her fawn.
>
> On the sky-line
> she moved round to watch,

[17] D. H. Lawrence, *Selected Literary Criticism*, edited by A. Beal (1955), pp. 495, 500.
[18] Sir H. Read, *The True Voice of Feeling* (1953), p. 100.

> she pricked a fine black blotch
> on the sky.
>
> I looked at her
> and felt her watching;
> I became a strange being,
> Still I had my right to be there with her.
>
> Her nimble shadow trotting
> along the sky-line, she
> put back her fine, level-balanced heaa.
> And I knew her.
>
> Ah yes, being male, is not my head hard-balanced, antlered?
> Are not my haunches light?
> Has she not fled on the same wind with me?
> Does not my fear cover her fear? [19]

Here, surely, the wonder is intrinsically present in the verse. The lightness and delicacy of the vision of the doe find perfect expression in the lightness and delicacy of the texture and movement of the language, and the changes in rhythm in the last two stanzas convey perfectly the elusive suggestion of sex in the relationship of the man to the animal and the dream or myth of his transformation into a stag. Jessie Chambers in her *Memoir* wrote that "a living vibration passed between" Lawrence and "wild things." [20] Here at last Lawrence has found a sort of verse that makes us feel that vibration.

This poem points the way to Lawrence's mature poetic achievements of his middle years in *Birds, Beasts and Flowers*. Here he found matter which was new to English poetry and which freed him from the trammels of autobiography. It was a subject matter that he was particularly well-qualified to treat: the immediate apprehension of the flux of life, especially of sexual life in nonhuman organisms. In Lawrence, as Blackmur rightly stresses, this was a religious apprehension: "the love of God for him was in the declaration of life in the flux of sex." [21] In his Preface to *The Grand Inquisitor*, Lawrence wrote that "*life* is the great reality . . . true living fills us with vivid life, the 'heavenly bread.' " [22] In the best of the poems he conveys the experience of immediate contact with this "vivid life," the actual taste of the "heavenly bread." Here he is carrying forward the work of the great Romantics, especially that of Wordsworth, in the exploration of what may be called the divine other-

[19] *The Collected Poems of D. H. Lawrence*, I, 211.
[20] *D. H. Lawrence: A Personal Record* by E. T. [Jessie Chambers] (London: Jonathan Cape, 1935), p. 223.
[21] Blackmur, *op. cit.*, p. 299.
[22] *Phoenix: The Posthumous Papers of D. H. Lawrence*, p. 285

ness of nonhuman life. The Romantics neglected the animal world and
the sexual element in nature, and tended to confuse the apprehension of
the life of nature with the quiet contemplation of landscape. Lawrence
aims at a more complete nature poetry which will include birds, beasts,
fishes and even insects as well as vegetable life. Blackmur complained that
Lawrence's "pious recognition of the substance of life" is tortured, and
that he lacks "the ultimate vision" and "orderly insight" of "the great
mystics." [23] Surely there is a confusion of thought here. Lawrence was not
a mystic but a poet and a poet's business is not necessarily to convey "an
orderly insight," but to give artistic (i.e., orderly) expression to his own
experience and the sensibility of his age. Sometimes Lawrence's apprehension of the mystery of life was tortured and his complete honesty as
an artist compelled him to exhibit this tortured apprehension as part of
his own sensibility and that of his age. But the word *tortured* has been
used far too freely with reference to Lawrence's poetry. *Birds, Beasts and
Flowers* is an extremely varied and uneven collection. There are poems
in it that may fairly be described as representing tortured states of mind
and passages that, perhaps, deserve the epithet "hysterical" that Blackmur
has applied far too glibly to the whole of Lawrence's poetry.[24] Too often
Lawrence succumbs to the worst part of Whitman's influence and mistakes strident statement for poetic expression. The best poetry in the
collection, however, is neither tortured nor hysterical nor strident. It is an
affirmation of the grandeur and mystery of the life of nature that, perhaps,
Wordsworth alone has equalled among English poets, and it is expressed
in an entirely original and un-Wordsworthian idiom. Such an affirmation
is to be found in the famous poem "Snake." This poem is based on that
complete truthfulness to the facts of common experience that Lawrence
shares with Wordsworth and Hardy, but here the common experience is
transformed and invested with mythical grandeur. This is a rare and
memorable achievement. Wordsworth did something similar in "Resolution and Independence," where the commonplace meeting with the old
leechgatherer is transmuted into a myth of overwhelming majesty. The
old man, while remaining a poor leechgatherer, is seen at the same time
as a gigantic natural force and the embodiment of transcendental strength
and majesty. Similarly the snake, which Lawrence saw one hot morning
drinking in his water trough at Taormina, remains in the poem an ordinary "earth brown, earth golden Sicilian snake," but at the same time
becomes a mythical, godlike lord of the underworld, an embodiment of
all those dark mysterious forces of nature which man ignobly fears and
neglects.

> Was it cowardice, that I dared not kill him?
> Was it perversity, that I longed to talk to him?

[23] Blackmur, *op. cit.*, p. 299.
[24] *Ibid.*, pp. 295, 296, 300.

Was it humility, to feel so honoured?
I felt so honoured.

And yet those voices:
If you were not afraid, you would kill him!

And truly I was afraid, I was most afraid,
But even so, honoured still more
That he should seek my hospitality
From out the dark door of the secret earth.

He drank enough
And lifted his head, dreamily, as one who has drunken,
And flickered his tongue like a forked night on the air, so black;
Seeming to lick his lips,
And looked around like a god, unseeing, into the air,
And slowly turned his head,
And slowly, very slowly, as if thrice adream,
Proceeded to draw his slow length curving round
And climb again the broken bank of my wall-face.[25]

This poem surely provides the answers to Blackmur's argument that
Lawrence's use of expressive form excludes craftsmanship and the control
of the rational imagination. There is no empty rhetoric or fake poetic
language here. The style is very simple, the diction mostly colloquial
and the word order that of common speech, and yet the effect is one of
grandeur and dignity. The verse, though free and rhymeless, moves easily
from the rhythms of common speech to formal iambics and back again,
but, nevertheless, has a subtle pattern expressing with curious felicity in
its alternation of short and long lines the relationship between the poet's
nagging thoughts and the sinuous majesty of the snake's movements.
"Snake" is a triumph of style and idiom, one of the very few English
poems in free verse where perception is embodied in rhythms that are an
essential part of the poem's meaning.

There are other triumphs of a different kind in *Birds, Beasts and
Flowers*. Blackmur speaks about a condition of "ritual frenzy" in some of
the poems that "carries them beyond the confines of poetry." [26] This may
be true of some passages in the collection but, if by "ritual frenzy" he
means an ecstasy of praise and adoration, there are poems in which this
ecstasy controlled by the rational imagination produces memorable
poetry. Such a poem is "Almond Blossom," a hymn to the miracle of
renewed life as revealed in the blossoming of the almond tree:

. . . the Gethsemane blood at the iron pores unfolds, unfolds,
Pearls itself into tenderness of bud

[25] *The Collected Poems of D. H. Lawrence*, II, 78, 79.
[26] Blackmur, *op cit.*, pp. 295, 296.

And in a great and sacred forthcoming steps forth, steps out in one stride
A naked tree of blossom, like a bridegroom bathing in dew, divested of cover,
Frail-naked, utterly uncovered
To the green night-baying of the dog-star, Etna's snow-edged wind
And January's loud-seeming sun.

Think of it, from the iron fastness
Suddenly to dare to come out naked, in perfection of blossom, beyond the sword-
      rust.
Think, to stand there in full-unfolded nudity, smiling,
With all the snow-wind, and the sun-glare, and the dog-star baying epithalamion.[27]

Here the poet is using images not as illustration or decoration but is
thinking in images, "recreating thought into feeling," to use T. S. Eliot's
phrase. There is wit here too, as well as magnificence. The image of the
"dog-star baying epithalamion" is a conceit which is at once witty and
imaginative, worthy of the seventeenth century masters, Donne and
Marvell. As Mr. Alvarez has written in his admirable study of Lawrence's
poetry, this kind of wit is "not a sparkle on top of intelligence; it is a
manifestation of intelligence." [28]

   The poems that Lawrence wrote at the end of his life have a peculiar
quality of freshness and directness. The Whitmanesque rhetoric and
the "ritual frenzy" that Blackmur condemns have now disappeared. We
hear in these poems the voice of a very wise man who is also humorous,
completely disillusioned yet never cynical, a man who loves life but is
saddened and embittered at the way in which it is being fouled and
violated by mass "civilization." In some of these poems, those written at
the very end of his life, the voice is that of a seer with a calm, majestic
vision of God and Death. In all these later poems of Lawrence one gets
the impression of a man who, like the Byron of *Don Juan,* is able to speak
out his whole mind in verse with complete ease and without any sort of
inhibition. Of the satiric poems in this last group Richard Aldington
wrote that "nearly all these Pansies and Nettles came out of Lawrence's
nerves, and not out of his real self." [29] This seems to me a gross exaggeration. Some of the Pansies and Nettles are written in a mood of exasperation, but many of them are brilliant and incisive satiric commentaries on
Western civilization, like the poem called "Wages":

      The wages of work is cash.
      The wages of cash is want more cash.

[27] *The Collected Poems of D. H. Lawrence,* II, 32. See the comments on this poem
by Dilys Powell in her valuable essay on Lawrence's poetry in *Descent from Parnassus*
(1934), p. 34-36.
[28] A. Alvarez, *The Shaping Spirit* (London: Chatto and Windus, 1958), p. 157.
[29] *The Collected Poems of D. H. Lawrence,* III, xl.

> The wages of want more cash is vicious competition.
> The wages of vicious competition is—the world we live in.
>
> The work-cash-want circle is the viciousest circle
> that ever turned men into fiends.
>
> Earning a wage is a prison occupation
> and a wage-earner is a sort of gaol-bird.
> Earning a salary is a prison overseer's job,
> a gaoler instead of a gaol-bird.
>
> Living on your income is strolling grandly outside the prison
> in terror lest you have to go in. And since the work-prison covers
> almost every scrap of the living earth, you stroll up and down
> on a narrow beat, about the same as a prisoner taking his exercise.
>
> This is called universal freedom.[30]

This poem has the quality of a great satire: it is at once witty and humorous and profoundly serious. The image of the gaol is the perfect symbol for industrial society, and that of the man with the private income strolling grandly outside "in terror lest you have to go in" is, like all the best satire, at once very funny and rather terrible. Some of the *Pansies* and *Nettles* are in riming doggerel, very like the doggerel that Blake used to send in his letters to his friends, with a similar mixture of mocking humor and penetrating insight. Blake would have delighted in "Modern Prayer," surely a prophecy of the affluent society of 1960:

> Almighty Mammon, make me rich!
> Make me rich quickly, with never a hitch
> in my fine prosperity! Kick those in the ditch
> who hinder me, Mammon, great son of a bitch! [31]

In the poems that Lawrence wrote at the last months of his life in the South of France his preoccupation is no longer with the flux of life but with God and death. He was thinking much about the Greeks at this time and had been reading Burnet's *Early Greek Philosophy* and Gilbert Murray's *Five Stages of Greek Religion*. For him as for a Greek poet there was no contradiction in a belief in God and the gods: sometimes God for him is the creative force in nature:

> God is the great urge that has not yet found a body
> but urges towards incarnation with the great creative urge.

[30] *Ibid.*, II, 255, 256.
[31] *Ibid.*, III, 19.

And becomes at last a clove carnation: lo! that is god!
and becomes at last Helen, or Ninon: any lovely and generous woman.[32]

At other times he feels the presence of the gods in the colors and shapes
of the visible world:

But all the time I see the gods:
the man who is mowing the tall white corn,
suddenly, it curves, as it yields, the white wheat
and sinks down with a swift rustle, and a strange, falling flatness,
ah! the gods, the swaying body of god! [33]

Lawrence is a mythological poet here, but his mythology is no elegant
fiction or learned reconstruction. The gods are realities to him as they
were to a Greek poet, and as they have been, perhaps, to no other English
poet since Keats. The greatest of his mythological poems is certainly
"Bavarian Gentians":

Reach me a gentian, give me a torch
let me guide myself with the blue, forked torch of this flower
down the darker and darker stairs, where blue is darkened on blueness
even where Persephone goes, just now, from the frosted September
to the sightless realm where darkness is awake upon the dark
and Persephone herself is but a voice
or a darkness invisible enfolded in the deeper dark
of the arms Plutonic, and pierced with the passion of dense gloom,
among the splendour of torches of darkness, shedding darkness on the lost
bride and her groom.[34]

Here Lawrence does not, as in his early poems, try to give the reader an
immediate apprehension of the life of the flowers; he uses them mytho-
logically, turning them into miraculous torches from the Halls of Dis
lighting us down stairs that lead to the underworld, where the spring
goddess goes to the embrace of Hades, the "arms Plutonic," and we are
made to feel she is the *anima,* the soul of man going to the embrace of a
death, which is not terrible but august and godlike. This is a use of
mythology not as decoration or allegory, but, like that of Keats in *The
Fall of Hyperion,* as a means to lead the reader to "a world of wonder
and reverence." [35]

Blackmur calls Lawrence's poems "ruins," though he admits that they

[32] *Ibid.,* III, 132.
[33] *Ibid.,* III, 86.
[34] *Ibid.,* III, 140.
[35] I owe this phrase as well as other things in this essay to Dr. F. R. Leavis.

are "ruins which we may admire and contemplate." [36] The word *ruin* implies that Lawrence aimed at great constructions in verse and failed. This is, surely, a misconception. To aim at great constructions would have meant assuming the mask of a master builder in verse and Lawrence saw that the age of masks (i.e., traditional form) in poetry was over. In his poetry we must look for "the insurgent naked throb of the instant moment," a poetry that is "neither star nor pearl, but instantaneous like plasm." [37] To convey this sort of experience with the greatest delicacy, the finest intelligence and the most complete honesty was his aim, and, after many unsuccessful and partly successful efforts he achieved it in such poems as "Snake," "Almond Blossom," and "Bavarian Gentians." Like Wordsworth he wrote a good deal of bad poetry, but, like Wordsworth's even his bad poems are important, because they are the experiments of a major poet groping his way towards the discovery of a new kind of poetic art.

[36] Blackmur, *op. cit.,* p. 300.
[37] *Phoenix: The Posthumous Papers of D. H. Lawrence,* p. 221.

The Plays of D. H. Lawrence

by Arthur E. Waterman

I

In 1913 D. H. Lawrence spoke of his plays as relaxation from the more arduous work of novel writing: "I enjoy so much writing my plays —they come so quick and exciting from the pen—that you mustn't growl at me if you think them a waste of time." [1] Although he wrote seven plays and a fragment,[2] Lawrence didn't take his dramatic work very seriously, and when two of his plays were given stage performances, he didn't bother to see them. *The Widowing of Mrs. Holroyd* was done in London in 1926 and *David* the following year, but Lawrence, who was living in Italy at the time, wrote that he couldn't come.[3] In fact, he rarely went to the theater, so his knowledge of the drama was fairly well limited to texts rather than stage presentations. Lawrence seldom talks about the theater in his letters, but does mention that he prefers Synge and Shakespeare above other playwrights.[4] Catherine Carswell sums up Lawrence's attitude toward his plays when she comments on his refusal to attend the performance of *David*: "But Lawrence would not risk the strain and disappointment. Though he always had a half a hope that one of his plays

"The Plays of D. H. Lawrence" by Arthur E. Waterman. From *Modern Drama*, II (February, 1960), 349-57. Copyright © 1960 by *Modern Drama*. Reprinted by permission of the author and *Modern Drama*. Minor changes have been made with the author's permission.

[1] *The Letters of D. H. Lawrence,* edited by Aldous Huxley, 2nd ed. (London: William Heinemann, 1934), p. 90.

[2] The plays in chronological order are: *A Collier's Friday Night* (1906-1907), *The Married Man* (1912), *Altitude* (1912), *The Merry-Go-Round* (1912), *The Widowing of Mrs. Holroyd* (1913), *Touch and Go* (1919), *David* (1925), and *Noah*, a fragment (1925?). *The Plays of D. H. Lawrence* (London: Martin Secker, 1933) contains *The Widowing of Mrs. Holroyd, Touch and Go,* and *David*. I have not been able to examine *Altitude*, published in *Laughing Horse. The Married Man* was published in *The Virginia Quarterly Review*, XVI, 524-47, and *The Merry-Go-Round* in volume XVII, 3-44. *Noah* can be found in *Phoenix: The Posthumous Papers of D. H. Lawrence* (New York: Viking, 1936).

[3] *Letters*, pp. 673 and 676.

[4] *Ibid.*, p. 7.

would succeed on stage, I doubt if he had much belief in them as stage plays, or if he felt their failure acutely." [5]

For the most part critics have ignored Lawrence's plays. They are justified in that none of them is very good drama and contains nothing new in dramatic technique. They are important, however, in their relationship to Lawrence's other work, as they do reflect and sometimes severely qualify the themes of his other forms. If we are to praise Lawrence as an important thinker as well as an artist, as Mr. Leavis does, then we had better know the plays where his ideas are not always the same as in his novels. In the differences between *Touch and Go* and *Women in Love,* which I shall treat later, we find that Lawrence has handled the theme of industrial England in opposing ways. A case, then, can be made for the plays, and in this paper I propose to discuss Lawrence's plays in relation to his other work, and to analyze their dramatic nature in order to show Lawrence's artistry, for better or worse, at work.

One last point before I turn to the plays themselves: they reflect a trait of Lawrence's character which has been often overlooked. Since the plays do qualify the ideas of his novels and short stories, they show that Lawrence never gave in to anything without a great deal of hedging. As Richard Aldington says: "Lawrence would not have been Lawrence if he had come at once to a clear decision and had acted upon it without hesitation," and he speaks of Lawrence's "chronic indecision and almost pathological self-mistrust." [6] I believe we need to examine Lawrence, not as a philosopher with a consistent system of thought, but as an artist whose ideas were continually being shaped by the demands of his art, sometimes even reversed. In his introduction to the American edition of *Lady Chatterley's Lover,* Mark Schorer writes: "Lawrence's greatness of mind shows in the necessity he felt to reject the abstraction when it would not work for the imagination." [7] The magnificence of Lawrence lies partly in this continuous qualification as abstractions are tested against the reality of art and life. The plays of D. H. Lawrence show this qualification in dramatic action.

II

Lawrence's first play, *A Collier's Friday Night* (1906), may be considered as an earlier and partial version of *Sons and Lovers.* The play covers

[5] Catherine Carswell, *The Savage Pilgrimage* (New York: Harcourt Brace and World, Inc., 1932), p. 253.

[6] Richard Aldington, *D. H. Lawrence. Portrait of a Genius But . . .* (New York: Duell, Sloane, and Pearce, Inc., 1950), p. 284.

[7] Mark Schorer, Introduction to *Lady Chatterley's Lover* (New York: Grove Press, 1957), p. xv.

roughly the same material in the novel up to the last half of the chapter "Strife in Love." The first act presents the major conflict between Mrs. Lambert and her collier husband; the second act presents the minor conflict between mother, son, and girl; and in the third act these two conflicts are resolved as Mrs. Lambert wins out over both husband and girl.

The difference between Mr. and Mrs. Lambert is essentially the same as in the novel: she resents her husband's lower-class background and her life as a collier's wife. The husband reacts to his wife's withdrawal by emphasizing the very qualities she objects to; however, the husband is not given sufficient treatment to develop his side of the domestic quarrel. Nor is the girl, Maggie, characterized carefully enough to make her correspond to Miriam of the novel. The son's awakening love for Maggie, his first act of independence from his mother, is superficially handled so that Mrs. Lambert can easily dismiss the young and helpless girl.

As an earlier version of the first parts of *Sons and Lovers,* then, *A Collier's Friday Night* oversimplifies conflict and character, presenting the mother's viewpoint one-sidedly without honestly treating the deeper issues. The novel qualifies the attitude toward the mother and examines the nature of love much more complexly than does the play.

Lawrence's next plays were three comedies, all written in 1912: *The Married Man, Altitude,* and *Merry-Go-Round. The Married Man* is a poor play; part witty dialogue, part situation comedy, part overt statement by the author's mouthpiece, Elsa Smith. The idea of the play is that love must be honest and frank, not hidden and toyed with like a game. The plot centers around George Grainger, a married man, who is carrying on with two other women, as he tries to play at marriage while he dabbles with love. The comedy comes in when George's friend tells his girlfriends that George is married, forcing him to hide under beds and lie his way out of his philandering. Finally, Elsa Smith calls for honesty in love which she says is better than "subterfuge, bestiality, or starvation and sterility." She advises George: "Don't make trouble in the world; try to make happiness." The quick, short scenes of the play indicate that it needs further development, but it is doubtful whether anyone could make of it a successful comedy.

Like *The Married Man, Merry-Go-Round* needs rewriting, but Lawrence never got around to reworking these "impromptus" as he called them. The exposition is rough and many scenes clearly need revision. The play has one good character, however. Old Mrs. Hemstock, grouchy and ill, speaks a wonderful dialect of homey images: "She melts herself into a man like butter in a hot tater. She ma'es him feel like a pearl button swimmin' away in hot vinegar." The plot is a Nottinghamshire *As You Like It,* with three pairs of lovers switching affections and partners for five acts. Harry T. Moore correctly criticizes the failure of the play: "*The Merry-Go-Round* . . . is crowded and disorganized . . . the situations often strain too hard after comic effects . . . in which most of the characters stiffly and incredibly take part." [8]

One of Lawrence's problems, which can be seen in *Merry-Go-Round*, was how to catch in creative language the words of love. In this play he stumbles around trying out witty dialogue, innuendo, and a touch of frankness. Only once, in Act IV, Scene 1, does he create the touch of tenderness, as Rachel expresses her love for Harry in terms of her anguish over his working in the mine. But in none of the plays does Lawrence create "lovers' talk" and not until *Lady Chatterley's Lover* does he truthfully, tenderly give us love in its fullest range of sensuous response. "We have no language for the feelings," he wrote, and in the plays we can see his futile attempts to create this language dramatically.

In both *The Married Man* and *The Merry-Go-Round* Lawrence tried to fuse a serious theme with a comedy of manners. The fact that he never finished his revisions of these plays would suggest that he realized how artificial they were. *The Widowing of Mrs. Holroyd* takes the serious element from the comedies and treats love in a working-class society much more effectively and dramatically than in the earlier *A Collier's Friday Night*. Like Mrs. Lambert, Mrs. Holroyd resents her collier husband's background and occupation, but the treatment of this conflict is both more dramatic and more honest than in the earlier play. Lawrence centers the conflict on the husband and wife, leaving out the son, and achieving a dramatic tension not unlike that of his favorite play, *Riders to the Sea*.

Mr. Holroyd is so driven by his wife that he brings home two drunken tavern wenches. In a very effective scene Mrs. Holroyd desperately tries to keep some semblance of dignity and decency in the face of a drunken husband and two giggling, outspoken chippies. But she, too, is tempted to infidelity as she almost runs off with the mine electrician. The miner's mother rebukes his wife, and we see his side of the quarrel as his mother says, "You thought yourself above him, Lizzie, an' you know he's not the man to stand it . . . what man wouldn't leave a woman that allowed him to live on sufferance in the house with her, when he was bringing the money home?" At this moment news comes that Holroyd has been killed in a mine accident.

In the last scene Mrs. Holroyd washes her husband's body and speaks to the corpse, trying to absolve her sin and confess her error:

My dear, my dear—oh, my dear! I can't bear it, my dear—you shouldn't have done it. Oh—I can't bear it, for you. Why couldn't I do anything for you? The children's father—my dear—I wasn't good to you. But you shouldn't have done this to me. Oh dear, oh, dear! . . . I can't bear it. No, things aren't fair . . . a shame for you! It was a shame. But you didn't

---

[8] Harry T. Moore, *The Life and Works of D. H. Lawrence* (New York: Twayne Publishers, 1951), p. 124.

—you didn't try. I *would* have loved you—I tried hard. What a shame for you! It was so cruel for you . . . and it hurt you so! (She weeps bitterly, so her tears fall on the dead man's face; suddenly she kisses him.) My dear, my dear, what can I do for you, what can I? (She weeps as she wipes his face gently.)

Essentially this is the same plot as in the short story "Odour of Chrysanthemums"; both were written about 1913. The major difference between the two is in Lawrence's treatment of the wife. In the play, the miner triumphs in death, forcing his wife to realize her situation and her responsibilities—as they were in relation to him, and as they will be in her life without him. It is as if the dead Holroyd had become a dark god to whom his wife offers herself in tears of atonement for killing him, that is, for destroying him in life and wishing his death. There is only a hint of this in the story where Mrs. Bates neither accepts nor realizes her guilt as she does in the play.

The Preface to *Touch and Go* (1919) is Lawrence's only stated theory of drama. Ostensibly it was written for The People's Theatre, but Lawrence is more concerned with the nature of tragedy and the specific example of tragedy found in the labor-capital strife:

> Granted that men are still men, Labour *v.* Capitalism is a tragic struggle. If men are no more than implements, it is non-tragic and merely disastrous. In tragedy the man is more than his part. . . . He may be killed, but the resistant, integral soul in him is not destroyed. He comes through, though he dies. . . . And it is in this facing of fate, this going right through with it, that tragedy lies. Tragedy is not disaster. It is a disaster when a cart-wheel goes over a frog, but it is not tragedy. Tragedy is the working out of some immediate passional problem within the soul of man.

The difference between disaster and tragedy is expressed another way, where we see that Lawrence is thinking not only of labor versus capitalism, but also of the war which had just ended:[9]

> If we really could know what we were fighting for, if we could deeply believe in what we were fighting for, then the struggle might have dignity, beauty, satisfaction for us. If it were a profound struggle for something that was coming to life in us, a struggle that we were convinced would bring us to a new freedom, a new life, then it would be a creative activity,

[9] Indeed, by 1915 he equated them, held that the war resolved itself into "a war between Labour and Capital" (*The Letters of D. H. Lawrence*, p. 235); and throughout the war he consistently hoped that the maimed and injured "soul of the people" would find a life after the war "wherein the struggle shall not be for money or for power, but for individual freedom and common effort towards good" (*Ibid.*, p. 220). These are the terms, too, of the Preface in *Touch and Go*.

a creative activity in which death is a climax in the progression towards new being. And this is tragedy.

If we could feel the tragedy in the struggle, we would know the happiness of creative suffering—a type of catharsis. *Touch and Go* is an example of a struggle which is both accidental and tragic. Using the characters from *Women in Love* (with different names), Lawrence creates a different version of Gerald Crich in Gerald Barlow, the industrial magnate. Gerald faces two problems: an impending strike at the mines he owns, and an emotional strife with Anabel, his former sweetheart.

The first of these conflicts is complicated by Gerald's family. As in the novel, Gerald's father had solved unrest among the miners by acts of Christian charity; he did what he could for the needy who came to him and sympathized with their poverty. Gerald does not repeat his father's easy patronage; he is closer to his mother who urges him to fight. Anabel has returned to Gerald after she had left him because their affair was unresolved passion, more like hate than love. She ran away with a Norwegian, but she couldn't stand the cold negation of passion with him, so she has returned to Gerald to fight out her love-hate struggle.

The final act of *Touch and Go* resolves both of Gerald's problems. His struggle with Anabel, he realizes, must be worked out from within, through a catharsis which will cleanse their hate and purify their love:

> Gerald: I've known you long enough—and known myself long enough—to know I can make you nothing at all, Anabel: neither can you make me. If the happiness isn't there—well, we shall have to wait for it, like a dispensation. It probably means we shall have to hate each other a little more—I suppose hate is a real process. . . . Nobody is more weary of hate than I am—and yet we can't fix our own hour, when we shall leave off hating and fighting. It has to work itself out in us. . . . It's a cleansing process—like Aristotle's Katharsis. We shall hate ourselves clean at last, I suppose.

At the end of the play Gerald and Anabel marry and this conflict is resolved.

The strike solution is neither so simple nor so final—it is touch and go. Speaking of one of the old clerks, who has been at the mines since his father's day, Gerald says, "they're so self-righteous. They think I'm a sort of criminal who has instigated the new devilish system which runs everything so close and cuts it so fine—as if they hadn't made this inevitable by their shameless carelessness and wastefulness in the past." This is a different Gerald from the one in *Women in Love*, with different reasons for modernizing the mine. He realizes that mechanization is evil, but he knows it is inevitable because of what the generations before him have done. He says that he hopes the miners will strike because "If they would, I'd have some respect for them." The strike parallels the hate-love conflict between Gerald and Anabel and there is hope of resolution in both conflicts.

By the end of the play Gerald has been able to reconcile his father's and mother's points of view. He has his father's purpose and his mother's method. His father failed because he would not respect the miners as men, and his mother would simply fight with no end in sight—no love growing from hate. We feel that the solution to the strike will come as it did with Anabel, through time and creative struggle.

The differences between *Touch and Go* and *Women in Love* are enormous. Not only are the characters portrayed differently, but even more striking is Lawrence's attitude toward the industrial owner and the machine world. Here Gerald's methods are given at least favorable bias, if not affirmation. Yet Harry T. Moore says of *Touch and Go*: "Lawrence might have done better if he had confined himself to the theme of the strike, or if he had invented a new set of characters to represent the mine owners and their friends instead of using several people from *Women in Love* with some of the problems of the novel, irrelevant here, still clinging to them." [10]

I don't think we can evade the relationship between *Touch and Go* and *Women in Love* this easily. I have tried to show that the conflict with Anabel and the strike problem are related, so that the solution to the one problem defines the kind of solution possible for the other, even though the play doesn't present a definite climax to the strike issue. Furthermore, as the preface to the play suggests, it is indirectly about the war. The struggle in *Touch and Go,* the working out of the *passional* problem, is for Gerald a consummation—as the preface calls it, a tragedy.

Lawrence's letters through this period reveal a state of shock with momentary flashes of hope and, at the end of the war, a sense of release from his confinement in England and the horror of the holocaust. Speaking of *Women in Love,* he wrote, "The book frightens me: it is end-of-the-world. But it is, it must be, the beginning of a new world." [11] This refers to the Ursula-Birkin relationship in the novel, but it also indicates Lawrence's attitude at the end of the war. In the play Gerald and Anabel do come through and marry, and the war between Gerald and the strikers can be resolved when their mutual hatred and violence lead to catharsis, that is to mutual respect and understanding. Discussing Lawrence's attitude after the war, Mark Schorer says, "he was still fairly desperate to find some means of satisfying what he himself called his 'societal impulse' and of making his novels end positively in this world." [12] This impulse finds dramatic expression in the tragic catharsis of *Touch and Go,* but a different kind of expression in the later novels like *Kangaroo* and *The Plumed Serpent.*

[10] Moore, *op. cit.,* p. 179.
[11] *Letters of D. H. Lawrence,* p. 376.
[12] Schorer, *op. cit.,* p. xiv.

I suggest that Lawrence, using the more limited play form, chose one problem—the strike—and made it representative of the war in order to show how such struggles might be beneficial. He was trying to find some meaning, some hope from the war. *Touch and Go* defines this meaning in dramatic terms, and this definition is quite different from that found in the novels. Later, after two trips to England in 1925 and 1926, where Lawrence was appalled at the industrial wasteland his beloved Nottingham had become, he restated his attitude to mechanization. *Lady Chatterley's Lover* requalifies *Touch and Go,* so that we might say that Clifford Chatterley is descended from Gerald Barlow as well as Gerald Crich.

Lawrence's last play *Saul* or *David* (1925) (the manuscript has *David* crossed out and *Saul* written across the top) is taken directly from the Old Testament, Samuel I:15-20. Like *The Plumed Serpent,* written two years earlier, *David* deals with one kind of religion supplanting another. Whereas *The Plumed Serpent* creates a new symbolic religion which returns to more primitive origins, *David* shows the decline of one kind of religious faith. But the two works complement each other. In *The Plumed Serpent* Doña Carlota says: "But man loses his connection with God. And then he can never recover it again, unless some new Saviour comes to give him his new connection. And every new connection is different from the last, though God is always God." In the play Saul has lost his connection with God (*why* is not clear) and David is going to establish a new connection. David's God is sometimes gods, plural and uncapitalized, but the emphasis in the play is on the decline of Saul's faith and his complex attitude—a mixture of fear, defiance, and acceptance—toward David the new prophet.

In *David* Lawrence created what the critics called a "cinemagraphic" technique, meaning that it is composed of sixteen short scenes rather than the conventional five-act structure. These scenes give a rapid plot movement and allow Lawrence to avoid a definite climax, which, in turn, shows the gradual, tenuous decline and replacement of God by gods. At the end of the play it is implied that David's God, in time, shall be replaced by another, as each new faith gradually succumbs to a newer one. *Noah,* which Lawrence abandoned for *David,* uses the more symbolic language of *The Plumed Serpent* and suggests that the new God Noah will bring will give man, not God, power and strength. Neither *Noah* nor *David* successfully dramatizes the tragic, but necessary, need for man to redefine and reaffirm his faith. Lawrence was unable to give them the care and scope that he lavished on *The Plumed Serpent.*

III

I have concentrated mainly on the ideas in Lawrence's plays rather than on their dramatic qualities. The plays do not stand up very well under conventional dramatic criticism. Only *Touch and Go* and *The Widowing of Mrs. Holroyd* show any intensity, or tension, which would give them stage possibilities. Only a few of the characters could be played well on stage, and the dialogue, especially in the comedies, is limited and frequently stilted. In short, Lawrence is not an important playwright.

But his plays do show an important part of Lawrence's vision and artistic process. They do attempt, for better or worse, to handle his ideas dramatically. If he does not create dramatic dialogue, character, or plot, he does, nevertheless, create an art form different from the novel, tale, or poem. What I mean is that Lawrence did write *plays;* he did shape his thought to dramatic necessity. The best example of this is *Touch and Go.* It is impossible to say whether the fact that Lawrence was writing a play forced the change in his ideas about industrial England, or whether he was using the play form as a scapegoat, pouring into *Touch and Go* the reservations he felt after *Women in Love.* But *Touch and Go* is a better play than if it had been simply a watered-down version of the novel. It is more consistent in its structure and characterization and more satisfying in its conclusion. The same is true of the other plays. They are not important as drama, but they are dramatic attempts to reshape and restate the same concerns to be found in Lawrence's other work.

When the plays qualify that work, as they often do, it is for two reasons. First is Lawrence's chronic indecision. The plays are the hedgings of the other forms. He needed some art form which would allow him the chance to work over his ideas. Second, the plays are different because their dramatic nature demanded changes in ideas as well as form. Reading Lawrence's plays we see more clearly how a great artist hammered out his thought on several anvils, reshaping and redefining it to fit the specific form—novel, tale, play—to produce the work of art.

Criticism as Rage: D. H. Lawrence

by Richard Foster

"The essential function of art is moral. Not aesthetic, not decorative, not pastime or recreation." This principle, stated in *Studies in Classic American Literature,* is perhaps the only general idea on which D. H. Lawrence and T. S. Eliot could have approached agreement. Eliot, spokesman for tradition and the disciplined sensibility, is certainly the leading critical spirit of our time; while Lawrence, prophet of rebellion and "the blood," is virtually unheard as a critic. Perhaps the band of dedicated apologists Lawrence has always had would say that this is because the times are now not right for the reception of a mind like Lawrence's. But this wouldn't help much, because the times are never right for men of his temperament. For he participates in an odd kind of subtradition of his own made up of intellectual renegades, of violently creative minds, of brilliant and angry men whom the ordering techniques of the historian never quite succeed in assimilating into the homogeneous textures of their "periods."

One thinks of Dante, of Milton, of Swift, of Voltaire, perhaps of Thoreau, and even of Dr. Johnson; and in our time, certainly of Gide, of Shaw, of Pound. It isn't sufficient simply to label such men "iconoclasts," for they are makers as well as breakers. They are indeed "originals," and they are that long after they have become part of cultural history; but they are toughly men of intellect also, and so one does not think of Shelley with these. They possess compulsively responsive moral natures that must be expressed: thus the sharp and special "insights" they seem to have while most of their contemporaries, small and great, go on confirming the historical process as history in its slow wisdom comes to see that process. Such men never achieve revolutions—never *make* history— though they make disciples as readily as they make enemies. They are too selfish and inconsistent to lead causes. They are never specialists, always instinctively amateurs. And their prejudices are queer, pronounced, grotesque, sometimes verging upon the insane.

"Criticism as Rage: D. H. Lawrence" by Richard Foster. From *A D. H. Lawrence Miscellany,* ed. Harry T. Moore. Copyright © 1959 by Southern Illinois University Press. Reprinted by permission of the author and the Southern Illinois University Press.

But these men have more perfectly "whole" sensibilities than their contemporaries, for almost nothing relating to the human condition in their times seems to escape them. Their wholeness consists in this personal moral confrontation of the whole range of possible and actual human experience; and if they survive history at all, they survive "alive" in this sense. I think this is the way Lawrence will survive—his wholeness as a man surviving more importantly and permanently than his novels or his poetry, or than himself as a fact and cause of literary history as such. The wholeness can be felt in the continuity (and this is a matter of *style* in the deepest and broadest sense, as well as of "ideas") of fiction and poetry with reminiscence and essay, of reminiscence and essay with criticism, and of the criticism—because it is also *art*—back round again with the fiction and poetry.

His criticism, which especially interests me because, with others of my time, I feel a need for a "return" to something like *moral* criticism, provides the sharpest and most direct expression of his moral nature. And by criticism I mean not only the essays and reviews and prefaces, but also the letters; and of course by implication all the confirmations of the criticism in his fiction and poetry. Literature was to Lawrence a vast expressive record of the intellectual and emotional—and so, to him, moral —errors of mankind. Perhaps the place to begin with Lawrence as critic, then, is with the essential Lawrence—those raw, uncut, and unspoiled responses to literature that take the form of sudden and fierce moral assaults upon it.

Classic figures, old or modern, were not sacred to Lawrence because of their status: Blake was to him one of those "ghastly, obscene knowers"; Richardson "with his calico purity and his underclothing excitement sweeps all before him"; *The Scarlet Letter* was a "masterpiece, but in duplicity and half-false excitement"; and *The Marble Faun* "one of the most bloodless books ever written." He called Dostoevsky "a lily-mouthed missionary rumbling with ventral howls of derision and dementia"; Chekhov, a "second-rate writer and a willy wet-leg"; and Proust, "too much water-jelly." Many of Lawrence's nearer contemporaries received the same kind of sudden vitriol. Wells's work showed "a peevish, ashy indifference to *everything*, except himself, himself as the center of the universe"; Galsworthy's novels, read together, "just nauseated me up to the nose"; Huxley was only "half a man" as a writer, "a sort of precious adolescent"; and Thomas Mann "is old—and we are so young . . . the man is sick, body and soul."

Such are the characteristic moments of frank rage, many of them yielded to in the privacy of personal letters. And some of these same writers— Huxley, for example—occupied more favorable positions in the longer run of Lawrence's judgment. For there were a number of writers that, though he regarded them as gravely flawed in some way or other, Law·

rence valued for some actual if unfulfilled capacity for feeling or seeing. They constitute an odd Limbo, when one begins naming them over— Melville, Whitman, Emerson, Shelley, George Gissing, Frederick Rolfe (alias Baron Corvo), whose *Hadrian the Seventh* he called "a clear and definite book of our epoch, not to be swept aside," and so on. Lawrence's strong literary enthusiasms were few. He seconded the greatness that tradition had conferred upon Shakespeare, Homer, and the Greek trage- dians, but he wrote nothing about them. Synge was apparently the only modern dramatist he cared for at all. There was Giovanni Verga, of course—a major and lasting literary love. And the one poet—perhaps the one writer in whatever medium—for whom Lawrence seems to have had an entirely unalloyed admiration was Robert Burns. He loved Burns "as a brother" because Burns despised "society," affirmed life, and accepted the flesh. Lawrence admired Burns so much, in fact, that he once con- sidered writing a novel about him.

This partial and hasty catalogue of his literary opinions illustrates no more, of course, than that Lawrence as a critic was subjective, capricious, dogmatic. It fails to show two very important things. One is that, as I have said, his criticism is also art. Not art in the sense of highly wrought and "formed," for Lawrence's expression, whether in letters or essays, is characteristically fragmented, repetitious, *dis*ordered. But art rather in the sense of effect: it is, as Lawrence would say of good art, overwhelm- ingly *alive*. His criticism has a breathless immediacy about it, an intensity of caring, a violent energy due in part to Lawrence's marvelously articu- late rage, and in part also to his marvelously articulate humor. For humor, sometimes felt to be lacking in his fiction, is abundant in the criticism, though its function is vituperative, to articulate the rage.

But conviction about the art of Lawrence's criticism may be allowed to accrue by itself as we pursue a second matter: the fact that, spontane- ous and subjective as his critical performance may seem, Lawrence knew quite consciously—that is to say, theoretically and philosophically— what he expected of art, and he knew how to use those expectations as principles, even as the basis and threshold for a general *method* of criticism peculiarly his own. Lawrence's principle was that the function of literature is moral. But, he wrote in *Studies in Classic American Literature,* it is a "passionate, implicit morality, not didactic"; it "changes the blood" before it changes the mind. Lawrence does not, then, intend to mean that poetry is a "meter-making argument." He means that the arts are enactments, not sermons; they are experienced discoveries of moral "facts" or "laws" inherent in the very substance of our living. If we can imagine a liberated Emerson whose Truth is *in* nature—not "beyond" at all, but wholly interinanimate with it—then we have imag- ined an approximate image of Lawrence's principle. Since Lawrence believed, for example, that sexual love was an enactment not only of biological and psychological but of moral and religious truth as well, a novel imitating the progress of sexual love in a man and woman could not but be, therefore, an actualization of moral and religious ideas.

These are the things Lawrence meant when he said, in *Assorted Articles,* that "art is a form of religion, minus the Ten Commandments business, which is sociological, . . . a form of supremely delicate awareness and atonement—meaning at-oneness . . ."; and in "Morality and the Novel" that "the business of the novel is to reveal the relation between man and his circumambient universe, at the living moment"; and in "Why the Novel Matters" that "if you're a parson, you talk about souls in heaven. If you're a novelist, you know that paradise is in the palm of your hand, and on the end of your nose, because both are alive. . . ." Lawrence, of course, believed his own work as a novelist to be a dedication of art to the moral experience of man. As early as 1913 he wrote in a letter of England's need for a "readjustment between men and women, and a making free and healthy of this sex. . . ." "Oh, Lord," he cried, "and if I don't 'subdue my art to a metaphysic,' as someone very beautifully said of Hardy, I do write because I want folk—English folk—to alter, and have more sense."

Lawrence necessarily had a view of criticism which prescribed that critics be "alive" in much the same sense as artists. This was a difficult affair, for it required in the critic both an intense moralism of purpose and a total freedom and openness of sensibility. Lawrence condemned all forms of academic and methodological criticism and frankly proposed an impressionistic substitute, but clearly only for those who had the moral wisdom to use it in truth and reverence. He wrote in his essay on Galsworthy that the critic must be not only "emotionally alive in every fibre," but also "intellectually capable and skillful in essential logic, and then morally very honest." It was this last quality that Lawrence seemed to feel most strongly about in modern criticism (he called critics "canaille" when he was angry at their moral blindness). "To my way of thinking," he once said in a review, "the critic, like a good beadle, should rap the public on the knuckles and make it attend during divine service. And any good book is divine service." There could be no more satisfactory image than this of Lawrence's own activity as critic, unless it were to be that of Lawrence as messianic scourge whipping out of the temple various perpetrators of literary fraud and sacrilege.

The arts, as Lawrence said of the novel, "can help us live, as nothing else can." But he believed that art first had to destroy, to wreck the forms and monuments of dead beliefs so that new life could take root in cleared ground. He valued writers as disparate as the Futurist poets, Huxley, and Baron Corvo for their destructive force. He respected "hate, a passionate, honourable hate," when he saw it in writers like Swift, Gogol, and Mark Twain. Even Galsworthy, who so suffocated Lawrence with his "faked feelings," was worth something as a destroyer, as a satirist

of the bourgeois "social being." "Satire," wrote Lawrence in the Galsworthy essay, "exists for the very purpose of killing the social being, showing him what an inferior he is and, with all his parade of social honesty,
how subtly and corruptly debased." But Lawrence distinguished between
the literature of repudiation, which in destroying the old makes a place
for new life, and the literature of negation, which in accepting defeat
makes room only for death. He could approve Dos Passos' *Manhattan
Transfer* as an honest but unreconciled vision of a whole civilization
going into a dark nowhere, and Hemingway's *In Our Time* where the
self of the stories rejects everything outside it only in order to preserve
its own identity and integrity. But he could not approve Arnold Bennett
("I hate Bennett's resignation. Tragedy ought really to be a great kick at
misery") and Conrad ("I can't forgive Conrad for being so sad and for
giving in") because they seemed to be reconciled to negation as its own
finality, because they had lost the moral passion of life.

If Lawrence saw in his own work the most nearly perfect realization
of a life-affirming literature, opposite to the literature of negation and
complement to the literature of repudiation, he certainly saw it nowhere
else. Perhaps Verga, with his sense of the "spirit of place" and his un-
affected primitivism, was the next closest, among the moderns, to Lawrence's ideal. But everywhere else Lawrence turned as a critic he was met
by attitudes and philosophies and programs that had about them the
charnel smell of death. All that was ideologically and psychologically
most noisome to him was related directly or indirectly to what I will call
the "bourgeois spirit." To Lawrence the bourgeois spirit was the life-
killing force of the modern mass-mentality that transformed living men
into empty and corpse-like "social beings." In 1927 he wrote to Donald
Carswell: ". . . You can't know Robert Burns unless you hate . . . all
the estimable bourgeois and upper classes as he really did—the narrow-
gutted pigeons." This tells us a great deal about Lawrence's affection for
Burns, about the themes of *Lady Chatterley's Lover*, about the Melvilles
in the story "Things," about Kate's difficult choice at the end of *The
Plumed Serpent*. But it is also a key sentence for the understanding of
Lawrence's moral rage at almost everything by other writers that he read.

As Lawrence saw it, literature under the influence of the bourgeois
spirit, instead of expressing "the relationship between man and his
circumambient universe," expressed him instead in a relationship of
mechanically prescribed responsibility to the organized mass of other
men, called "society." All forms of society-worship, from Galsworthy's
middle-class conscience to Shaw's polemic socialism to Tolstoy's and
Dostoevsky's evangelical Christianity to Whitman's metaphysical impulse
to merge his identity with that of others, were to Lawrence disease symptoms of the bourgeois spirit, and were thus heresies against the life-force
and the sacredness of man alive. For though Hardy instinctively recognized, as Lawrence put it in his "Study of Thomas Hardy," "a great back-

ground, vital and vivid, which matters more than the people that move upon it," he compulsively defeated his "aristocrats" of the blood, his great individuals in quest of fulfillment, by forcing upon them some defeating attachment to community and convention. Hardy shows the weakness of modern tragedy, "where transgression against the social code is made to bring destruction, as though the social code worked our irrevocable fate."

The abstract social reason merges into another dimension of the bourgeois spirit: sentimental humanitarianism. Lawrence once jeered at the social pity of Wells, Middleton Murry, and J. M. Barrie for "all other unfortunates" as "elderly bunk": "It's courage we want, fresh air, not suffused sentiments." But he found little courage in 1914 in the War Number of *Poetry:* "Your people have such little pressure," he wrote to Miss Monroe. "Their safety valves go off at a high scream when the pressure is still so low. Have you no people with any force in them?" Things were even worse when in 1923 he reviewed *A Second Contemporary Verse Anthology:* "The spirit of verse prefers now a 'composition salad' of fruits of sensation, in a cooked mayonnaise of sympathy." He quotes: " 'For after all, the thing to do/Is just to put your heart in song—' " and comments, "Or in pickle." And he dismisses his friend Amy Lowell, who once gave him a typewriter, as "sounds sweetly familiar, linked in a new crochet pattern. . . . 'Christ, what are patterns for?' But why invoke deity? Ask the *Ladies' Home Journal.*"

But Lawrence saw the most serious ravages of the humanitarian pathos in realistic and naturalistic fiction, which had destroyed the idea of the hero and taught its readers to identify instead with pathetic and helpless little Emma Bovary. The trouble with realism, Lawrence wrote in a preface to Verga's *Mastro-Don Gesualdo,* was that serious writers could now do no more than pour their own perhaps "deep and bitter tragic consciousness into the little skins" of trivial people, mere husks and nothings like the Bovarys, until the "seams of pity" show. Even with Verga one must discount, he says, as one must with Balzac, Hawthorne, Dickens, and Charlotte Brontë, "about twenty per cent of the tragedy." Lawrence seems to have regarded humanitarian sympathy, whether in life or art, as a kind of moral false coin passed between social beings who fear the *real* experience of living.

"Spunk is what one wants," Lawrence once wrote to Murry, "not introspective sentiment. This last is your vice. You rot your own manhood at the roots with it." As the social reason begets humanitarian sympathy, humanitarian sympathy begets self-sympathy—a state where the self abandons the divine business of living and turns a fascinated mental eye inward upon the actions and reactions of its own consciousness. *Self*-consciousness was to Lawrence the last station of the bourgeois spirit's progress toward death. In men it brought about the kind of softness he believed was overcoming Murry, and the complete psychic degeneration he saw in Poe. In art it had produced a set of perversions ranging from the ludicrous to the ghastly. The modern serious novel, as portrayed in the essay "Surgery for the Novel—Or a Bomb," was "self-consciousness picked into such fine bits that the bits are most of them invisible, and you have to go by smell." It is dying "in a very long-drawn-out fourteen-volume death-agony, and absorbedly, childishly interested in the phe-nomenon. 'Did I feel a twinge in my little toe, or didn't I?' asks every character of Mr. Joyce or of Miss Richardson or of M. Proust." And as the stepchildren of T. S. Eliot, we can but listen when Lawrence warns us, "One has to be self-conscious at seventeen . . . but if we are going it strong at thirty-seven, then it is a sign of arrested development. . . . And if it is still continuing at forty-seven, it is obviously senile precocity."

It was this quest for self-consciousness that had brought about the mentalization of sex, the subtle perversion of genuine passional instincts into nasty conceptualizations—what in "Pornography and Obscenity" Lawrence called "the dirty little secret"—until writers and their readers alike had come to despise the body's health with the dirtiness of their own minds. Richardson, George Eliot, Hawthorne, Charlotte Brontë, Goethe (one of the "grand orthodox perverts"), Tolstoy, Dostoevsky, Strindberg—these were some of the older writers Lawrence accused of playing with mentalized sex, and then either rarefying it into bloodless ideality or scourging it as ineluctable sin. But the moderns, scorning the perfumery and prudery in which sex had been traditionally veiled by art, plunged straight into it like pigs into a wallow. It was still sex mentalized, but now in a worse form of perversion—that of parading the "dirty little secret" out in the open. It was sensationalism—Joyce ("What a clumsy *olla putrida*") was one of Lawrence's "serious" examples—and thus a viler kind of sacrilege against life. "The tragedy is," he wrote of *Fantazius Mallare,* a now forgotten book by Ben Hecht, "when you've got sex in your head, instead of down where it belongs. . . ." It was perhaps just such books that caused his own to be misunderstood. "Anybody who calls . . . *Lady Chatterley's Lover* a dirty sexual novel is a liar," he wrote to his agent, Curtis Brown. "It's not even a sexual novel: it's phallic. Sex is a thing that exists in the head, its reactions are cerebral, and its proc-esses mental. Whereas the phallic reality is warm and spontaneous."

Lawrence seems to have believed that self-consciousness had desiccated not only the life-content of literature but its life-form as well. He hated, for example, any and all conscious rules for metrical scansion, and he found the poetry of Poe, one of the most relentless of mentalizers, hope-lessly "mechanical." He also deplored ideas of the "art" of the novel as strangling its natural life in the bonds of willed artistic precision, and particularly condemned the French for their creed of artistic "self-efface-ment," which he traced directly to an inverted form of the sin of "self-consciousness." Part of the reason he could not stomach Thomas Mann was that he saw him as compensating for a sick vision of life by seeking to perfect the statement of his disgust—a trick of perversely conscious and mental "art" learned from Flaubert and the "Paris smarties." "Theorise, theorise all you like," he advised painters in the essay "Making Pictures," "but when you start to paint, shut your theoretic eyes and go for it with instinct and intuition." Rhyme, he told Catherine Carswell, must be "accidental," and rhythm in poetry, he wrote to Edward Marsh, "all depends on the *pause*—the natural pause, the natural *lingering* of the voice according to the feeling—it is the hidden *emotional* pattern that makes poetry, not the obvious form." As for the novel, he wrote to J. B. Pinker, "all rules of construction hold good only for novels which are copies of other novels. A book which is not a copy of other books has its own construction."

Lawrence's artistic faith, like that of the great Romantics, clearly centered on the idea of "organic" or "expressive" form—a faith, alas, that can cover a multitude of incompetencies. We know that Lawrence "rewrote" his novels and poems, some of them several times; but there is reason to believe that the rewriting was more than anything else a matter of further outpourings from the "passional self." And we also know from some early letters to Edward Garnett that on occasion he felt in himself a lack ("Trim and garnish my stuff I cannot. . . . I have always got such a lot of non-essential stuff in my work") of craftsmanship in the "French" sense. But he believed in the long run in the principle of expressive freedom and in the special *instinctual* skills, as he said, "much finer than the skill of the craftsman," that such a freedom requires. And such a principle of form, whether or not it served to excuse Lawrence's insufficiencies as a craftsman, was of course wholly consistent with his demand that art be a spontaneous discovery of life-truths untrammeled by limiting and dead conventions, a dynamic and revealing "divine service" in honor of life.

With these ideas and—in his critical use of them—"principles" before us, something yet remains to be said of what is perhaps most interesting about Lawrence as a critic: his *method*. For he did have a method, though it was really half unconscious, or more accurately, instinctive. His instinctive judgments of art by the standard of his personal moral vision, which of course he believed to be objectively "true," become at least a kind of quasi-method when we put them into alignment with two of Lawrence's fundamental assumptions. The first assumption, amply illustrated in all that has been said so far, is that nearly every modern writer, great and small, has been so infected by what has been called here the "bourgeois spirit" that he is unable to tell false from true, good from bad, living from dead. The second assumption is suggested by Lawrence in the first chapter of *Studies in Classic American Literature*: "Never trust the artist. Trust the tale. The proper function of the critic is to save the tale from the artist who created it." Lawrence's method may be described, then, as a kind of literary psycho-interpretation in which the critic goes beneath

the surface excrescences of a writer's distorted psyche in order to illuminate the life-truths inevitably present in the subconscious levels of his
work. Lawrence the critic thus discovers in literary works the "real"
truths that their creators were themselves unaware of.

But it must not be concluded that Lawrence was merely an eccentric
subjectivist who perversely misunderstood everybody else's work in terms
of his own. He knew perfectly well, for example, when he wrote his
essay on *The Grand Inquisitor* what Dostoevsky's intentions had been;
he was only pointing out that Dostoevsky in a sense misunderstood his
own materials, that there were inherently truer truths in them than in
Dostoevsky's intentions, and that these truths come forward of their own
power if we are alive as we read. When Lawrence said in the introduction
to his book of paintings that "even to Milton, the true hero of *Paradise
Lost* must be Satan," he didn't mean at all what Shelley appears to have
meant; he was only saying, really, that Satan is too much alive for the
willed moral abstractions of Milton's theology to contain dramatically.
Perhaps no one has shown as well as Lawrence how and why Satan and
the Grand Inquisitor are so powerful, how and why they seem to break
loose from the intentions of their creators and set up such an overwhelming counterforce of meaning and feeling of their own.

Studies in Classic American Literature, one of the few great works of
modern literary criticism, I believe, is the same sort of psycho-interpretation applied to a whole culture through its literature as seen in extended
historical perspective. Historical consciousness is functional in nearly all
of the criticism, and though it is stamped always with Lawrence's own
personality, it is far more dynamically and dramatically operative—a
felt presence of history—than in, say, Eliot's essays. In the *Studies* Lawrence reads American literature as an instinctive projection of America's
sloughing-off of the humanistic European consciousness and dying into the
self-annihilation of the democratic consciousness, the whole process seen
as promising a Phoenix rebirth of "It"—the life of the blood renewed,
and the true individuality of the fulfilled "deepest self" refound. Lawrence seems sometimes to have believed that he was on the threshold of
some kind of latter day, and so all this sounds a little bizarre in the saying. But the energy with which he applied his unusual convictions to our
literature yields illuminations that can be matched nowhere else in
criticism.

As is his habit, Lawrence works dialectically—sometimes with contrasting authors, sometimes with conflicting impulses within individual
authors. He pairs Franklin and Crèvecoeur, for example, as representative
respectively of two basic aspects of the dying American psyche: Franklin,
with his apothegmatic directives on self-reliance, is the dry little architect
of the practical mental machinery of "Americanizing and mechanizing
. . . for the purpose of overthrowing the past"; and Crèvecoeur, who
blinked at the bloody Indians in order to thrill the English romantics

with "a new world . . . of the Noble Savage and Pristine Nature and Paradisal Simplicity and all that gorgeousness that flows out of the unsullied fount of the ink bottle," becomes the emotional prototype of the American by mentalizing "the blood" into characteristic sentimentality.

Cooper's "white" novels comprise both of these archetypes: sex is just sentiment, and living human beings get "pinned down . . . transfixed by the idea or ideal of equality and democracy, on which they turn loudly and importantly, like propellers propelling." But there is a counterimpulse in Cooper's Leatherstocking novels, an impulse which is prophetic of the coming Natural Man: "Natty was Fenimore's great Wish. . . . Fenimore, in his imagination, wanted to be Natty Bumppo, who, I am sure, belched after he had eaten his dinner." In Cooper, then, there is both the "sloughing-off of old consciousness" and the forming of a new one.

Poe shows only one of these—that of the dying consciousness, projected through a fascinatedly morbid mental dissection of diseased love. But Lawrence seems to see Hawthorne's *The Scarlet Letter* as a kind of sociological counterpart to Poe's more purely psychological "Ligeia." He sees Hawthorne's novel as an unconscious but "colossal" satire on male-female relationships in America; it is "one of the greatest allegories in all literature," an allegory—unwitting, of course—of how the honest fact of sexual passion turns to "sin" through "self-watching, self-consciousness."

Dana and Melville, who came so close to the life-force in their dealings with the sea, were also led astray by "self-consciousness." As Tolstoy and Hardy and Verga ultimately failed with the soil-male principle, Dana fails with the sea-female principle. He wants to "know" the sea: "Dana sits and Hamletizes by the Pacific—chief actor in the play of his own existence." Similarly, Moby Dick is the "deepest blood-being of the white race . . . hunted by the maniacal fanaticism of our white mental consciousness."

But Lawrence sees Whitman, finally, as the great unconscious prophet of a new life for the race. Though Whitman's merging is a kind of death-agony of the old, specifically because it confuses love with salvation in a societal "charity," it is also an unconscious recognition of a new morality that smashes the old moral idea that "the soul of man is something 'superior' and 'above' the flesh." After Whitman's death-rhapsodies we have only to await the Phoenix-fires.

This is, of course, only the barest sort of summary. The book is a major critical work rich with historical, sociological, psychological, and mythic perceptions. It is sensitively aware of symbolism: just as an example, Lawrence is critically at home with the polar symbolism of dark and light ladies in American fiction some years before Professor Matthiessen and others were to make it critical coin of the realm. It is also notable, I think, that he is discussing American "classics" almost before we knew we had such things, at least of the sort he interests himself in: the book was published in 1923, and some of the chapters were written much in advance of Professor Weaver's inauguration of the Melville industry, which led a spate of discoveries and rediscoveries of a number of important writers from the American past.

But while the book is historically significant, it is also a permanent contribution to criticism and an extraordinarily vital piece of literature. It is written with enormous verve and color, and the management of the whole is rhythmic, contrapuntal, climactic. And it is an antidotal book—destructive, purgative, creative. The chapters on Poe, Hawthorne, Melville, and Whitman ought to be prescribed counterreading to the overwhelming quantity of academic, formalistic, and mythographic commentary we have on these writers—if only because Lawrence will be satisfied with none of them on *moral* grounds. And his lively chapters on such more dimly historical figures as Franklin, Crèvecoeur, Cooper, and Dana, refresh them amazingly. One can only regret that he wrote nothing on Thoreau, and that he did not live to tackle Faulkner, as he almost certainly would have. The occasional essays, the prefaces, and the "Study of Thomas Hardy" are full of the same sort of wrathfully brilliant insights vividly and wittily expressed. The essay on "Art and Morality" alone, for example—better, I think, than the more familiar "Pornography and Obscenity"—is indispensable as a profound and superbly written study in the sociology of modern taste.

It is perhaps a commonplace about Lawrence that one is either for him, like F. R. Leavis, or against him, like T. S. Eliot. But no one can mistake the fact that everywhere in his work mind and conscience are in strenuous encounter with the blank neutrality of existence. It is Lawrence's fierce integrity that makes him so necessary to us now—necessary perhaps especially as a critic, because in our time critics characteristically choose or are taught to be less than he is: a man alive who illuminates literature in an infinity of directions with his powerful vision of its moral relationship to all our human experience.

Lawrence's Social Writings

by Raymond Williams

It is easy to be aware of Lawrence's great effect on our thinking about social values, but it is difficult, for a number of reasons, to give any exact account of his actual contribution. It is not only that the public projection of him is very different from his actual work, and that this has led to important misunderstandings (that he believed that "sex solves everything"; that he was "a precursor of the Fascist emphasis on blood"). These, in the end, are matters of ignorance, and ignorance, though always formidable, can always be faced. The major difficulties are, I think, two in number. First, there is the fact that Lawrence's position, in the question of social values, is an amalgam of original and derived ideas. Yet, because of the intensity with which he took up and worked over what he had learned from others, this is, in practice, very difficult to sort out. Secondly, Lawrence's main original contribution is as a novelist, yet his general writing, in essays and letters, which for obvious reasons expresses most clearly his social ideas, cannot really be separated or judged apart from the novels. For example, his vital study of relationships, which is the basis of his original contribution to our social thinking, is naturally conducted in the novels and stories, and has constantly to be turned to for evidence, even though it is very difficult, for technical reasons, to use it just as evidence. Again, he has certain clear positives, which appear in a central position in his general arguments, yet which again depend on what he learned, and shows, in the writing of the novels. We can quote him, for example, on vitality, or on spontaneity, or on relationship, but to realize these, as the matters of substance which for him they were, we can only go, as readers, to this or that novel.

The thinker of whom one is most often reminded, as one goes through Lawrence's social writings, is Carlyle. There is more than a casual resemblance between the two men, in a number of ways, and anyone who has read Carlyle will see the continuity of such writing as this, in Lawrence:

"Lawrence's Social Writings." (Originally entitled "D. H. Lawrence.") From *Culture and Society, 1780-1950* by Raymond Williams. Copyright © 1958 by Raymond Williams. Appeared also in *A D. H. Lawrence Miscellany*. Reprinted by permission of the author, the Columbia University Press, and Chatto & Windus Ltd.

The Pisgah-top of spiritual oneness looks down upon a hopeless squalor of industrialism, the huge cemetery of human hopes. This is our Promised Land. . . . The aeroplane descends and lays her eggshells of empty tin cans on the top of Everest, in the Ultima Thule, and all over the North Pole; not to speak of tractors waddling across the inviolate Sahara and over the jags of Arabia Petraea, laying the same addled eggs of our civilization, tin cans, in every camp-nest. . . . It is the joy for ever, the agony for ever, and above all, the fight for ever. For all the universe is alive, and whirling in the same fight, the same joy and anguish. The vast demon of life has made himself habits which, except in the whitest heat of desire and rage, he will never break. And these habits are the laws of our scientific universe. But all the laws of physics, dynamics, kinetics, statics, all are but the settled habits of a vast living incomprehensibility, and they can all be broken, superseded, in a moment of great extremity. ("Climbing down Pisgah")

The bitter sweep of this critique of industrialism; this vibrant repetitive hymn to the "vast incomprehensibility": these, across eighty years, belong uniquely to Lawrence and Carlyle, and the resemblance, which is not only imitation, is remarkable. Lawrence takes over the major criticism of industrialism from the nineteenth century tradition, on point after point, but in tone he remains more like Carlyle than any other writer in the tradition, then or since. There is in each the same mixture of argument, satire, name-calling, and sudden wild bitterness. The case is reasoned and yet breaks again and again into a blind passion of rejection, of which the tenor is not merely negative but annihilating—a threshing after power, which is to be known, ultimately, only in that force of mystery at the edge of which the human articulation breaks down. The impact of each man on the generation which succeeded him is remarkably similar in quality: an impact not so much of doctrines as of an inclusive, compelling, general revelation.*

The points which Lawrence took over from the nineteenth century tradition can be briefly illustrated. There is, first, the general condemnation of industrialism as an attitude of mind:

The industrial problem arises from the base forcing of all human energy into a competition of mere acquisition. ("Nottingham and the Mining Country")

Then, when narrowed to competitive acquisitiveness, human purpose is seen as debased to "sheer mechanical materialism":

* I have read, since writing this paragraph, Dr. Leavis' censure (in *D. H. Lawrence: Novelist*) on a comparison of Lawrence with Carlyle. He traces the comparison to Desmond MacCarthy, and predicts that it will "recur." Well, here it is, but not, so far as I am concerned, from that source. As my comparison stands, I see no reason for withdrawal.—Au.

When pure mechanization or materialism sets in, the soul is automatically pivoted, and the most diverse of creatures fall into a common mechanical unison. This we see in America. It is not a homogeneous, spontaneous coherence so much as a disintegrated amorphousness which lends itself to perfect mechanical unison. ("Democracy")

Mechanical, disintegrated, amorphous: these are the continuing key words to describe the effect of the industrial priorities on individuals and on the whole society. It is this condition of mind, rather than industry as such, which is seen as having led to the ugliness of an industrial society, on which Lawrence is always emphatic:

The real tragedy of England, as I see it, is the tragedy of ugliness. The country is so lovely: the man-made England is so vile. . . . It was ugliness which betrayed the spirit of man, in the nineteenth century. The great crime which the moneyed classes and promoters of industry committed in the palmy Victorian days was the condemning of the workers to ugliness, ugliness, ugliness: meanness and formless and ugly surroundings, ugly ideals, ugly religion, ugly hope, ugly love, ugly clothes, ugly furniture, ugly houses, ugly relationship between workers and employers. The human soul needs actual beauty even more than bread. ("Nottingham and the Mining Country")

Or again:

The blackened brick dwellings, the black slate roofs glistening their sharp edges, the mud black with coal-dust, the pavements wet and black. It was as if dismalness had soaked through and through everything. The utter negation of natural beauty, the utter negation of the gladness of life, the utter absence of the instinct for shapely beauty which every bird and beast has, the utter death of the human intuitive faculty was appalling. . . . (*Lady Chatterley's Lover*)

Lawrence is here carrying on a known judgment, yet with his own quick perception and in his own distinctive accent. This kind of observation has to be made again and again, in every generation, not only because the atmosphere of industrialism tends to breed habituation, but also because (in ironic tribute to the strength of the tradition of protest) it is common to shift the ugliness and evil of industrialism out of the present, back into the "bad old days." The reminder that the thing is still here has repeatedly to be issued. Lawrence is little concerned, historically, with the origins of industrialism. For him, in this century, it is a received fact, and at the center of it is the "forcing of all human energy into a competition of mere acquisition"—the common element in all the diverse interpretations of which the tradition is composed.

Lawrence's starting point is, then, familiar ground. The inherited ideas were there to clarify his first sense of crisis. When we think of Lawrence, we concentrate, understandably, on the adult life, in all its restless dedication. That he was the son of a miner adds, commonly, a certain pathetic or sentimental interest; we relate the adult life back to it, in a personal way. But the real importance of Lawrence's origins is not and cannot be a matter of retrospect from the adult life. It is, rather, that his first social responses were those, not of a man observing the processes of industrialism, but of one caught in them, at an exposed point, and destined, in the normal course, to be enlisted in their regiments. That he escaped enlistment is now so well known to us that it is difficult to realize the thing as it happened, in its living sequence. It is only by hard fighting, and, further, by the fortune of fighting on a favorable front, that anyone born into the industrial working class escapes his function of replacement. Lawrence could not be certain, at the time when his fundamental social responses were forming, that he could so escape. That he was exceptionally gifted exacerbated the problem, although later it was to help towards solving it. Yet the problem of adjustment to the disciplines of industrialism, not merely in day-to-day matters, but in the required basic adjustments of feeling, is common and general. In remembering the occasional "victories"—the escapes from the required adjustment—we forget the innumerable and persistent defeats. Lawrence did not forget, because he was not outside the process, meeting those who had escaped, and forming his estimate of the problem from this very limited evidence. For him, rather, the *whole* process had been lived, and he was the more conscious of the general failure, and thus of the general character of the system:

> In my generation, the boys I went to school with, colliers now, have all been beaten down, what with the din-din-dinning of Board Schools, books, cinemas, clergymen, the whole national and human consciousness hammering on the fact of material prosperity above all things. ("Nottingham and the Mining Country")

Lawrence could not have written this, with such a phrase as "all been beaten down," if the pressures had not been so intensely and personally felt. In the early stages of the imposition of the industrial system, an observer could see adult men and women, grown to another way of life, being "beaten down" into the new functions and the new feelings. But once industrialism was established, an *observer* could hardly see this. Tension would be apparent to him only in those who had escaped, or half-escaped. The rest, "the masses," would normally appear to him fully formed—the "beating down" had happened, and he had not seen it. It thus became possible for men in such a position to believe, and with a show of reason to argue, that the residual majority, the "masses," had essentially, got the way of life they wanted, or, even, the way of life they deserved—the way "best fitted" for them. Only an occasional generous spirit could construct, from his own experience, the vision of an alternative possibility; even this, because it had to be vision, was always in danger of simplification or sentimentality. The outstanding value of Lawrence's development is that he was in a position to know the living process as a matter of common rather than of special experience. He had, further, the personal power of understanding and expressing this. While the thing was being lived, however, and while the pressures were not theoretic but actual, the inherited criticism of the industrial system was obviously of the greatest importance to him. It served to clarify and to generalize what had otherwise been a confused and personal issue. It is not too much to say that he built his whole intellectual life on the foundation of this tradition.

A man can live only one life, and the greater part of Lawrence's strength was taken up by an effort which in terms of ideas achieved perhaps less than had already been reached by different paths. Lawrence was so involved with the business of getting free of the industrial system that he never came seriously to the problem of changing it, although he knew that since the problem was common an individual solution was only a cry in the wind. It would be absurd to blame him on these grounds. It is not so much that he was an artist, and thus supposedly condemned, by romantic theory, to individual solutions. In fact, as we know, Lawrence spent a good deal of time trying to generalize about the necessary common change; he was deeply committed, all his life, to the idea of re-forming society. But his main energy went, and had to go, to the business of personal liberation from the system. Because he understood the issue in its actual depth, he knew that this liberation was not merely a matter of escaping a routine industrial job, or of getting an education, or of moving into the middle class. These things, in Lawrence's terms, were more of an evasion than what he actually came to do. Mitigation of the physical discomforts, of the actual injustices, or of the sense of lost opportunity, was no kind of liberation from the "base forcing of all human energy into a competition of mere acquisition." His business was the recovery of other purposes, to which the human energy might be directed. What he lived was the break-out, not theoretically, nor in any Utopian construction, but as it was possible to him, in immediate terms, in opposition alike to the "base forcing" and to his own weakness. What he achieved, in his life, was an antithesis to the powerful industrial thesis which had been proposed for him. But this, in certain of its aspects, was never more than a mere rejection, a habit of evasion: the industrial system was so strong, and he had been so fiercely exposed to it, that at times there was little that he or any man could do but run. This aspect, however, is comparatively superficial. The weakness of the exclusively biographical treatment of Lawrence, with its emphasis on the restless wanderings and the approach to any way of life but his own, lies in the fact that these things were only contingencies, whereas the dedication, and the value, were in the "endless venture into consciousness," which was his work as man and writer.

Lawrence is often dramatized as the familiar romantic figure who "rejects the claims of society." In fact, he knew too much about society, and knew it too directly, to be deceived for long by anything so foolish. He saw this version of individualism as a veneer on the consequences of industrialism.

> We have frustrated that instinct of community which would make us unite in pride and dignity in the bigger gesture of the citizen, not the cottager. (*Ibid.*)

The "instinct of community" was vital in his thinking: deeper and stronger, he argued, than even the sexual instinct. He attacked the industrial society of England, not because it offered community to the individual, but because it frustrated it. In this, again, he is wholly in line with the tradition. If in his own life he "rejected the claims of society," it was not because he did not understand the importance of community, but because, in industrial England, he could find none. Almost certainly, he underestimated the degree of community that might have been available to him: the compulsion to get away was so fierce, and he was personally very weak and exposed. But he was rejecting, not the claims of society, but the claims of industrial society. He was not a vagrant, to live by dodging; but an exile, committed to a different social principle. The vagrant wants the system to stay as it is, so long as he can go on dodging it while still being maintained by it. The exile, on the contrary, wants to see the system changed, so that he can come home. This latter is, in the end, Lawrence's position.

Lawrence started, then, from the criticism of industrial society which made sense of his own social experience, and which gave title to his refusal to be "basely forced." But alongside this ratifying principle of denial he had the rich experience of childhood in a working-class family, in which most of his positives lay. What such a childhood gave was certainly not tranquillity or security; it did not even, in the ordinary sense, give happiness. But it gave what to Lawrence was more important than these things: the sense of close quick relationship, which came to matter more than anything else. This was the positive result of the life of the family in a small house, where there were no such devices of separation of children and parents as the sending-away to school, or the handing-over to servants, or the relegation to nursery or playroom. Comment on this life (usually by those who have not experienced it) tends to emphasize the noisier factors: the fact that rows are always in the open; that there is no privacy in crisis; that want breaks through the small margin of material security and leads to mutual blame and anger. It is not that Lawrence, like any child, did not suffer from these things. It is rather that, in such a life, the suffering and the giving of comfort, the common want and the common remedy, the open row and the open making-up, are all part of a continuous life which, in good and bad, makes for a whole attachment. Lawrence learned from this experience that sense of the continuous flow and recoil of sympathy which was always, in his writing, the essential process of living. His idea of close spontaneous living rests on this foundation, and he had no temptation to idealize it into the pursuit of happiness: things were too close to him for anything so abstract. Further, there is an important sense in which the working-class family is an evident and mutual economic unit, within which both rights and responsibilities are immediately contained. The material processes of satisfying human needs are not separated from personal relationships; and Lawrence knew from this, not only that the processes must be accepted (he was firm on this through all his subsequent life, to the surprise of friends for whom these things had normally been the function of servants), but also that a common life has to be made on the basis of a correspondence between work relationships and personal relationships: something, again, which was only available, if at all, as an abstraction, to those whose first model of society, in the family, had been hierarchical, separative, and inclusive of the element of paid substitute labor—Carlyle's "cash-nexus." The intellectual critiques of industrialism as a system were therefore reinforced and prepared for by all he knew of primary relationships. It is no accident that the early chapters of *Sons and Lovers* are at once a marvellous re-creation of this close, active, contained family life, and also in general terms an indictment of the pressures of industrialism. Almost all that he learned in this way was by contrasts, and this element of contrast was reinforced by the accident that he lived on a kind of frontier, within sight both of industrial and of agricultural England. In the family and out of it, in the Breach and at Haggs Farm, he learned on his own senses the crisis of industrial England. When the family was broken by the death of his mother, and when the small world of the family had to be replaced by the world of wages and hiring, it was like a personal death, and from then on he was an exile, in spirit and later in fact.

The bridge across which he escaped was, in the widest sense, intellectual. He could read his way out in spirit, and he could write his way out in fact. It has recently been most valuably emphasized, by F. R. Leavis, that the provincial culture which was available to him was very much more rich and exciting than the usual accounts infer. The chapel, the literary society attached to it, the group of adolescents with whom he could read and talk: these were not the "drab, earnest institutions" of the observers' clichés, but active, serious, and, above all, wholehearted in energy. What they lacked in variety and in contact with different ways of living was to a large extent balanced by just that earnestness which is so much larger and finer a thing than the fear of it which has converted the word into a gesture of derision. Lawrence's formal education, it must be remembered, was also by no means negligible.

This then, in summary, is the background of Lawrence's inherited ideas and social experience. It remains to examine his consequent thinking about community, at the center of his discussion of social values. This depends on what was his major "venture into consciousness": the attempt to realize that range of living, human energy which the existing system had narrowed and crippled. He put one of his basic beliefs in this way:

> You can have life two ways. Either everything is created from the mind, downwards; or else everything proceeds from the creative quick, outwards into exfoliation and blossom. . . . The actual living quick itself is alone the creative reality. ("Democracy")

Lawrence's exploration was into this "creative reality," not as an idea, but in its actual processes:

> The quick of self is *there*. You needn't try to get behind it. As leave try to get behind the sun. (*Ibid.*)

This "quick of self," in any living being, is the basis of individuality:

> A man's self is a law unto itself, not unto *himself*, mind you. . . . The living self has one purpose only: to come into its own fulness of being. . . . But this coming into full, spontaneous being is the most difficult thing of all. . . . The only thing man has to trust to in coming to himself is his desire and his impulse. But both desire and impulse tend to fall into mechanical automatism: to fall from spontaneous reality into dead or material reality. . . . All education must tend against this fall; and all our efforts in all our life must be to preserve the soul free and spontaneous . . . the life-activity must never be degraded into a fixed activity. There can be no ideal goal for human life. . . . There is no pulling open the buds to see what the blossom will be. Leaves must unroll, buds swell and open, and *then* the blossom. And even after that, when the flower dies and the leaves fall, *still* we shall not know. . . . We know the flower of today, but the flower of tomorrow is all beyond us. (*Ibid.*)

Lawrence wrote nothing more important than this, although he wrote it differently, elsewhere, using different terms and methods. The danger is that we recognize this too quickly as "Lawrencean" (that "gorgeous be-feathered snail of an *ego* and a personality" which Lawrence and his writing could be at their worst), and accept it or pass it by without real attention. For it is quite easy to grasp as an abstraction, but very difficult in any more substantial way. In all Lawrence's writing of this kind one is reminded of Coleridge, whose terms were essentially so different, and yet whose emphasis was so very much the same: an emphasis, felt towards in metaphor, on the preservation of the "spontaneous life-activity" against those rigidities of category and abstraction, of which the industrial system was so powerful a particular embodiment. This sense of life is not obscurantism, as it is sometimes represented to be. It is a particular wisdom, a particular kind of reverence, which at once denies, not only the "base forcing of all human energy into a competition of mere acquisition," but also the dominative redirection of this energy into new fixed categories. I believe that it sets a standard, in our attitudes to ourselves and to other human beings, which can in experience be practically known and recognized, and by which all social proposals must submit themselves to be judged. It can be seen, as a positive, in thinkers as diverse as Burke and Cobbett, as Morris and Lawrence. It is unlikely to reach an agreed end in our thinking, but it is difficult to know where else to begin. We have only the melancholy evidence of powerful and clashing movements that begin elsewhere. When this is so, every renewed affirmation counts.

For Lawrence, the affirmation led on to an interesting declaration of faith in democracy, but this was something rather different from the democracy of, say, a Utilitarian:

> So, we know the first great purpose of Democracy: that each man shall be spontaneously himself—each man himself, each woman herself, without any question of equality or inequality entering in at all; and that no man shall try to determine the being of any other man, or of any other woman. (*Ibid.*)

At first sight, this looks like, not democracy, but a kind of romantic anarchism. Yet it is more than this, essentially, even though it remains very much a first term. Our question to those who would reject it must rest on the phrase "no man shall try to determine the being of any other man." We must ask, and require the answer, of anyone with a social philosophy, whether this principle is accepted or denied. Some of the most generous social movements have come to fail because, at heart, they have denied this. And it is much the same, in effect, whether such determination of human beings is given title by the abstractions of production or service, of the glory of the race or good citizenship. For "to try to determine the being of any other man" is indeed, as Lawrence emphasized, an arrogant and base forcing.

To Lawrence, the weakness of modern social movements was that they all seemed to depend on the assumption of a "fixed activity" for man, the "life activity" forced into fixed ideals. He found this

> horribly true of modern democracy—socialism, conservatism, bolshevism, liberalism, republicanism, communism: all alike. The one principle that governs all the *isms* is the same: the principle of the idealized unit, the possessor of property. Man has his highest fulfilment as a possessor of property: so they all say, really. (*Ibid.*)

And from this he concludes:

All discussion and idealizing of the possession of property, whether individual or group or State possession, amounts now to no more than a fatal betrayal of the spontaneous self. . . . Property is only there to be used, not to be possessed . . . possession is a kind of illness of the spirit. . . . When men are no longer obsessed with the desire to possess property, or with the parallel desire to prevent another man's possessing it, then, and only then, shall we be glad to turn it over to the State. Our way of State-ownership is merely a farcical exchange of words, not of ways. (*Ibid.*)

In this, Lawrence is very close to the socialism of a man like Morris, and there can be little doubt that he and Morris would have felt alike about much that has subsequently passed for socialism.

Lawrence's attitude to the question of equality springs from the same sources in feeling. He writes:

Society means people living together. People *must* live together. And to live together, they must have some Standard, some *Material* Standard. This is where the Average comes in. And this is where Socialism and Modern Democracy come in. For Democracy and Socialism rest upon the Equality of Man, which is the Average. And this is sound enough, so long as the Average represents the real basic material needs of mankind: basic material needs: we insist and insist again. For Society, or Democracy, or any Political State or Community exists not for the sake of the individual, nor should ever exist for the sake of the individual, but simply to establish the Average, in order to make living together possible: that is, to make proper facilities for every man's clothing, feeding, housing himself, working, sleeping, mating, playing, according to his necessity as a common unit, an average. Everything beyond that common necessity depends on himself alone. (*Ibid.*)

This idea of equality is "sound enough." Yet when it is not a question of material needs but of whole human beings:

We cannot say that all men are equal. We cannot say $A = B$. Nor can we say that men are unequal. We may not declare that $A = B + C$. . . . One man is neither equal nor unequal to another man. When I stand in the presence of another man, and I am my own pure self, am I aware of the presence of an equal, or of an inferior, or of a superior? I am not. When I stand with another man, who is himself, and when I am truly myself, then I am only aware of a Presence, and of the strange reality of Otherness. There is me, and there is *another being*. . . . There is no comparing or estimating. There is only this strange recognition of *present otherness*. I may be glad, angry, or sad, because of the presence of the other. But still no comparison enters in. Comparison enters only when one of us departs from his own integral being, and enters the material-mechanical world. Then equality and inequality starts at once. (*Ibid.*)

This seems to me to be the best thing that has been written about equality in our period. It gives no title to any defense of material inequality, which in fact is what is usually defended. But it removes from the idea of equality that element of mechanical abstraction which has often been felt in it. The emphasis on relationship, on the recognition and acceptance of "present otherness," could perhaps only have come from a man who had made Lawrence's particular "venture into consciousness." We should remember the emphasis when Lawrence, under the tensions of his exile, falls at times into an attitude like that of the later Carlyle, with an emphasis on the recognition of "superior" beings and of the need to bow down and submit to them. This "following after power," in Carlyle's phrase, is always a failure of the kind of relationship which Lawrence has here described: the impatient frustrated relapse into the attempt to "determine another man's being." Lawrence can show us, more clearly than anyone, where in this he himself went wrong.

I have referred to the tensions of exile, and this aspect of Lawrence's work should receive the final stress. In his basic attitudes he is so much within the tradition we have been following, has indeed so much in common with a socialist like Morris, that it is at first difficult to understand why his influence should have appeared to lead in other directions. One reason, as has been mentioned, is that he has been vulgarized into a romantic rebel, a type of the "free individual." There is, of course, just enough in his life and work to make this vulgarization plausible. Yet it cannot really be sustained. We have only to remember this:

Men are free when they are in a living homeland, not when they are straying and breaking away. (*Studies in Classic American Literature*)

And again:

Men are free when they belong to a living, organic, believing community, active in fulfilling some unfulfilled, perhaps unrealized purpose. (*Ibid.*)

But this in practice was the cry of an exile: of a man who wanted to commit himself, yet who rejected the terms of the available commitments. Lawrence's rejection had to be so intense, if he was to get clear at all, that he was led into a weakness, which found its rationalization. He kept wanting to see a change in society, but he could conclude:

Every attempt at preordaining a new material world only adds another last straw to the load that already has broken so many backs. If we are to keep our backs unbroken, we must deposit all property on the ground, and learn to walk without it. We must stand aside. And when many men stand aside, they stand in a new world; a new world of man has come to pass. ("Democracy")

This is the end of the rainbow: the sequel to that Rananim which had been one more in the series of attempts to evade the issues: an idealized substitute community, whether Pantisocracy, New Harmony, or the Guild of St. George. Lawrence's point is that the change must come first in feeling, but almost everything to which he had borne witness might have shown how much "in the head" this conclusion was. He knew all about the processes of "beating down." He knew, none better, how the consciousness and the environment were linked, and what it cost even an exceptional man to make his ragged breathless escape. There is something false, in the end, in the way he tries to separate the material issues and the issues in feeling, for he had had the opportunity of knowing, and indeed had learned, how closely intermeshed these issues were. It is not a question of the old debate on which conditions are primary. It is that in actuality the pressures, and the responses creating new pressures, form into a whole process, which "is *there*. You needn't try to get behind it. As leave try to get behind the sun." Lawrence came to rationalize and to generalize his own necessary exile, and to give it the appearance of freedom. His separation of the material issues from the issues in consciousness was an analogy of his own temporary condition. There is something, in the strict sense, suburban about this. The attempt to separate material needs, and the ways in which they are to be met, from human purpose and the development of being and relationship, is the suburban separation of "work" and "life" which has been the most common response of all to the difficulties of industrialism. It is not that the issues in consciousness ought to be set aside while the material ends are pursued. It is that because the process is whole, so must change be whole: whole in conception, common in effort. The "living, organic, believing community" will not be created by standing aside, although the effort toward it in consciousness is at least as important as the material effort. The tragedy of Lawrence, the working-class boy, is that he did not live to come home. It is a tragedy, moreover, common enough in its incidence to exempt him from the impertinences of personal blame.

The venture into consciousness remains, as a sufficient life's work. Towards the end, when he had revisited the mining country where the pressures of industrialism were most explicit and most evident, he shaped, as a creative response, the sense of immediate relationship which informs *Lady Chatterley's Lover,* and which he had earlier explored in *The Rainbow, Women in Love,* and *St. Mawr.* This is only the climax of his exploration into those elements of human energy which were denied by the "base forcing," and which might yet overthrow it. It is profoundly important to realize that Lawrence's exploration of sexual experience is made, always, in this context. To isolate this exploration, as it was tempting for some of his readers to do, is not only to misunderstand Lawrence but to expose him to the scandal from which, in his lifetime, he scandalously suffered. "This which we are must cease to be, that we may come to pass in another being": this, throughout, is the emphasis. And, just as the recovery of the human spirit from the base forcing of industrialism must

lie in recovery of "the creative reality, the actual living quick itself," so
does this recovery depend on the ways in which this reality can be most
immediately apprehended: "the source of all life and knowledge is in
man and woman, and the source of all living is in the interchange and
meeting and mingling of these two." It is not that sexual experience is
"the answer" to industrialism, or to its ways of thinking and feeling. On
the contrary, Lawrence argues, the poisons of the "base forcing" have
extended themselves into this. His clearest general exposition of this
comes in the essay on Galsworthy, where he derides the proposition of
"Pa-assion," and its related promiscuity, as alternatives to the emphasis
on money or property which follows from men being "only materially
and socially conscious." The idea of sex as a reserve area of feeling, or as
a means of Byronic revolt from the conventions of money and property
(a Forsyte turning into an anti-Forsyte), is wholly repugnant to Lawrence.
People who act in this way are "like all the rest of the modern middle-
class rebels, not in rebellion at all; they are merely social beings behaving
in an anti-social manner." The real meaning of sex, Lawrence argues, is
that it "involves the whole of a human being." The alternative to the
"base forcing" into the competition for money and property is not sexual
adventure, nor the available sexual emphasis, but again a return to the
"quick of self," from which whole relationships, including whole sexual
relationships, may grow. The final emphasis, which all Lawrence's convincing explorations into the "quick of self" both illumine and realize, is
his criticism of industrial civilization:

> If only our civilization had taught us . . . how to keep the fire of sex
> clear and alive, flickering or glowing or blazing in all its varying degrees
> of strength and communication, we might, all of us, have lived all our lives
> in love, which means we should be kindled and full of zest in all kinds of
> ways and for all kinds of things. ("Sex versus Loveliness")

Or again, as an adequate summary of the whole "venture into consciousness":

> Our civilization . . . has almost destroyed the natural flow of common
> sympathy between men and men, and men and women. And it is this that
> I want to restore into life. ("The State of Funk")

Chronology of Important Dates

September 11, 1885	Born in Eastwood, Nottinghamshire, to coal miner and his middle-class wife.
1901	Leaves school to work for surgical-appliance manufacturer; falls ill when older brother dies.
1903-1908	Becomes pupil-teacher; studies at Nottingham College; begins teaching in Surrey.
1909	Publishes first poems through intercession of childhood sweetheart, Jessie Chambers.
December 1910	His mother dies.
January 1911	Publishes *The White Peacock*, his first novel.
April-May 1912	Meets Frieda Weekley-Richthofen, wife of former professor, daughter of German Baron, mother of three. Leaves with Frieda for the continent. Publishes *The Trespasser*.
1913	Publishes *Love Poems* and *Sons and Lovers*. Begins work on *The Rainbow* and *Women in Love*.
1914	Marries Frieda (now divorced) in England. Publishes *The Prussian Officer* (tales).
1915	Publishes *The Rainbow* in September; it is suppressed in November. Embarks on a series of joint lectures against war with Bertrand Russell which dissolves in philosophic quarrel.
1916	Publishes *Twilight in Italy* (travel) and *Amores* (poems).
1917	Quarrels with J. M. Murry and Katherine Mansfield; he and his wife are ordered out of Cornwall as suspected spies.
November 1919	Leaves England (with his wife) for Italy and years of global travel.
1917-19	Publishes *Look! We Have Come Through! New Poems, Bay*.
1920	Publishes *Women in Love* (New York subscription edition) and *The Lost Girl*.
1921	Publishes *Movements in European History, Psychoanalysis and the Unconscious, Sea and Sardinia*.
1922	Travels to Ceylon, Australia, and New Mexico. Publishes *Aaron's Rod, Fantasia of the Unconscious, England, My England*.
1923	Publishes *The Captain's Doll, Studies in Classic American Literature, Kangaroo*, and *Birds, Beasts and Flowers*. Begins

work on *The Plumed Serpent* in Mexico. When he follows Frieda to England in winter, the famous "Last Supper" occurs: his friends refuse to join him in America.

1924   Returns together with Frieda and one disciple, Dorothy Brett, to Luhan ranch, Taos, New Mexico. *The Boy in the Bush* (with M. L. Skinner) appears. Begins public squabble with Norman Douglas. His father dies.

1925   Completes *The Plumed Serpent* on uncertain note; falls ill in Mexico. *St. Mawr, Reflections on the Death of a Porcupine* appear. Returns to England and Italy.

1926   Publishes *The Plumed Serpent* and tales. Writes and paints in Florentine wood.

1927   Publishes *Mornings in Mexico*.

1928   Publishes *Lady Chatterley's Lover* (subscription edition), which causes journalistic furor, piracy, confiscations. Tales, *Collected Poems* appear.

1929   *Pansies* seized in the mail; exhibited paintings seized in London. *The Escaped Cock*, "Pornography and Obscenity" appear.

March 4, 1930   Dies of tuberculosis at Vence, France.

Notable posthumous volumes: *Nettles*, "Apropos of *Lady Chatterley's Lover*" (1930); *Apocalypse* (1931); *Etruscan Places, The Letters* (1932); *The First Lady Chatterley* (1944).

Notes on the Editor and Authors

MARK SPILKA, editor of this volume, is the author of *The Love Ethic of D. H. Lawrence* and *Dickens and Kafka: A Mutual Interpretation.* He is Assistant Professor of English at the University of Michigan and a Fellow in the Indiana School of Letters.

MONROE ENGEL teaches English at Harvard University. He is the author of *A Length of Rope, The Visions of Nicholas Solon,* and *Voyager Belsky;* a critical study, *The Maturity of Dickens;* and a forthcoming critical biography of Lawrence.

RICHARD FOSTER, Associate Professor of English at the University of Minnesota, has written one of the finest reappraisals of New Criticism: *The New Romantics.* He contributes to such journals as *Hudson Review, Minnesota Review, ELH,* and *Toronto Quarterly.*

GRAHAM HOUGH, a Fellow of Christ's College, Cambridge, is the author of *The Last Romantics, The Romantic Poets,* and *The Dark Sun: A Study of D. H. Lawrence.* He contributes poems and essays to *Critical Quarterly* and other journals.

HARRY T. MOORE, now teaching at the University of Colorado, is general editor of a modern literature series published by the Southern Illinois University Press. He is the author of *The Novels of John Steinbeck,* the author and editor of numerous books on Lawrence, and a frequent reviewer for *The New York Times, Saturday Review,* and other periodicals.

JULIAN MOYNAHAN, Assistant Professor of English at Princeton University, has written a book on Lawrence called *The Deed of Life.* His work appears in *Essays in Criticism, ELH,* and other journals.

MARVIN MUDRICK teaches English at Santa Barbara University. He is the author of a book on Jane Austen and a forthcoming study of Colette, and contributes frequently to *Hudson Review, Kenyon Review,* and other prominent journals.

VIVIAN DE SOLA PINTO, retired Professor of English at Nottingham University, has written *D. H. Lawrence: Prophet of the Midlands* and is now editing the collected poems of Lawrence. He is a poet, Restoration scholar, and Fellow of the Royal Society of Literature.

MARK SCHORER, widely known novelist, critic, and biographer, has written books on William Blake and Sinclair Lewis. He teaches at the University of California at Berkeley, and is now writing a biography of Stephen Crane. He is the editor of the volume on Sinclair Lewis in the Twentieth Century Views series.

W. D. SNODGRASS, a Hudson Review Fellow in poetry, now teaches English at Wayne State University. His book of poems, *Heart's Needle,* won the Pulitzer Prize for poetry in 1960.

DOROTHY VAN GHENT, former Professor of English at the University of Kansas and the University of Vermont, is author of the well-known study, *The English Novel: Form and Function.*

ARTHUR E. WATERMAN, Associate Professor of English at Georgia State College, has contributed essays to *Critique, Walt Whitman Review,* and *Modern Drama.* He is currently writing on the novels of Wright Morris.

RAYMOND WILLIAMS, a tutor at Oxford, is the author of several books of literary and social criticism. His most recent works are *Culture and Society, The Long Revolution,* and an autobiographical novel, *Border Country.*

Selected Bibliography

Biographical Studies

Aldington, Richard. *D. H. Lawrence: Portrait of a Genius But . . .* New York: Duell, Sloan & Pearce, Inc., 1950. The most balanced of the memorial biographies.

Moore, Harry T. *The Life and Works of D. H. Lawrence.* New York: Twayne Publishers, 1951. Still the best critical biography.

————. *The Intelligent Heart: The Story of D. H. Lawrence.* New York: Farrar, Straus, and Cudahy, 1954. A straight biography containing new material on Lawrence's youth.

Nehls, Edward, ed. *D. H. Lawrence: A Composite Biography.* Madison, Wisc.: University of Wisconsin Press, 1957-59. 3 vols. Brief memorial fragments arranged as lenses on the author's life—a superb job of editorial artistry.

Wood, Jessie Chambers (pseud. E.T.). *D. H. Lawrence: A Personal Record.* London: Jonathan Cape, Ltd., 1935. An invaluable account of Lawrence's early intellectual development though unreliable in its analysis of his youthful conflict; by the model for Miriam in *Sons and Lovers*.

Critical Studies

Hough, Graham. *The Dark Sun: A Study of D. H. Lawrence.* London: Gerald Duckworth and Co., 1956. A complete critical survey, especially good on the poems and the general "doctrine."

Leavis, F. R. *D. H. Lawrence: Novelist.* London: Chatto and Windus, 1955. The best critical book on Lawrence, concentrating on *The Rainbow, Women in Love* and the finest tales.

Spilka, Mark. *The Love Ethic of D. H. Lawrence.* Bloomington, Ind.: Indiana University Press, 1955. A study of the "life-morality" as concretely developed in five major novels.

Tindall, William York. *D. H. Lawrence and Susan His Cow.* New York: Columbia University Press, 1939. A generally unsympathetic study of Lawrence's primitivism, valuable for its anthropological scholarship.

Tiverton, Father William (Martin Jarrett-Kerr). *D. H. Lawrence and Human Existence.* New York: Philosophical Library, Inc., 1951. Preface by T. S. Eliot. An excellent account of Lawrence's Christian existential propensities.

Vivas, Eliseo. *D. H. Lawrence: The Failure and the Triumph of Art*. Evanston, Ill.: Northwestern University Press, 1960. Less valuable for its criticism (which labors obvious failures and adds little to established triumphs) than for its attempt to define symbolic form in Lawrence's fiction.

Anthologies

D. H. Lawrence Number. *Modern Fiction Studies*, V (Spring, 1959). A collection of somewhat pedestrian essays, chiefly valuable for its complete and up-to-date bibliography.

Moore, Harry T. and Frederick J. Hoffman, eds. *The Achievement of D. H. Lawrence*. Norman, Okla.: University of Oklahoma Press, 1953. A good historical sample of Lawrence criticism.

Moore, Harry T., ed. *A D. H. Lawrence Miscellany*. Carbondale, Ill.: Southern Illinois University Press, 1959. An uneven collection of critical essays, letters, memoirs and original documents.

Essays on Major Novels

Bertocci, Angelo. "Symbolism in *Women in Love*," in the *Miscellany*. An impressive attempt to explain the novel in strictly *symboliste* terms. See Spilka, "Was D. H. Lawrence a Symbolist?" *Accent*, XV (Winter, 1955), 49-60, for a different view.

Engelberg, Edward. "Escape from the Circles of Experience: D. H. Lawrence's *The Rainbow* as a Modern *Bildungs-roman*." PMLA, LXXVIII (March, 1963). A convincing justification of the problematic ending in terms of the *Bildungs-roman* tradition.

Fraiberg, Louis. "The Unattainable Self: D. H. Lawrence's *Sons and Lovers*," in *Twelve Original Essays on Great English Novels*, edited by Charles Shapiro. Detroit: Wayne State University Press, 1960. A persuasive and consistent Freudian reading of the novel. See opposing views by Seymour Betsky in *The Achievement* anthology and Spilka in *The Love Ethic*.

Tindall, William York. Introduction to *The Plumed Serpent*. New York: Alfred A. Knopf, Inc., 1951. An approach to the novel's unity through symbol and myth. See Jascha Kessler's similar approach in the *Miscellany*.

Knoepflmacher, U. C. "The Rival Ladies: Mrs. Ward's 'Lady Connie' and Lawrence's *Lady Chatterley's Lover*." *Victorian Studies*, IV (December, 1960), 141-58. Tracing Lawrence's plot to this fag-end novel in the drawing-room tradition (1916), the author credits Lawrence with transforming and revivifying the old Victorian ethos.

Genre Studies

Aldington, Richard. Introduction to *The Spirit of Place*. London: William Heinemann, 1935. The first of many essays on Lawrence's unusual gift for travel writing. See similar essays by Edward Nehls in *The Achievement of D. H. Lawrence* and Mark Schorer in the *Miscellany*.

Amon, Frank. "D. H. Lawrence and the Short Story," in *The Achievement of D. H. Lawrence*. An account of "symbolic *rites de passage*" in three tales. See also Anthony West's "The Short Stories" in the same anthology, and H. E. Bates' chapter on Lawrence in *The Modern Short Story: A Critical Survey* (London and New York: Thomas Nelson, 1943).

Blackmur, R. P. "D. H. Lawrence and Expressive Form," in *The Double Agent*. New York: Arrow Editions, 1935. The famous attack on Lawrence's "demonic" approach to poetry. See opposing views by Harold Bloom and A. Alvarez in the *Miscellany*.

Huxley, Aldous. Introduction to *The Letters of D. H. Lawrence*. New York: The Viking Press, Inc., 1932. Reprinted in *The Achievement of D. H. Lawrence* and more recently in *The Collected Letters of D. H. Lawrence* (ed. Moore), this important early essay remains one of the finest introductions to Lawrence and his letters. Compare Diana Trilling's characteristically destructive introduction to *The Selected Letters of D. H. Lawrence*, reprinted in the *Miscellany*.

Rieff, Philip. Introduction to *Psychoanalysis and the Unconscious* and *Fantasia of the Unconscious*, by D. H. Lawrence. New York: The Viking Press, Inc., 1960. A sympathetic and perceptive account of Lawrence's "pollyanalytics."

Controversies

Bantock, G. H. "D. H. Lawrence and the Nature of Freedom," in *Freedom and Authority in Education*. London: Faber, 1952. A sympathetic study of Lawrence's controversial views on educating and rearing children.

Caudwell, Christopher. "D. H. Lawrence: A Study of the Bourgeois Artist," in *The Critical Performance*, edited by Stanley Edgar Hyman. New York: Vintage Books, Inc., 1956. A famous Marxist attack of the Thirties. For a sounder view of Lawrence's social thinking, see Raymond Williams in this anthology.

Freeman, Mary. "Lawrence and Fascism," in *D. H. Lawrence: A Basic Study of His Ideas*. Gainesville, Fla.: University of Florida Press, 1955. An intelligent defense of Lawrence against the charge of fascism.

Hoffman, Frederick J. "Lawrence's Quarrel with Freud," in *Freudianism and the Literary Mind*. Baton Rouge, La.: Louisiana State University Press, 1945. On Lawrence's use (and abuse) of Freud to establish his own vitalistic psychology.

Myers, Neil. "Lawrence and the War." *Criticism*, IV (Winter, 1962), 44-58. A justification of Lawrence's vitriolic response to World War I—a response often attributed to mere neuroticism.

Rolph, C. H., ed. *The Trial of Lady Chatterley*. Baltimore: Penguin Books, Inc., 1961. This transcript of the trial in England, Regina *v.* Penguin Books, Ltd., summarizes the censorship issue in superbly dramatic form.

Spilka, Mark. "Lawrence in No Man's Land," in *The Love Ethic*. An exploration of Lawrence's changing views on the vexed question of *Blutbrüderschaft*.

Widmer, Kingsley. *The Perverse Art of D. H. Lawrence*. Seattle: University of Washington Press, 1962. A distorted view of Lawrence's satanism, countering "prevailing academic-moral views."

TWENTIETH CENTURY VIEWS

British Authors

TWENTIETH CENTURY VIEWS

American Authors